SHIVA

GOD OF GODS

SHIVA

NILIMA CHITGOPEKAR

CONTENTS

Foreword — 8
The sacred masculine — 10

1
THE IDEA OF SHIVA

A cryptic deity	18
The lord of animals	22
His emerging identity	24
The one who listens	26
Ravananugraha	30
Kiratarjuniyam	32
Shiva's transformation	36
Shiva Sahasranama	38
The divine trinity	40
Harihara	46
Sharabha	50
Tripundra and trident	52
Hariharapitamahasurya	54
The aniconic Shiva	56
Forms of the icon	60
Gudimallam Lingam	64
Jyotirlingas	66

2
SHIVA, THE FIERCE ONE

The god who destroys	72
Rudra	74
The third eye	78
Destroyer of Kama	80
Daksha's folly	84
Veerbhadra	86
Cosmic renewal	90
The cosmic dance	92
Nataraja	98
Drum of creation	102
Nadatanumanisam Sankaram	104
The timeless lord	106
Kaal Bhairava	108
Markandeya's devotion	112
Divine justice	114
Tripurasura slayed	118
An Asura transformed	120
Coiled around his neck	122
Churning of the ocean	124
Kumbh Mela	128
Moon in his embrace	130
Khandoba	132
The boon that became a curse	134
Flame and fury	136

3
SHIVA, THE HOUSEHOLDER

The ascetic householder	142
Cosmic companions	144
The tragedy of Sati	148
Parvati's sacred trials	150
Kalyanasundarmurti	152
A call for Shiva	154
Where gods wed	156
The eternal couple	160
And it started to rain	164
Ardhanarishvara	166
Protector and guide	172
Shankara	174
Birth of Ganesha	176
Karttikeya's birth	178
Kumarasambhava	180
Somaskanda	182
The descent of Ganga	184
Wild and untamed	186
Those closest to Shiva	192
Devout, but imprudent	196
The loyal Nandi	200
Mount Kailasha	202

4
SHIVA, THE YOGI

The supreme ascetic	208
The seven wise men	210
The power of austerity	212
Bhikshatanamurti	216
Nirvana Shatakam	218
The flowing locks of Shiva	220
Dakshinamurti	222
A home for Shiva	224
Pancha Bhuta temples	228
Panchamukha	232
He who has no form	234
Maha Mrityunjaya mantra	236
Many Bhairavas	240
Secrets from the guru	242
Stirring the serpent	246
Shiva and Shakti	248
Kashi	250

5
SHIVA, THE DEITY

God of those who seek	**256**
Tamil Shaivism	**258**
Karaikkal Ammaiyar	**260**
The heroic worshippers	**262**
Verses of mystique	**264**
The guru and the sanyasi	**268**
Shivanandalahari	**270**
The Nathas	**272**
Transcending the mind	**274**
Lal Ded	**278**
The esoteric sects	**280**
The Aghoris	**284**
From ashes to ashes	**288**
Parallel traditions	**290**
Vankeshvara	**294**
Amarnath	**296**
Lord of the herbs	**300**
Gateways to the gods	**302**
The muse divine	**304**
The modern icon	**308**
Panch Kedar	**310**

Glossary	**314**
Index	**316**
Bibliography	**322**
Acknowledgments	**324**

▷ **This miniature portrays Tantric Shiva**, whose body embodies the elements of nature – space on his forehead, the Moon in his left eye, the Sun in his right, fire in his throat, air in his torso, and water in his lower body. He holds a trident and *damaru* in his upper hands, while his lower hands cradle the Earth, brimming with life. An ascetic rests in his matted locks, from which the Ganga flows, and in the foreground stands a lingam.

Foreword

By Professor Gavin Flood FBA

The great god Shiva has been a major focus of worship, poetry, and art through a long history of Indian civilization especially from the 7th to 13th centuries, although hymns to Rudra, an earlier form of Shiva, are found in the ancient *Rig Veda*. Rivalling the tradition of Vishnu, the religion focused on Shiva produced a remarkable flourishing of scripture, philosophy, poetry, and the plastic arts in a culture from Kashmir through to Khmer in Southeast Asia.

Dr Nilima Chitgopekar presents us with the different forms of Shiva from this long history. For example, we find here Shiva as Pashupati, the Lord of Animals, as Sharabha, the lion-bird who calms the rage of Narasimha, and as the killer of the demon Gajasura, illustrating the great diversity of his representations and the emergence of Shiva as a major focus that dominated the medieval religious landscape.

This is a complex history that Dr Chitgopekar brings to life through the various portrayals of Shiva in painting and sculpture that illustrate important texts such as the *Shivasahasranama*, the hymn to the thousand names of Shiva found in the Puranas and *Mahabharata*.

This book shows the interface between scriptural and visual representations of Shiva, how he is the family man as husband to Parvati and the ferocious Bhairava whose bulging eyes represent his immersion in the world of the senses. Dr Chitgopekar explains this history with reference to contemporary scholarship. For example, Pashupati was initially a protector of domestic animals and only later was this extended to wild animals too. In this wonderful book we learn how the enigmatic deity Shiva has been of central importance at all social levels through a long history, emerging from the margins of society to the heart of the social and political order, and how Shiva continues to inspire contemporary art and life too.

Gavin Flood is Professor of Hindu Studies and Comparative Religion at Oxford University, Academic Director of the Oxford Centre for Hindu Studies, and Senior Research Fellow at Campion Hall. His publications include *Religion and the Philosophy of Life* (2019), *The Truth Within: A History of Inwardness in Christianity, Hinduism, and Buddhism* (2013), *The Importance of Religion: Meaning and Action in Our Strange World* (2012), and *The Ascetic Self: Subjectivity, Memory, and Tradition* (2004). He is also the General Editor of the series "The Oxford History of Hinduism" and is a Fellow of the British Academy.

> The tongue that speaks of Shiva's stories is the real tongue; the eyes that see His image, the real eyes; the hands that always worship Him, the real hands; and he who ever remembers Him, the attainer of the true end of life.
>
> Verse 94, *Shivanandalahari*, from *Sivanandalahari of Sri Sankaracarya* by Swami Tapasyananda

THE SACRED MASCULINE

Shiva is multiple. Shiva is plural. No neat binary can hold him. The mind must deepen, the heart must widen, to love a god who slips every definition. With Shiva comes divine messiness, divine peccadilloes. Upon his shoulders he carries the weight of time, the yearnings of ardent devotees, lores of peoples, and the multitude of figures. This is Shiva – ever one, ever many.

I was 10 when I first encountered Shiva, at Tapkeshwar Mahadev Temple in Dehradun, Uttarakhand. Wandering into the cave shrine, I witnessed a prayer service. I was not alarmed by the dark, incense-filled atmosphere – the smoke, the clang of the metal bell, the intent recitation of mantras. Looking back, I can see that, at some subconscious level, the wonder and fascination stayed with me. How else can I explain an abiding interest that has lasted more than 40 years? Over this time, I have realized that whenever I turn my mind to Shiva – whether through reading texts, writing, or contemplating his sculptures – I feel a sense of autonomy, fulfilment, and a curiosity that never ceases.

This is because the essence of Shiva is built upon pluralities. Over centuries, both his character as a deity and Shaivism as a tradition have moved like a rolling stone gathering much moss. There was no unilinear progression from Rudra to Shiva; instead, complex, multiple, and parallel traditions converged into him, giving him a robust character and offering his devotees a panacea for their varied afflictions.

Regional deities into Shaivism

Shiva's character and worship have undergone centuries of transformation – some aspects eroding, others flourishing – yet Shiva's popularity has never eclipsed. A most fascinating dimension in the history of early and medieval India is the cultural interaction between priestly or Sanskritic and tribal or non-Sanskritic elements. This process, variously labeled as "Brahmanization" or "Sanskritization", is in fact a two-way process, with the reverse phenomenon sometimes referred to as "indigenization". It is worthwhile to capture this process as embedded in the Shaiva story, highlighting how acceptable, legitimate, Brahmanical deities became affiliated with the "lesser" gods of the autochthonous substrata.

One of my favourite discoveries goes back to the time I was pursuing my doctorate on the expansion of Shaivism in 6th-century Madhya Pradesh. While working through a book called *Corpus Inscriptionum Indicarum*, a compilation of ancient Indian inscriptions, I came across a fascinating inscription from the Kalachuri Dynasty, who ruled in parts of central India during the 6th and early 7th centuries. The inscription mentioned a deity named Vankeshvara, a Prakrit name unfamiliar to me. It recorded that the king had washed the "resplendent feet of the god" on the occasion of constructing a temple in Tummana, their capital.

What struck me was that the object of worship was not a lingam – as one would expect in most Shaiva temples of the region – but an image. Even more intriguing, I could not find this name, Vankeshvara, in any recognized Hindu scriptures. Curious, I dug further and, to my surprise, discovered a photograph in the archives in Varanasi. The image was from a temple complex a few kilometres from Tummana. Examining it closely, I realized that Vankeshvara (*See pp294–95*) was likely a form of Rudra-Shiva. The facial features resembled Shiva in his Bhairava aspect, while the rest of the body was composed of animals and human faces. The image was also ithyphallic, a common feature in 6th-century representations of Shiva. His very name meant "lord of vagabonds", and who but Shiva roamed with a band of outcasts and spirits?

It became evident to me that Vankeshvara had once been a local deity, worshipped by the people of the region before the Kalachuris arrived. Being newcomers, the dynasty seems to have adopted him, perhaps to win local acceptance or to guard against offending a powerful local god.

This encounter showed me, perhaps more vividly than any theory, how local deities could be absorbed into the larger fold of Shaivism – reshaped, renamed, and ultimately woven into the complex identity of Shiva himself.

The Hindu pantheon has always made room for the old gods if they retained their relevance, and for new gods if they offered favours or boons. Historically, as the population expanded, village after village came under the influence of Vedic culture, and regional gods of various kinds gradually assimilated into Shiva. Some were mountain gods, others were associated with snakes or bulls, and still others were linked as consorts to primitive mother goddesses such as Uma, Parvati, Durga, or Kali, or to the alluring Chaunsatha Yoginis, the 64 esoteric attendants of the Goddess Shakti. Some deities became associated with Shiva because they were adept at yoga, while others for their wildness and fondness for meat, wine, dancing, death, and ghosts. Brahmanical disdain no longer kept the ancient mother goddesses in fuzziness. They emerged as the wives of Shiva, brought together from many regions. Their former consorts faded into obscurity as they joined the retinue of the single, powerful Shiva.

Myth after myth was created to justify and provide a purpose for the peculiarities of some of these erstwhile regional or local divinities incorporated under the Shaivic umbrella. In this manner, Shaivism, as a developing and complex socio-religious tradition encompassing diverse cults and beliefs, changed over the centuries and across different geographical areas.

The blending of traditions and philosophies

Shaiva theology developed from Rudra's appearances in Vedic literature, from Advaita Vedanta in the Upanishads, from Shaiva revelations as the lingam and married god in the Puranas, but also from the extreme practices and radical thoughts expressed in the Tantras and Agamas. At the macro level, it was part of the highbrow Sanskrit tradition; at the micro level, it exhibited cultic features endemic to specific geographical and socio-economic conditions. Between these two levels, there was a continuous traffic of give and take, a process of osmosis exemplified in sculpture, rituals, and mythology. Ultimately, a composite godhead emerged, with multifarious functions.

The process of syncretism functioned without distorting Shiva's core principles. He retained his essential character of being wrathful, marginalized, and appeased through prayers while simultaneously absorbing local traditions, rituals, and ideology. Murugan became identified with Shiva's son Skanda, and deities such as Khandoba and Mallara were assimilated into Shiva's fold. In this way, regional traditions expressed in vernacular languages, local deities, local mythologies, ritual forms, and possession cults were universalized through Sanskritization. There is no linear development in Shaivism proceeding in an orderly sequence from animism through polytheism to monotheism. Animism, often considered primitive, exists alongside the most complex, abstruse, and sophisticated philosophies. All are part of Shaivism, as are the simplest stories recited during a fast. What is striking is that the Shiva imaginary upholds the values and goals of mainstream, orthodox Brahmanism, cheek by jowl with the unkempt Shiva, unburdened by civilization. This is why he appeals equally to the youth, the transvestic, the marginalized, and the "strange". Rebellious individuals have relished Shiva's form; some adopt his dreadlocked hairstyle, and many bear tattoos of his figure, his trishula, or the oft-used invocation, *Aum Namah Shivaya*. Just as Shiva is myriad in his projections, so are his devotees – from Naga Sadhus to individuals steeped in abstruse Advaita philosophies, to those content fasting on Shiva's chosen day, Monday.

Folk, elite, and scriptural traditions

In *Shiva: God of Gods*, I aim to highlight that one of the most significant elements in the evolution of Shiva is the diversity arising from Shaivism's vitality and its willingness to accommodate innumerable personal proclivities and tastes. In doing so, I analyze the process of interaction and assimilation, delineating the incorporative aspect of Brahmanical religion through synthesis and absorption. Accompanying the narrative is a rich array of visuals.

I have always been captivated by Indian art, so much so that I examine it with a magnifying glass, studying the smallest details – the mudras, the subtle expressions on Shiva's face, the fangs of his Bhairava form, or the intensity of his wife Kali's bulging eyes. Even worn and weathered sculptures hold a fascination, revealing layers of meaning in their age and imperfection.

Wherever my research has taken me – whether in my office at the Oxford University or at home in India – I have always felt the need to keep an image of Shiva before me while I study him. Modern Indian painter Nandalal Bose's depiction of the dead Sati cradled in Shiva's lap was a constant companion while I wrote one of my earlier books, as was Upendra Maharathi's depiction of Ganga flowing through Shiva's hair. I returned to these images again and again, letting my gaze linger, letting them speak beyond words. For this book, I placed a Shiva bust before me, a focal point for meditation as I wrote. These visual sources remind me that studying Shiva extends far beyond texts.

Paintings, sculptures, and objects are not mere illustrations; they are living encounters with the divine that deepen the experience in ways that words alone cannot capture.

The sources I have in this book are not semantically imprisoned. Apart from sculptures and paintings, they include local oral stories, folk songs, dance, chants, and practices – the popular, the elite, the oral, and the folk all existing simultaneously. Yet the dividing lines and defining features are always tricky, and one steps into murky waters the moment one attempts to set definitions or boundaries. The book shows that a diffusion takes place between the folk and the "high" religion; in the process, neither is left untouched. Over the course of this development, some traits remain local, while others come to be pan-Indian.

This book demonstrates that nowhere else do we find such seamless cohesion between tribal religion, folk religion, and scriptural religion as in the study of Shaivism. The story unfolds in five chapters, divided thematically. The first sets the stage, exploring the historical developments that shaped Shaivism. The second examines Shiva's first characteristic, his fierceness, and gradually reveals the calm that lies beneath. This leads into the third chapter, which focuses on him as the householder, surrounded by his vast and varied entourage. In the fourth chapter, Shaiva ideas expand from the Puranic to the Tantric through his profound connection with asceticism. Finally, the fifth chapter presents Shiva as seen through the eyes of his devotees in the modern world.

The outsider

In its early days, Shaivism comprised several sects, but not many have survived to the present. Few were sanctioned by the Vedas and practised mild forms of worship. Many were considered outside, or even opposed to, the Vedas and engaged in shocking or extreme rites. Their lifestyles provided an "anti-structure," so to speak.

This was also the time when Shiva was known as Rudra. From the very beginning, he was held at a cautious distance. He was the outsider, representing all that was to be dreaded. In keeping with this early perception, many later sculptures depict a bell in one of his hands, signalling his "low-class" status.

The transition

However, centuries later, Shiva appeared adorned with the highest attributes, at home among the Brahmanical gods. He asserted his claim to equal sovereignty alongside Brahma, the creator, and Vishnu, the preserver.

Then came the Puranas, the mythological matrix, where recurrent episodes, reinforced through frequent repetition across texts and visual reminders in sculpture, helped solidify key ideas and characteristics of Shiva in the minds of devotees. Even though one is loath to essentialize or reify the notion of a continuous linear development, it is undeniable that many characteristics from his earliest appearances persisted – unfiltered and unbridled. This continuity is vividly evident in imagery depicting frenzied worship, long-haired followers, antinomian practices, animal-skinned clothing, the thrill of dread, and the euphoria born of fear.

One could say that the memory of his past still clung to him. He was a powerful, wrathful, impetuous god, always associated with disease and destruction, but with the Puranas, in addition, he became generous and bountiful – a beneficent protector, a fulfiller of desires, a giver of food. His terrible might and relentless strength became a shield against all evils for those who knew how to trust him. He retained his old reputation for a love of cremation grounds and austere practices – the divine yogi, surpassing all in rigid asceticism. In the Puranas, for the first time, the lingam appears in literature as the symbol of his creative power, and the skull as the sign of his activity as a destroyer.

In Shiva, two phases of nature's way with humankind are combined in stark realism: one bringing all things into existence through the passionate fires of creative reproduction, the other driving life inexorably toward the dark halls of death. Master of life and lord of death, he became a god of grace and blissful salvation for those who entrusted him with perfect faith and love.

The slayer

When Shiva was incorporated into the Brahmanical fold, his primary characteristic was that of the destroyer. The Puranas presented him as the ultimate slayer of Asuras. The story often started with an Asura, such as Tripurasura, Gajasura, or Bhasmasura, causing chaos in the celestial realm, prompting Shiva to step in as the rescuer.

Psychology also plays an important role in these stories. Ultimately, it is the ego that must be subdued. The episode of Daksha's decapitation demonstrates that mere intellectual knowledge is insufficient; one must also learn the Shaiva way through experience – and, if necessary, punishment.

At a philosophical level, Shiva as the destroyer is not associated with the negative connotations normally tied to "destruction". There is nothing perverse in Shiva's act of destruction.

Indian scholar of comparative religion Arvind Sharma suggests that consummation or transformation, rather than destruction, better captures the essence of Shiva. Destruction, in this sense, can be beneficial: just as evil can be eliminated, so too can illness, misfortune, radical metaphysical ignorance, and the cycle of birth and rebirth.

Thus, Shiva is far from being merely a doomsday god; he is also salvific. The positive role of destruction and annihilation is more clearly defined in Shaiva theology than in the theologies of most other religions. For Shaivites, destruction cleanses, renews, and constructs. It grants the boon of life even as it brings doom and death.

The family man
When Parvati draws Shiva into the household, the domestic life they share is unlike that of any other celestial couple. While there are pairs such as Vishnu and Lakshmi or Radha and Krishna, Shiva is the only divine being who has a fully realized family with whom he resides. He is exceptional, not only in possessing a family, but also in the nature of his interactions with his spouses. His core identity as a renunciant, craving isolation, inevitably disrupts the peace of his married life. Yet many can relate to this trait – most of us seek solitude from time to time to reflect on our thoughts, purpose, or adjustments to changing circumstances. In modern terms, a couple that allows each other space is considered to have a healthy relationship; Shiva had already embodied this practice.

One of the myths that has always moved me is the story of Sati dying at her father's sacrifice. At the end of this story, Shiva, often powerful, virile, and intensely masculine, is shown in one of his most vulnerable forms – overwhelmed with grief, mourning his wife for centuries. As a woman, this affects me strongly, especially knowing how, in the past, men were taught to be stoic, unfeeling, and never shed tears. That vulnerability makes him deeply relatable – a reminder that even the strongest can experience profound loss. I see in him an icon that modern men could emulate, one who embodies strength and the courage to feel.

O Gaura (Parvati), tell us, why should we not
solemnize your wedding with Bhola (Shiva)?
You need not worry about light, dear one,
for Bhola bears a lamp (the Moon) on his forehead.
You need not worry about vehicles,
for Nandi (the bull) is always ready at his door;
you can make him run as much as you like.
You need not worry about water,
for Bhola has a pipeline (the River Ganga) fitted on his head;
you can spill and bathe as much as you wish.
You need not worry about servants,
for ghosts and phantoms are always on hand to serve him;
they will clean your place and attend to you just as you desire.

A folk song in Bundelkhandi

The ascetic

The genius of Shaivism lies in its renouncer traditions. The asceticism that Shiva embodies and proclaims is exceptional, appealing to those who seek a personal, unique path to meditation or stillness – they turn to Shiva as their guide.

Shaiva ideals of asceticism stand in contrast to the Brahmanical, as they are less concerned with situating themselves strictly within the Vedic tradition of elaborate rituals. For those seeking personal salvation, greater credence is given to private norms. The mundane social world and Vedic ritualism is often viewed as synonymous with attachment and bondage. Ritual action, long held in paramount importance in Vedic literature, now faced a rival: knowledge.

In Shaivism, asceticism offers a path to individual mobility and may be the only viable alternative for those wishing to escape the rigid confines of caste society. When Shiva errs by beheading a brahman, he must adopt the life of a mendicant. Yet even in this guise, he remains thoroughly Shaivic: as Bhairava, he frightens all he encounters, almost mocking the punishment in his nude garb and fangs. On one level, he carries out the necessary act of humbling the arrogant; on another, the Brahmanical world reasserts itself, creating the myth of his long penitence for such a grave sin. In this way, Shiva continually moves between two realms, bridging asceticism and society.

From past to present

Over time, Shiva has become one of the most important deities of India. Worship and belief in him grew like a mammoth organism across centuries. During this process of evolution and development, he was alternately enriched and attenuated, culminating in the composite deity we encounter today. The ability of gods like Shiva to encompass such myriad beliefs rests on a historical process of assimilation and a human psychology that allows for this remarkable adaptability.

This is the story of how he endured through the long history of Hinduism. This is the story of how he mutated in order to survive. This is the story of how he was feared. This is the story of how he is loved. This is the story of the making of a god who incorporates this country's key cultural ideas – dance, yoga, music, art, and asceticism. Spanning the esoteric, the psychological, the mundane, and the most obvious to the completely embedded – that is Shiva.

It is all there in Shiva. So I stand, astonished at the humanity that succeeded in putting together the approximation of a godhead so pragmatic in his life stories, so celestial in his being, so abiding for the faithful, so enchanting for the dilettante. If my readers can experience even a glimpse of this, I will be deeply gratified.

Mind–intellect–thought–ego am I not

Nirvana Shatakam, Adi Shankaracharya

1 | THE IDEA
OF SHIVA

△ **A Mohenjo-daro seal** featuring a yogic figure adorned with bangles, believed to represent Shiva.

A CRYPTIC DEITY

Faint seals and cryptic motifs from the ancient Indus Valley Civilization hint at Shiva's primordial form. Yet, the past offers only tantalizing fragments, and no certainties, opening these up for debate and conjecture.

Shiva's appearance in the Indian subcontinent has long been a subject of scholarly discord among historians, archaeologists, and mythologists alike. Even so, one could say that Shiva's origins go back to the Indus Valley Civilization, one of the earliest urban cultures, which flourished in the northwestern region of the Indian subcontinent from c.3300 to 1300 BCE. Excavations at Indus sites have brought to light the representations of what appear to be the earliest foreshadowing of Shiva, and in fact, the first anthropomorphic representation of any Hindu deity. This may very well be the era in which Shiva first became known to humankind. If one were to accept that these are indeed depictions of Shiva, then he becomes the oldest living, worshipped god in the world. Unfortunately, 12 centuries of that history remain obscured, as the Indus script remains undeciphered. The symbols engraved on seals and artefacts are so minute and contextually elusive that a consensus remains out of reach. Therefore, in this process, memory, material evidence, and modern analysis interact in ways that often complicate rather than clarify.

The god of Mohenjo-daro

The depictions appear on steatite seals, the most celebrated being from Mohenjo-daro (in present-day Pakistan), one of the cities of the Indus Valley. Much has been made of this single steatite seal, barely an inch high. Pithily encapsulated, it depicts what appears to be a three-faced figure, seated cross-legged on a low platform, with three eyes and a trident. The figure also appears to be *urdhvalinga*, or ithyphallic. Originally designated as seal number 420, it later became known as the "Pashupati Seal" after English archaeologist Sir John Marshall, who served as the Director-General of the Archaeological Survey of India from 1902 to 1928, identified its central figure as a proto form of Pashupati, a form of Shiva connected to animals.

Shadow of the ascetic

The central figure on the seal is nude and reminiscent of later representations of Shiva, especially his 28th incarnation Lakulisha, who is also always represented nude. The "Pashupati" on the seal is seated in the yogic *Mulabandhasana*, a squatting position with heels joined and knees on the ground, traditionally used to control sexual energy. This yogic identity corresponds with later conceptions of Shiva as Mahayogi, or the Great Ascetic – an epithet found in later texts. Supporting the theory of Shaivic association are other small, independent terracotta figures from the Indus Civilization that also appear in yogic postures.

The horns

The personage on the "Pashupati Seal" seems to have horns, another element that echoes Shaiva symbolism. This is not an isolated rendering as similar motifs appear elsewhere – for instance, a horned mask from Mohenjo-daro; a terracotta bull atop a terracotta cake from Kalibangan (in present-day Rajasthan), another Indus site; and the depiction of a horned deity on a water pitcher from the archaeological site of Kot Diji, in Sindh, Pakistan. Bulls are frequently depicted on Indus seals, and in later tradition, Shiva's mount is Nandi, the bull. This has led many to associate the figure on the seal with Shaivism. British scholar of comparative religion Gavin Flood, a specialist in Shaivism and phenomenology, highlights the theory of Finnish Indologist Asko Parpola, an expert on the Indus script, in his notable work *An Introduction to Hinduism*. Parpola convincingly suggests that the figure on the "Pashupati Seal" is, in fact, a seated bull – almost identical to figures of seated bulls found on early Elamite seals from southwestern Iran, from c.3000–2750 BCE. The Elamite civilization was a contemporary of the early Indus civilization and one of earliest urban

THE IDEA OF SHIVA

△ **A sculpture of a bull,** from the later period of the Indus Valley Civilization.

cultures of ancient Iran. There are, however, alternative Shaivite interpretations regarding the object atop the figure's head on the seal. For some, it appears to be a plant, possibly pointing to a fertility deity. Others see it as a trishula – the trident that later becomes Shiva's primary weapon. The shape of the object has also led some to interpret it as a crescent Moon, linking it to one of Shiva's epithets, Chandrashekhara, meaning "he who wears the Moon on his head". In later iconography, Shiva is often depicted with the crescent Moon, an intriguing resemblance, perhaps, to the bull's horns.

The phallic imagery

The figure on the "Pashupati Seal" also appears to be ithyphallic, that is, depicted with an erect phallus, similar to Shaivic sculptural representations from later periods. However, this remains contentious. Some scholars argue that it could represent something different, such as a belt or the end of a waistband. Given the minuscule scale of the depiction, it is difficult to determine with certainty – so it could be ithyphallic, or just the knot of a dhoti.

Phallic-shaped stones have been found in Indus archaeological contexts. Some are highly polished and oblong, while most are small, and some measure up to 25 inches (2 feet) in height. It remains unclear whether these objects were symbolic representations of the lingam or served more mundane purposes, such as grinding grain.

According to Jan Gonda, a Dutch Indologist and the first Utrecht professor of Sanskrit, certain small, cone-shaped objects made of semi-precious stones, like lapis lazuli, found in the Indus context could plausibly be interpreted as lingams, similar to those still carried by members of the Lingayat tradition (*See pp262–63*) in present-day Hinduism. There are, of course, other interpretations, such as perhaps they were pieces from ancient board games.

A female divinity

However, some scholars have completely rejected the idea of the figure being a male deity, let alone an ithyphallic one. Indian historian Upinder Singh, in her seminal work *A History of Ancient and Early Medieval India*, highlights the theories of Indian historians such as MK Dhavalikar and Shubhangana Atre, who question the figure's gender and suggest it may, in fact, represent a female divinity.

One of the key arguments is that the so-called erect or exposed phallus might actually be a tassel hanging from the waistband, a feature observed in many female terracotta figurines from the Indus Valley. It has been conjectured that the figure on the "Pashupati Seal" represents a mistress of animals, a goddess of beasts and vegetation, possessing the quality of regenerative biological power. Atre even suggests that the figure could embody the archetypal mother, who has the singular command over the existence and destruction of the world. The two extra faces flanking the central visage may not be faces at all, but stylized ears. Atre also says that in Indus terracotta figures, males are typically shown nude, whereas the jewellery worn by the figure on the proto-Pashupati seal is more characteristic of female figurines.

The many faces

Some historians believe the figure on the seal could be tricephalic, further suggesting a connection to Shaivite iconography. This is because an epic-Pauranic epithet of Shiva is Tryambaka, or the "three-eyed", and Shiva is also often referred to as Panchamukha, or "five-faced".

There are, however, two other seals from Mohenjo-daro that depict horned deities wearing bangles and seated in a yogic position. Although the frontal visage is unclear, there appear to be additional faces on each side, making them a second example of a three-faced deity, possibly Shiva, in the Indus Valley Civilization.

▽ **In the background, the remains of a stupa-like stone tower** rise above the urban layout of Mohenjo-daro in southeastern Pakistan. This ancient site holds significance in Shaiva studies, as archaeologists have uncovered several seals and artifacts connected to the god.

A CRYPTIC DEITY | 21

. . . the earliest foreshadowing of Shiva, and in fact, the first anthropomorphic representation of any Hindu deity. . . . the oldest living, worshipped god in the world.

◁ **The Pashupati Seal from Mohenjo-daro** depicting a three-faced, Shiva-like figure in a yogic posture, surrounded by wild animals such as a tiger, elephant, bull, and rhinoceros. It also features prominent horns that are considered precursors to the crescent moon symbol in later Shaiva iconography.

THE LORD OF ANIMALS

Shiva first enters his mythology as a watchful hunter – camouflaged in the wilderness, draped in animal hide. He carries the bow and arrows, or the trident – weapons from a world shaped by the hunt. In him, the divine is not separate from the wilderness.

△ **An 1830 painting of an eight-armed Shiva** dancing within a red, oval-shaped background, representing the flayed hide of Gajasura. He wields multiple weapons, with his hair styled in a *jatamukuta*, from which three strands of hair fly loose on each side.

As the lord of animals, Shiva is Pashupati. The very first time we come across this label or name, chronologically, is when a personage, surrounded by animals, on a small Indus seal is declared to be Pashupati – or at the most, proto Pashupati. The animals include wild species such as the rhinoceros, water buffalo, tiger, and elephant, as well as domesticated ones like the deer and goat. The identification appears to be based entirely on the fact that, in later texts, Pashupati is an epithet of Shiva associated with a particular sect.

Protector or punisher

While Shiva's connection with animals is well-established, interpretations vary. One view suggests that Rudra (*See pp74–77*), the early form of Shiva, in Vedic literature, does not protect wild animals. Instead, his predominant trait toward them is wrath. In contrast, Indian archaeologist Shereen Ratnagar, known for her work on early Indian history, states that the Vedic figure of Pashupati is the protector of domestic cattle, safeguarding them while they graze, and that he was not associated with dangerous creatures of dense forests.

Draped in animal skin

Shiva's proximity to animals evolved over time, starting from the *Rig Veda*, the oldest Sanskrit text composed between 1500 BCE and 1000 BCE, where he is identified as a hunter. By the 6th century, this process seems complete, with paintings and sculptures showing all possible animal creatures gathered on his very being. For instance, he is shown seated on or wearing animal skin. It symbolizes many aspects – his mastery over primal instincts and harmony with nature's raw power, but also that he is on par with, and yet imbibing the power of, the creature by keeping it so close to himself.

This can be seen in the visuals called Gajaha or Gajasamharamurti – Shiva dancing on an elephant's head while holding up the animal skin. The story goes that once there was an Asura named Gajasura – *gaja* means "elephant". Shiva fought, slayed, and tore off Gajasura's skin, wrapping it around his body. It was crumpled, dripping blood and fat, and unfit to be tanned to be used as leather. Indian mythologist Devdutt Pattanaik, in his work *Devlok with Devdutt Pattanaik*, states that while originally it was elephant skin, over the years artists changed it to deer or tiger skin, as the yellow colour of the deer and tiger was more attractive than black.

There is another episode that explains the animal skin connection. Once, in the hidden pine forest of Daruvana, sages and their wives were meditating. Suddenly Shiva appeared and attracted the wives with his beauty. Alarmed, the sages ignited a fire and created a tiger out of it, flinging it at Shiva. He tore it to pieces with his little finger and wore its skin as a lower garment.

Association with snakes

In countless depictions, Shiva has a snake on his body. It is believed that once, the snake species was in danger and they approached Shiva for shelter. Compassionate as ever, Shiva allowed them to reside at his mountain abode, Kailasha. However, due to the extreme cold of the region, the snakes sought the warmth of Shiva's body. As their protector, Shiva allowed them to coil around his chest, where they now slither up and

THE LORD OF ANIMALS | 23

◁ **A 20th-century bronze sculpture of a triumphant Shiva** standing on the defeated Gajasura. He wields six weapons in his six hands, even as his other two hands hold up the elephant's skin. This depiction of Shiva encapsulated within the elephant's hide is typical of South Indian painting traditions from the 19th century onwards, particularly from the Mysore, Tiruchirapalli, and Tanjore schools.

down freely. As Pashupati, the lord of animals, Shiva has complete control over their behaviour. Since the snake is one of the most feared and dangerous creatures in the world, the garland of snakes around Shiva's neck symbolizes his supreme power – even the snakes, embodiments of fear themselves, are under his command.

The mount

Shiva's bond with animals is also seen in his entourage, especially his vahana, mount. The bull Nandi, ever-present in Shiva temples, sits facing the Shiva lingam, gazing at it with devotion, like a guardian. In fact, the only known Shiva temple in India without a Nandi statue is the Kapaleshwar Shiva Temple in Nashik, Maharashtra – though even here, a separate Nandi temple stands nearby. Nandi represents patience, strength, and unwavering devotion. Shiva's other forms are also linked to animals. For instance, Bhairava (*See pp240–41*), his fierce form, is depicted with a dog as his vahana. In keeping with this association, the practice of feeding stray dogs near Bhairava temples continues even today, as the dog is regarded as sacred and has a close bond with Shiva.

… his mastery over primal instincts and harmony with nature's raw power, but also that he is on par with, and yet imbibing the power of, the creature by keeping it so close to himself.

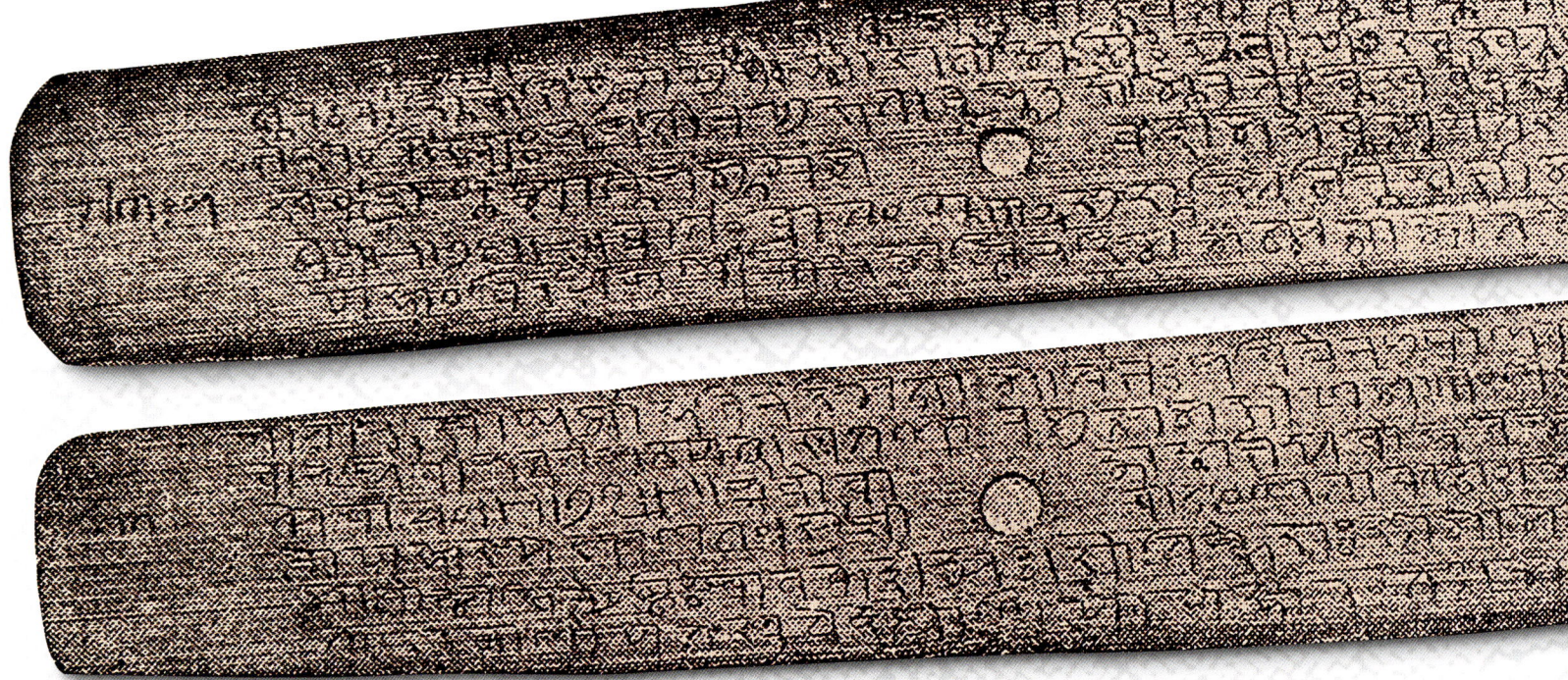

HIS EMERGING IDENTITY

First, Shiva was Rudra – *ghora*, or terrifying. He was a god of contradictions – destroyer and healer, wrathful and compassionate. Over time, the Vedic Rudra evolved into the complex cosmic force known as Shiva, but the seeds of that transformation were sown in the early Hindu texts – Vedas and Upanishads.

When analyzing early Vedic literature by the number of hymns dedicated to each deity, Shiva, as Rudra, appears to be a relatively minor figure compared to deities such as Indra, the god of thunder and rain, and Agni, the god of fire. Yet, he holds an arresting presence, particularly in the *Rig Veda*. The hymns that invoke him emphasize his terrifying nature. Dreadful and destructive forces of nature – violent storms, howling winds, raging fires, piercing thunderbolts, devastating epidemics, and sweeping floods – inspired awe among the Vedic seers, who personified these forces as the formidable Rudra.

He is referred to as *asau devata*, or "that god", a euphemism reflecting the dread of even saying his name. The sages often avoided naming him directly, using the adjective "rudric" instead. He was never invited to their sacrifices, as they feared his presence might provoke disaster – that the fire might suddenly flare up and engulf them. And yet, paradoxically, they also called Rudra the "king of the sacrifice". The fearsome Rudra, however, could transform into a benign force – Shiva – through human prayer. This transformation is first evident in the *Rig Veda*. In the Vedas, Rudra is not merely a god of destruction but a cosmic force of transformation and healing. Known as Sharva, the divine archer wielding bow and arrows, he shoots shafts of disease and death, yet devotees also implore him for healing. This dual role illustrates the Hindu belief that the deity that inflicts a sickness, is also the one who cures it. This connection extends to a later date Shiva, who is also revered as Vaidyanathan, the best physician of physicians and bearer of a thousand cures.

Beginnings of his form

Another important reference is a hymn called "Shatarudriya" of the *Yajur Veda*. It is, in fact, the oldest document of rising Shaivism. It contains

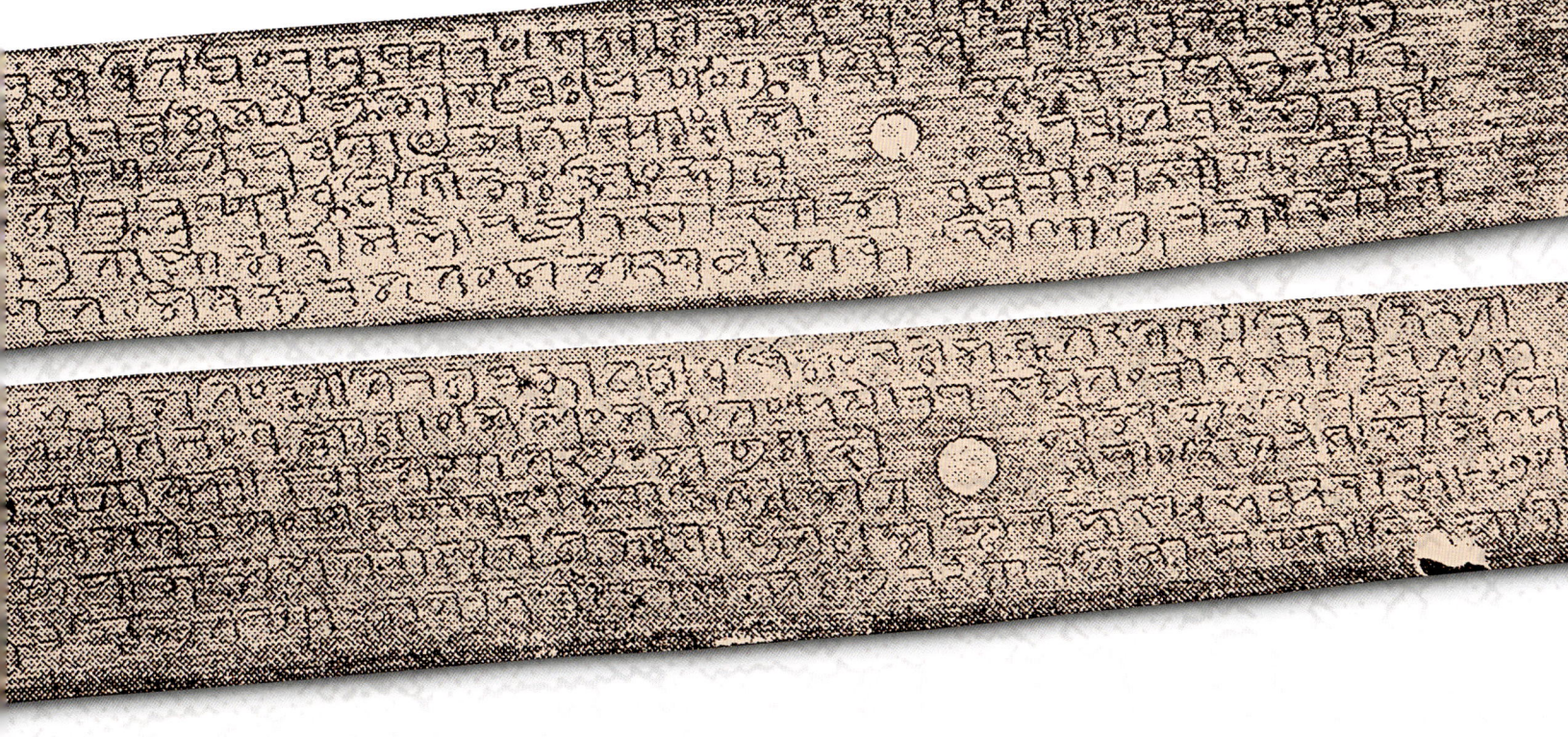

△ **A *Rig Veda* manuscript** from the 16th century.

100 names of Shiva, many of which form the roots of myths later elaborated in the Puranas. This hymn brings together various conceptions of Shiva and is an early example of enumerating a deity's divine names to establish a connection with them. It was likely composed by those who found little satisfaction in Vedic ritualism and instead sought bliss and salvation through a personal god, a deity who transcended schematic approximation and could be vocalized and visualized as an image.

Shiva's supreme role

The final part of the Vedas is the Upanishads. In the Shaivite context, the *Shvetashvatara Upanishad* is perhaps the most important as it identifies Rudra as the Supreme Deity. As Indian spiritual teacher Eknath Easwaran notes in *The Upanishads*, it begins by addressing the Supreme Being with the Shaivic Vedic terms "Rudra", "Isha", or "Ishvara", and soon introduces the name Shiva. Indian monk Swami Gambhirananda, in his translation of the text, notes that it explores Shiva's role in creation, sustenance, destruction, and spiritual liberation. Twice in the text, the same verse states Rudra as the origin and source of the divine powers of the gods, protector of the universe, and the great seer. Two verses claim Ishana, another name of Shiva, presides over all forms of yonis – an allusion to the physical fact of lingam and yoni connected together. The *Shvetashvatara Upanishad* also seems to provide the first instance of bhakti, or devotion. For the first time, Rudra appears as an object of monotheistic devotion.

In the minor Upanishads

There are five other Upanishads – *Atharvashiras*, *Atharvashikha*, *Nilarudra*, *Kalagnirudra*, and *Kaivalya* – that extol Shiva as a symbol of Atman, or self. They emphasize Shiva as the Supreme God, the one without beginning, middle, or end, and the source of all creation and existence.

The *Kaivalya Upanishad* delineates the all-pervasive nature of Shiva. Its first chapter answers the question, "Who is Rudra?" He is introduced as that which existed at first, exists now, and shall exist in the future, the east and the west, masculine and feminine, appearance and reality, water and fire, cow and buffalo, within and without, the inner essence of everything. The text asserts that all gods are Rudra, everyone and everything is Rudra, and Rudra is the principle in all things.

The *Kaivalya Upanishad* underscores the yogic aspects of Shiva. The Sanskrit word *kaivalya* means "aloneness, isolation" and therefore, this text highlights detachment from the world and the attainment of inner peace and bliss through realizing one's identity with Shiva.

△ **The blue-skinned Vishnu** decides to incarnate as Rama during a feast of the gods as depicted in this Pahari painting from c.1810 that recreates a scene from the Bala Kanda chapter of the *Ramayana*. Shiva can be seen in the foreground with a snake around his neck, eating with his Ganas.

THE ONE WHO LISTENS

Shiva's role within the *Mahabharata* and the *Ramayana* is integral to the story. He brings balance and harmony. He protects and empowers, forgives and absolves, and even administers justice, irrespective of who they may be – Rama or Ravana, Pandavas or Kauravas, Devas or Asuras.

Vishnu may be the titular deity in India's greatest epics – the *Ramayana* and the *Mahabharata* – but Shiva's presence and influence in these stories is undeniable. Devas and Asuras, kings and Rakshasas, all turn to him as his ardent devotees, praying for divine, indestructible weapons, victories in battles, strength, and sometimes, even redemption. In turn, Shiva, though gracious with boons, acts as the greatest of levellers, who keeps them in check, cuts through arrogance, breaks down egos, and maintains the cosmic balance.

One of the most unusual, yet fascinating of such relationships, not just in the epics but Hindu mythology as a whole, is the one Shiva shared with Ravana, the mighty king of Lanka and chief antagonist in the *Ramayana*. Foe to Rama, an

. . . Shiva, though gracious with boons, acts as the greatest of levellers . . . cuts through arrogance, breaks down egos, and maintains cosmic balance.

avatar of Vishnu and one of the Trinity, he is also one of Shiva's greatest devotees. His devotion was so intense that he composed the *Shiva Tandava Stotram*, a powerful hymn praising Shiva's cosmic dance. There are myriad stories of Ravana, of his devotion to Shiva, and his attempts to outdo the god, only to be put in his place of subservience.

In fervent prayer

Among them is the myth of Ravana who tried to uproot Mount Kailasha, Shiva's place of residence, when it came in the way of his Pushpak Vimana or aerial vehicle. His arrogant attempt was thwarted when Shiva pressed down with his toe, crushing the king. Shiva released him only when he sang his praise and became a devotee. There are several variations to this story, of course. One of them tells of Ravana wanting to move the mountain as he found it troublesome to go there every day to pray to his favourite lord. He tried to save himself the daily arduous journey and also demonstrate his strength. Shiva allowed him to lift Kailasha so that Parvati would hold him tight out of fear, thus providing him the pleasure of an unusual embrace. Then, amused and unperturbed, Shiva pressed the mountain and Ravana with his toe. The king shrieked in pain, acquiring the name Ravana or the Shrieker.

Another legend tells of a time when Ravana, desiring immortality, performed intense penance to obtain the Atmalinga, a divine representation of Shiva's essence. Satisfied with his devotion, Shiva granted it to him so that he could take it to his island kingdom to install. With it, both Ravana and his kingdom Lanka would be unconquerable. Shiva warned him against placing the lingam on the ground before reaching his destination. However, Ravana was tricked and once on the ground it became rooted at Gokarna in Karnataka.

There is also the instance when Ravana, to express his devotion for Shiva, fashioned a lute using one of his 10 heads as the gourd, one of his arms as the neck, and his nerves as the strings. He called this the Rudra Vina and used it to compose music for the *Rudra stotra*.

HANUMAN

Hanuman is believed to be the son of Kesari and Anjana with the wind god Vayu playing a significant role in his birth. However, some regard him as an incarnation of Shiva, or the Rudra Avatara. In the *Shiva Purana*, Shiva's seed shed at the sight of the enchanting nymph Mohini, which the seven rishis gathered and placed in the ear of a monkey woman who then gave birth to Hanuman. Unlike an ordinary *tapasvi*, or one who practices austerities, who uses the power of *tapas* – siddhi or spiritual powers – for personal gain, Hanuman uses it to help those who come to him, notes mythologist Devdutt Pattanaik.

▽ **A devotee dressed as Hanuman** gets ready to attend a religious procession in Prayagraj, India to commemorate the god.

Today, temples dedicated to Shiva often paint their walls with images of Ravana to demonstrate that even villains, Asuras, and Rakshasas seek the grace of the god.

The great leveller

Shiva's grace can turn like it did during the battle between Rama and Ravana. Rama found that he was losing ground, because of Ravana's protective sheath, a gift from Shiva. So, he prayed to the god and performed many austerities while begging Shiva to abandon his devotee. The story goes that the god told Rama that Ravana would fall on the seventh day of the final battle. So readily did Shiva give in to Rama's request, that Parvati became furious at the god's fickle nature. Ravana did fall – all the fruits of his asceticism were used up – just as Rama struck him with a magic arrow, notes ethnologist Wolf-Dieter Storl in his book, *Shiva: The Wild God of Power and Ecstasy*.

Despite his unwavering devotion, Ravana's pride and unchecked ambition led to his downfall. His story serves as a powerful reminder that true devotion requires humility, and even the most powerful beings must respect divine forces.

Religious studies scholar, Diana L Eck notes in her book *India: a Sacred Geography* that there are several references to Rama being a Shiva devotee as well, perhaps not in Valmiki's *Ramayana*, but in some vernacular versions, such as the Sanskrit *Adhyatma Ramayana*, Tulsidas' *Ramacharitamanas*, and Bengali poet Krittibas Ojha's *Krittibasi Ramayana*, which is dated around the 15th and 16th century, when devotion towards Rama flourished. This relationship, Eck notes has been best articulated in a popular saying at Chitrakut, Madhya Pradesh, one of the many locations associated with Rama's exile. Attributed to Tulsidas, the saying goes, "Shiva's best bhakta is Rama and Rama's best bhakta is Shiva."

From a place of righteousness

Shiva has a place of reverence within the *Mahabharata* as well – not only among the two warring families, Pandavas and Kauravas – but also as one who grants boons. He makes appearances as a hunter or Kirata, as the lingam, and even as a dancer. While not directly involved in the great war at Kurukshetra, he plays a crucial role in shaping its events and his blessings and influence are felt throughout. His role as the destroyer and cosmic force aligns with the themes of war, destruction, and renewal, which the Kurukshetra war embodies. He is revered as a divine guide and protector, often appearing to test and bless warriors. His role highlights the importance of devotion, humility, and righteousness in the epic.

Different characters in the epic often invoke Shiva in prayers and rituals. The myth of Kiratarjuniya *(See pp32–33)* is one such instance where Arjuna, the great warrior, appealed to Shiva to obtain powerful arrows that would turn the tide of the battle. The god, disguised as a Kirata or hunter, assessed Arjuna's character to see if he was worthy before granting him the celestial weapon.

Shiva's influence extended beyond the war. After the Pandavas defeated the Kauravas, they wished to atone for their sins and searched for Shiva to seek his blessings. Shiva ignored their prayers as he was incensed by the death and dishonesty during the war. Instead, he assumed the form of a bull and hid in the Himalayas. They built the Panch Kedar temples in his honour *(See pp310–11)* before meditating at Kedarnath for salvation.

Towards the end of the epic in the *Mahaprasthanika Parva*, as the Pandavas embarked on their final journey, Shiva, it is believed, accompanied them in the form of a dog, as a way of testing their virtue before granting them liberation.

▷ **A scene from the *Mahabharata*,** c.1825–40, from the Indian School, titled "Arjuna's Penance". It depicts the warrior in armour, while Shiva, holding a bow, can be seen in the distance with his trusted companion, Nandi.

▷ **Ravana, with his many heads and holding the musical instrument veena,** lifts Mount Kailasha on his back in this sculpture from the Annamalaiyar Temple in Thiruvannamalai, Tamil Nadu.

RAVANANUGRAHA

OF BENEVOLENCE AND REDEMPTION

Shiva sat with Parvati on top of Mount Kailasha, their home, but the moment of quiet was broken when the many-armed, 10-headed Ravana began lifting the mountain. The king of Lanka attempted to uproot it to use it as a magic dynamo of energy in his great battle against Rama. But, Shiva pressed down his big toe and imprisoned Ravana.

This myth is a popular theme in Indian sculptures and temple carvings from the Gupta–Pallava era, dated around 300–600 CE. Called Ravananugraha, it often features in manuscript paintings and temple sculptures, especially Hoysala art, from southern India, known for its ornate, detailed sculptures.

The composition of the sculpture is often divided into two sections. The upper section depicts Shiva and Parvati seated on Mount Kailasha, with the lower focusing on Ravana lifting the mountain.

The details vary. Some renditions depict Parvati clinging to her husband, arms flung around him. Shiva is calm, comforting her with one or two arms. In some, he holds a trishula or makes the *abhayamudra* symbolizing divine protection. The couple are seated on a lotus pedestal and some versions depict Shiva holding Parvati's chin in an affectionate manner. The mountain itself is a pile of rocks or an elaborate multi-tiered structure. Sometimes, attendants and Ganas accompany the couple, as do the divine children Ganesha and Karttikeya. Ravana is shown as a strong man lifting the mountain with all his might, and occasionally with an expression of frustration or pain.

A classic rendition of this myth is seen at the Kailasha Temple in the Ellora caves from the fifth century. In it, the upper section has a seated four-armed Shiva seated with Parvati, with a 10-headed, multi-armed Ravana in the lower section. Art historian Vidya Dehejia, in *Indian Art*, notes the marvellous theatrical effect where the image of Ravana in one relief panel is detached from its background so that the action takes place on a deeply shadowed stone stage.

Meaning

Ravananugraha means "Shiva's grace upon Ravana", revealing the god's more benevolent aspect. It also symbolizes the power of devotion and the possibility of redemption. Ravana's attempt to lift the mountain ends in failure and he remains imprisoned for a thousand years. Ravana, a devotee of Shiva, sings hymns in praise of the lord who, pleased, blesses and releases him.

△ **Ravananugrahamurti** or a statue depicting Shiva quelling Ravana from the last quarter of the 10th century.

◁ **Shiva, dressed as a hunter**, and Parvati, bless Arjuna with divine weapons in this 1913 lithograph titled "Kirat Arjuna" by pioneering modern Indian artist Nandalal Bose.

KIRATARJUNIYAM

THE DIVINE IN THE UNEXPECTED

Nothing could distract Arjuna, the great warrior, as he practised severe austerities seeking divine weapons from Shiva. He remained unmoved, focused in his devotion, until Shiva decided to test his might and skill. Mookasura, disguised as a wild boar, attacked Arjuna and the warrior felled him with his arrow, as did Shiva, dressed as a hunter. A battle broke out between the two, until Arjuna, realizing that the hunter was Shiva in disguise, surrendered, and the pleased god blessed him.

This story, a part of 6th-century poet Bharavi's Sanskrit *mahakavya* or epic poem *Kiratarjuniyam*, is a masterclass in layered symbolism – where every character, action, and setting becomes a metaphor for inner transformation. At its heart, it dramatizes the tension between ego and surrender, human effort and divine grace, and the illusory duality between the self and the absolute.

If Arjuna's penance, the intense *tapasya* or austerity he practises in the forest represents the disciplined seeker's journey inward, his one-legged stance and stillness reflects the yogic ideal of unwavering focus and detachment from worldly distractions.

Mookasura, the Asura disguised as a wild boar, stands for the primal, instinctual forces that disrupt spiritual focus. Arjuna and the Kirata or Shiva as they kill the Asura simultaneously are symbolic of the convergence of human will and divine intervention in overcoming inner obstacles. Shiva's disguise as a tribal hunter is meaningful as well. The Kirata, often seen as uncivilized or outside the Vedic fold, represents the wild, untamed aspect of divinity – a reminder that the sacred is not confined to temples or rituals. It also challenges Arjuna's ego – would he be able to recognize the divine in the unexpected? And so, the setting itself becomes a metaphor for inner transformation.

Iconography

This test of devotion is a favourite subject in Indian temple sculpture, especially in South India. One striking example is found at the Ulsoor Someshwara Temple in Bengaluru. The sculptural sequence begins with Arjuna in deep penance, standing on one leg with matted hair and arms raised. Mookasura disturbs his meditation. Both Arjuna and the Kirata (Shiva) shoot the boar, leading to the confrontation and eventual realization of the hunter's true identity. The scene culminates in Shiva and Parvati bestowing the Pashupatastra, a divine weapon, upon Arjuna.

In Kerala, exquisite wooden panels in temples depicting this tale often include rare iconographic elements like Harihara, emphasizing the unity of divine forces and the layered nature of Arjuna's spiritual journey.

▽ **A 12th-century relief depicting** Arjuna worshipping Shiva and killing Mookasura.

Maha Shivaratri, the sacred night of Shiva, commemorates several important events, including his divine wedding, the cosmic Tandava dance, and the swallowing of Halahala poison. Devotees perform *Rudrabhishekam*, a ritual where the lingam is bathed with water, milk, honey, and ghee, as sacred mantras echo, honouring Shiva in his Rudra form. Here, a priest pours milk over Shiva's idol, decorated with rudrakshas, during Maha Shivaratri prayers.

SHIVA'S TRANSFORMATION

Once a shadowy figure on the fringes of the Vedic pantheon, Shiva rose from obscurity to become one of the most revered deities in the Hindu cosmic tapestry. His ascendancy reached its zenith in the Puranas, where he emerges in full glory – majestic and awe-inspiring amidst a multitude of celestial beings.

The Puranas embody the received tradition of Hindu mythology. They were informally memorized as compared to the precision of the Vedas and were frequently added to and were converted to their present textual form in the early millennium CE. Intended for those who could not read the text, many times they are written in the form of queries and answers, explanations, and episodes, with simple analysis.

Like other major divinities, Shiva also has specific Puranas dedicated to him, such as the *Linga Purana*, composed in the 5th–10th centuries and the *Shiva Purana*, composed in the 10th–11th centuries. The fully developed portrayal of Shiva in the Puranas is most clearly seen in a section of the *Linga Purana* called the *Shiva Sahasranama* (See pp38–39). This hymn is a litany of a thousand epithets that encapsulate Shiva's cosmic role, mythology, and philosophical dimensions. Some of these appear to be names of numerous regional and local deities as epithets of Shiva, emphasizing his all-encompassing and universal nature.

Shiva and Shakti

The Puranas essentially serve to characterize and conceptualize Shiva, outlining key ideas central to his divine persona and worship. Through these narratives, Shiva's identity becomes more fully developed, both in his solitary ascetic form and in relation to other powerful deities. One of the most imperative elements that the Puranas bring forth in Shiva's mythology is his association

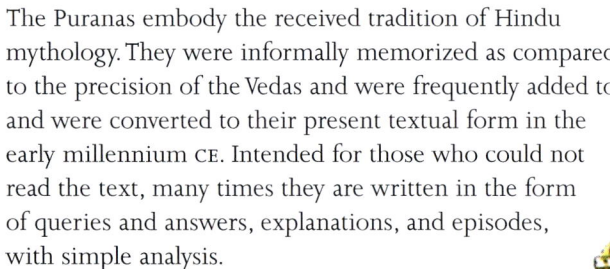

SHIVA'S TRANSFORMATION

... Through these narratives, Shiva's identity becomes more fully developed, both in his solitary ascetic form and in relation to other powerful deities.

with the powerful and influential Goddess Shakti. Through various episodes, Shakti – first as Sati and later as Parvati – plays a vital role in the evolution and glorification of Shiva. It is the Puranas that establish Uma, another name for Parvati, and Shankar, a form of Shiva, as the primordial parents of the world. The idea projected is that their relationship is about the dynamic interplay of energies – their union reflects not just harmony, but also moments of tension and friction. The underlying tension can be seen in several Puranic episodes such as their game of *chausara*, or dice, and the circumstances surrounding the birth of their son Ganesha (See pp176–77).

Apart from the mythological developments, the Puranas, especially the *Linga Purana*, also delve into philosophical discussions around Shiva and Shakti, embodied in the lingam. Together, the two are presented as custodians of cosmic balance and their union is understood to be the fundamental principle of creation.

The symbol of the lingam

Over the centuries, the lingam has become the most ubiquitous emblem of Shiva. The Puranas were significant in inducting and legitimizing this icon – which may have been a novel theological idea at the time – by putting forth numerous explanations and stories of the greatness of the phallus emblem. Apart from details on holy sites, pilgrimage routes, and temples associated with Shiva, the *Shiva Purana* makes clear that the worship of the lingam is the simplest and most uncomplicated way to attain salvation. It also emphasizes that while the other deities are worshipped only in their embodied form, Shiva is unique as he is worshipped both in his anthropomorphic or embodied form, and in the phallic or lingam form.

The *Linga Purana* glorifies the lingam with great ingenuity and fervour as well. It outlines the detailed rituals associated with its worship. To establish the supremacy of the lingam, the text recounts many compelling narratives. Among them is the dramatic episode in which Shiva seeks to demonstrate the might of the lingam by castrating himself in front of the sages of Daruvana. In the aftermath, the lingam becomes fiery and uncontrollable, only to be calmed once consecrated through obeisance in the rightful manner.

The fiery link

As the phallic symbolism was unpalatable to some, the Puranas presented an alternate interpretation by associating it with *agni*, or fire. Fire was chosen for its prominence in Vedic tradition, where it served as the mouth of the gods, carrying offerings to them. This symbolic connection provided legitimacy and validation. In the Puranic context, Shiva became the divine recipient of these offerings, thus reinforcing a ritualistic and theological unity between the two. This is elaborated in the myth of Shiva's son, Karttikeya's birth, (See pp178–79) where Agni carried Shiva's seed, but found it scorching hot and deposited it in the waters of Ganga. In another celebrated tale from the *Linga Purana*, Shiva manifested as an infinite pillar of fire to settle a dispute between Brahma and Vishnu.

This adaptation facilitated the dissemination of Shaiva philosophy across diverse social and cultural groups. The Puranas established Shiva's supreme authority and ensured that he was revered as Mahadeva – the God of Gods – in ways that were accessible and relatable to all.

◁ **A painting depicting the tale of Lingodbhava.** Vishnu, on the right, and Brahma, on the left, are engaged in a fierce contest for supremacy. At the centre, Shiva manifests as an infinite pillar of light, and challenges them to find its extremes. Brahma transforms into a swan, soaring upwards to find its peak, while Vishnu takes the form of a boar, burrowing deep into the earth to reach its base.

SHIVA SAHASRANAMA

A HYMN CARVED FROM ETERNITY

951. The Atman of the deities
952. The self-born
953. One who has come up
954. One who has taken three steps
955. Physician
956. Granter of boons
957. Born of Vishnu
958. In the form
959. Worthy of being worshipped
960. Elephant
961. Tiger
962. Lion among Devas
963. Great bull
964. Leader among Devas
965. God
966. Excellent
967. Lord of the heaven
968. The most excellent one
969. United
970. Splendid
971. Eloquent speaker

From *The Linga-Purana*, edited by JL Shastri

The *Shiva Sahasranama*, a sacred Sanskrit *stotram* or hymn of praise, has 1000 names for Shiva, capturing his divine attributes and mythology, and revealing his multiple facets. Each name is a mantra, a beautiful expression of divine paradox – fierce but compassionate, formless yet all-encompassing. This sacred litany is more than just a devotional chant – it draws the seeker into Shiva's mystery – a path of inner transformation, transcendence, and surrender. As the names unfold, they reflect the soul's journey through creation, destruction, and rebirth, eventually fading into the quiet where only Shiva remains.

More than a hymn

In Hindu tradition, a *Sahasranama* is more than a litany – it is a devotional cascade of 1000 names, each a facet of the divine. It offers not just praise but a deep, meditative immersion into the nature of a deity. The *Shiva Sahasranama* unfolds Shiva's luminous forms – fierce, gentle, cosmic, and transcendent. Every name carries layers of myth, philosophy, and power, evoking Shiva's vast presence in the universe and within the seeker. Reciting it becomes a spiritual journey, mapping the infinite through sacred sound.

More than names

The *stotram* appears in sacred texts such as the *Shiva Purana*, *Linga Purana*, *Vayu Purana*, and most notably, the *Mahabharata*. Far from a fixed canon, this hymn unfolds in at least eight distinct variations – each reflecting a unique vision of Shiva's boundless nature. Yet, it is the version found in Book 13, Anushasana Parva of the *Mahabharata* that is revered as the most authoritative. Chanted in temples, whispered in solitude, or recited in ritual, the hymn becomes a living act of devotion. These names, though, are not mere titles. They are a rich tapestry that draws in a multitude of traditions, deities, and local beliefs, unifying them under Shiva's expansive, divine persona. Some names such as Tripurasurasamhara or Gajasamhara, evoke his cosmic battles, while others reveal his profound symbolism. Ardhanarishvara, symbolizes the union of masculine and feminine while Bholenatha means "the innocent lord". Still more paint vivid images from his iconography – Kamandaludhara meaning "holder of the water pot", Banahasta meaning "archer," and Kapalavan, "bearer of skulls".

Unlike Vishnu, Shiva may not be known for a structured set of avataras – but his transformations are no less profound. In moments of cosmic crisis, Shiva emerges in fierce, unexpected forms – raw, primal expressions of divine will. These manifestations, often terrifying and awe-inspiring, reflect not just destruction, but a deeper, transformative power. For the devout, their meaning runs deeper than fear; they are symbols of protection, justice, and the annihilation of inner darkness. Each form, though seemingly wild or wrathful, reveals the limitless ways in which Shiva is envisioned – shaped not by doctrine, but by the imagination, devotion, and need of the worshipper.

▷ **A devotee worshipping the lingam** enshrined in the sanctum of the Mahakuteshwara Temple in Badami, Karnataka, where it is continuously bathed by the waters of a natural spring-fed tank.

△ **A gouache painting of the three-headed Trimurti,** with Shiva in the centre, Vishnu on the left, and Brahma on the right. Shiva's prominence is evident from the presence of his mount, Nandi, unlike that of the two other deities.

THE DIVINE TRINITY

The concept of multiple deities coming together in one body is an interesting characteristic in Hindu religious art and myth. The idea is for the worshipper to recognize the oneness of the divine. Among the most well-known examples of this divine convergence is the Trimurti, in which Shiva holds a central and indispensable place.

Depicting the "three forms" of God, the Trimurti shows divinity as a three-faced figure. It is represented as one body with three heads branching from one neck, each gazing in a different direction. These three faces represent God's responsibility for the cosmic functions of *srishti*, or creation; *sthiti*, or preservation; and *samhara*, or destruction, which are associated with Brahma, the source or creator, who is at the centre; Vishnu, the preserver, to the left; and Shiva, the destroyer and transformer, to the right. What makes them unique is that they are separate, yet interconnected. These three personae are thought to represent different modalities of the same one supreme divinity and, therefore, considered three forms of the same God.

Since time is looked upon as being cyclical, each phase follows the other, in what appears a natural continuum. The Trimurti symbolizes the cycle of existence where everything is created, maintained, and eventually transformed and dissolved to make way for new beginnings. At the existential individual level, the Trimurti represents aspects of human existence – birth, life, and death.

At the same time, there are several other frameworks through which their relationship can be understood. One such framework makes Brahma the embodiment of *rajas guna*, that is the passions and desires by whose means the world came into being; Vishnu the embodiment of *sattva guna*, that is the qualities of mercy and goodness by means of which the world is maintained; and Shiva the embodiment of *tamas guna*, that is the qualities of darkness, rage, and destructive force by which the world will be destroyed. British historian John Dowson describes the Trimurti in his *A Classical Dictionary of Hindu Mythology and Religion* as three in one and one in three.

The beginning

The emergence of the concept of Trimurti was perhaps a deliberate attempt to reconcile the major Hindu deities of the time into one universal Godhead. It was hoped that this would alleviate and minimize the spiritual competition among devotees, and hopefully promote unity and harmony.

Until the creation of the Trimurti, Vishnu, Shiva, and to a lesser extent, Brahma, were recognized under varying names dependent upon the particular locality in which they were being worshipped. The resultant forms of Shiva and Vishnu were the amalgamation of scattered folk cult traditions mixed with Vedic inspiration. Through a process of mutual osmosis, this fusion helped keep the popularity of most gods intact. Eventually, they came to subsume the names and traits of deities with whom they shared a similar nature through the agency of popular mediums such as poetry, mythology or art. For example, several of Shiva's alternative monikers, such as Veerbhadra and Bhairava, have been identified with Shiva-like regional deities, such as Khandoba of Maharashtra and Mallara of Andhra Pradesh. As these local gods rose to pre-eminence within the popular traditions in various regions, their attributes became coordinated with the powers which had been attributed

△ **A sandstone Brahman Stela** depicting the Trimurti, from the 2nd–7th century.

to Upanishadic Vedantic Brahman, the ultimate reality beyond all duality, and they too came to represent the Supreme Personal Being.

From fluid beliefs to Puranic doctrine

It was not until the arrival of the Puranas that the Trimurti became a standard doctrine. There is little specific mythology associated with this form, but it is briefly mentioned in this corpus. The first explicit reference of the three gods' essential oneness as constituents of the supreme principle comes from the *Vishnu Purana*. It describes how the supreme reality entity manifests in three forms to fulfil different cosmic functions. As Romanian historian Mircea Eliade notes in the *Encyclopedia of Religion*, even *Padma Purana*, which accords prominence to Vishnu, states that at the onset of creation, as the supreme Vishnu wished to form the entire world, he became threefold – the creator, the maintainer, and the destroyer. In order to form this world, the supreme spirit produced Brahma from his right side.

The rise and retreat

Even though the Puranas solidified the concept of Trimurti, there were limits to accommodation and syncretism, and relations between different religious communities were not always harmonious. Indian historian DD Kosambi in *The Culture and Civilization of Ancient India in Historical Outline* says that this image apparently failed to reconcile the growing antagonism between the two different classes of larger and smaller landholders, which appeared as a theological quarrel between the worshippers of Shiva and Vishnu. Moreover, at no time was the Trimurti itself actually worshipped. Since the 16th century the god Dattatreya – a deity who has historically been associated with yoga practice and often depicted with three heads representing Brahma, Vishnu, and Shiva – has been considered to be an avatar of the Trimurti, but the concept never became popular. Individual deities continued to be worshipped rather than the singular Trimurti.

This is probably because each individual feels their chosen deity is capable of all the three tasks. In Hinduism, each individual has the freedom to know the Supreme Truth in the best way they prefer. The individual freedom to know God negates such forced amalgamation.

Since the concept never gained much popularity, there are few ground-level depictions of the Trimurti. It is more common to find the image of the Devi. In the rare cases when the Trimurti is depicted, Brahma's head is replaced by that of the Devi.

Brahma, the silent pillar

The fact that the Trimurti never gained widespread devotional traction is reflected in the marginal role of Brahma as creator. It became an empty honour once the universe came to be seen as an eternal recurrence of vast cycles of change governed by karma. Priests might praise Brahma as the Supreme One, the Mighty, the All-Seeing, the Lord of All, the Maker, the Creator, but the ordinary folk, whose eyes were open to the sorrows of life, expressed doubt and distrust of his worthiness as a god. His worship was shadowed by doubts: why does Brahma not set his creatures right if he is indeed powerful. Why are his creatures condemned to pain, why is everyone not happy? Why do fraud, lies, and ignorance prevail? The prevailing idea that gained ground was that no god created or controlled the world. This is one of the reasons why Brahma fell back into a place of relative unimportance, while Vishnu and Shiva rose to take their places among the few who have been able to weather the storms of history until modern times. They knew how to kindle the fires of devotion in the hearts of people. The sickness of karma could not touch them, for their worship offered the promise of release from earthly suffering and the hope of eternal joy in heaven. As British mythologist A Eustace Haydon notes in *Biography of the Gods*, Shiva's role is particularly significant because destruction in Hindu thought is not considered negative. Instead, it is considered a necessary force for renewal and transformation.

In combining the three deities in this way, however, the doctrine elides the fact that Vishnu is not merely a preserver and Shiva is not merely a destroyer. Moreover, while Vishnu and Shiva are widely worshipped in India, very few temples are

THE DIVINE TRINITY | 43

... the Trimurti represents aspects of human existence – birth, life, and death.

dedicated to Brahma, who is expressly said to have lost his worshippers as the result of telling a lie and is merely entrusted with the task of creation under the direction of one of the two other gods.

The divine dichotomy

While Brahma slipped into oblivion, in appearance, in deed, in myth, in philosophy, Vishnu and Shiva became contrasting elements of the Hindu celestial playground – "high" gods in the brahmanical stream. They came together in many mythological episodes and yet they were in their individual orbits, helping humankind in their own prolific ways.

The two gods were in origin and in essence inimical, deriving from radically different social backgrounds and religious attitudes. The idiom of Vaishnavism was essentially orthodox and professedly based on the Vedas. Shaivism was kind of rebellious and often appeared to be apocryphal. Broadly speaking, Vishnu's religion was based on a thoroughly patriarchal ideology reflecting a settled varna-conscious community, or caste-based hierarchy.

Shiva's religion was an independent quest with a strong ascetic creed and rare display of pomp, splendour, and grandeur, especially in the temples of North India. The contrast between Shiva and Vishnu is also blatantly clear by looking at the roles their spouses play in their mythology and from their portrayal in iconography. The first main difference to understand is that Vishnu is known through his avatars, such as Rama and Krishna, and Shiva is known through his manifestations of just himself and his powerful entourage of family and followers. As the preserver of the world, Vishnu appears to be world-affirming, while Shiva is world-renouncing. Shiva's philosophy is expressed forcefully in various myths, yet it is psychologically appealing to those who can deal with extremes. Vishnu faces

△ **Dattatreya**, a personification of the Trimurti, represented by his three heads and six arms, is shown here holding objects attributed to the respective deities.

> ... Shiva teaches the inescapable truth of life. The cool comfort of rationale gives way to Shiva's wrath ...

disputes and conflicts as well, but resolves them by example, moral superiority, and, when necessary, war. Albeit all this is done with an acceptable mien of equanimity, barring Narasimha, the fourth avatar, depicted as half-human and half-lion. Vishnu, as Rama, is a prince; as Krishna, he frolics in verdant meadows – lovable and accessible. Cremation grounds are liminal spaces – bridges between the world of the spirits and the world of the living – and it is here that Shiva presides. These powerful locations, where humans arrive vulnerable and fearful, are where Shiva teaches the inescapable truth of life. The cool comfort of rationale gives way to Shiva's wrath, as his anger bursts forth, claiming his victim and teaching them a lesson, often in macabre ways.

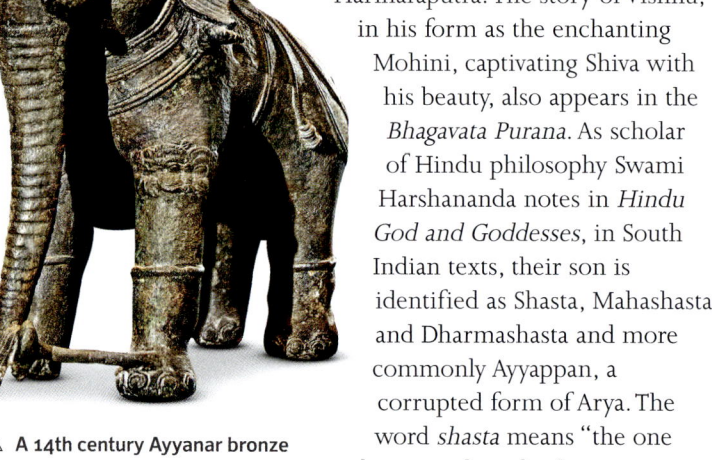

△ **A 14th century Ayyanar bronze sculpture** from Thogur, Thanjavur.

Vishnu bedecks himself with ornaments, silks, sandalwood paste, and flowers. Shiva smears himself with ashes, wraps himself in animal skin, and lets serpents slither around his neck. While Vishnu is associated with domestic cattle – cows specifically – Shiva is inseparable from the virile, untamed bull. Shiva is linked with snowcapped mountains, caves, and cremation grounds, while Vishnu is surrounded by symbols of pleasure and prosperity, by all things auspicious. Shiva, in contrast, is surrounded by things inauspicious, such as ghosts and dogs.

Vishnu is clearly a member of society, distinguishing between the appropriate and inappropriate, while Shiva is the eternal outsider, even refusing to discriminate between gods and Asuras.

Ayyappan, their offspring

While Shiva and Vishnu embody contrasting aspects, their bond remains deeply intertwined. During the Samudramanthan, or the churning of the ocean (*See pp124–25*), when Vishnu transformed into the enchantress Mohini, Shiva spilled his seed and the outcome was their son Hariharaputra. The story of Vishnu, in his form as the enchanting Mohini, captivating Shiva with his beauty, also appears in the *Bhagavata Purana*. As scholar of Hindu philosophy Swami Harshananda notes in *Hindu God and Goddesses*, in South Indian texts, their son is identified as Shasta, Mahashasta, and Dharmashasta and more commonly Ayyappan, a corrupted form of Arya. The word *shasta* means "the one who controls and rules over the whole world" and the other names are used for him as he is considered the protector of dharma. Sometimes, he is also referred to as Ayyanar or Ayyappan and Manikantha.

Although Shaivites and Vaishnavites have historically been in conflict, both groups ultimately reached a compromise, declaring him as their son. As Indian mythologist Devdutt Pattanaik delineates in *Myth = Mithya*, in most versions of his story, Ayyappan descends to Earth, given in the care of a childless Chera king in Kerala, where he grew up a great ascetic–warrior. The king gave him the name Manikantha. Ayyappan defended the land against Asuras but refused any material rewards. He could tame wild beasts such as tigers and lions. He captained the king's army. Everyone realized he was a manifestation of God. Like Vishnu, he fought Asuras and made the Earth a safer place. Like Shiva, he renounced his claim to the throne and eventually retreated to a shrine in the mountains and lived a celibate existence atop a hill.

In praise of Ayyappan

In images, Ayyappan is shown squatting, with a cloth tied just below his knees. Local lore in Kerala, Pattanaik states, has it that his father, the king, tied him thus, to prevent him from running away from the world. He thus stays atop a hill known as Sabarimala, protecting and providing for all those who come to him.

Today, Sabarimala is the main sanctuary and is in thickly wooded Shabari Hills of Kerala, near the western coast of South India. There the lord Ayyappan protects his followers from evil spirits and endows them with knowledge that leads to salvation. The ritual pilgrimage to his shrine in Sabarimala is considered highly auspicious. Swami Harshanand notes that the pilgrimage has to be preceded by 41 days of austerity, during which strict celibacy and restrictions regarding food, speech, and sleep are to be observed.

In South India, almost every Tamil village has a shrine of Ayyanar. Sometimes, in tribal regions, just a large rough stone, without any carving and set up under a tree, stands for his presence. Generally, however, his sanctuary is on the banks of a pond. In some, Ayyanar is represented in human shape, a kingly figure riding a horse or an elephant. Large terracotta horses are offered to him, – at least two every year – so that he does not lack a mount during night watches when he rides around the villages and looks after its safety. Over the years, horses accumulate in the sacred groves. As many as 500 large clay horses, some reaching up to 3 metres (10 feet) or more, may be prepared in a single sanctuary for the nocturnal rides. New horses are added, while the old and broken ones are left to decay and return to the Earth. Ayyanar is also worshipped in the form of a hunter. His devotees dance wildly when they worship him. Neither the wisdom aspect nor the orgiastic one are overtly part of the divinity of Ayyanar in the eastern Tamil part of South India, but the mystery of his birth from the two great gods is passed on to the potency of the waters and the earth of any particular area or locality, where Ayyanar is worshipped. While he is the same everywhere, art historian Stella Kramrisch says that each time, it is a different Ayyanar who is worshipped.

▽ **A lithograph showing Vishnu and Lakshmi** riding an elephant, encountering Shiva, Parvati, and Ganesha on a bull, while Brahma and other gods look down from heaven above.

◁ **An early 20th century watercolour painting by** Indian artist Kailash Raj depicts Harihara, two powerful deities, Vishnu and Shiva, joined into a single form. On the left is the blue-skinned Vishnu holding a conch and discus, while the right features the ascetic Shiva, with the moon, third eye, and snake around his neck.

HARIHARA

THE SYMBOL OF UNITY

"May the form, the form of Hari-Hara or Vishnu and Shiva, grant you both enjoyment and salvation which is both passionless and passionate, wearing both a wreath of human skulls and flower garlands, clad both in tiger and elephant skins and in costly garments, adorned with both serpents and with pearl strings and other ornaments and both smeared with ashes and with perfume, Shiva is fearful as well as auspicious."

This devotional verse from the *Epigraphia Indica*, II, 1892–93, offers a vivid portrayal of the striking contrast and profound unity between two major deities of the Hindu pantheon. The concept of two distinct gods merging into a single, composite form is a powerful and recurring motif in sacred Hindu art and mythology.

Such syncretic representations reflect a deeper philosophical synthesis, where seemingly opposing divine forces are not in conflict, but in harmony. In sculptures, this unity is often depicted with symmetrical precision: two deities fused as equal halves. One of the most iconic examples is Ardhanarishvara, the half-male, half-female form of Shiva and Parvati, embodying the cosmic balance of masculine and feminine energies. In a similar spirit, the figure of Harihara (or Haryardhamurti) blends the attributes of Vishnu and Shiva into a single, composite deity, with Vishnu occupying the left half and Shiva the right. This image, often linked to Shiva's gentler, *saumya* aspect, symbolizes a reconciliation not only of form but of ideology – an acceptance of unity amidst diversity.

The portrayal of Harihara resonates with the imagery of Ardhanarishvara, each offering a visual testament of harmony between seemingly divergent paths. By placing two prominent gods side by side, the sculptural form becomes a statement of reconciliation within the Brahmanical tradition.

The philosophy of Harihara

Philosophical texts of the time reflect the dynamic interplay of religious rivalry, often driven by questions of doctrinal authority and patronage. These tensions found occasional expression in visual art and iconography.

While Harihara does not dominate any one mythology, references to this composite form appear in various texts, including the, *Vayu Purana*, *Kurma Purana*, *Linga Purana*, *Padma Purana*, and *Bhagavata Purana*. In a passage from the Sanskrit epic text, the *Harivamsha*, the sage Markandeya tells Brahma that Vishnu manifests as Shiva, and Shiva as Vishnu, and that ultimately, they are one. The distinctions, he says, are illusions born of *avidya* – ignorance. The *Vishnu Purana* echoes this sentiment, affirming the essential oneness of these two great deities. According to the *Vamana Purana*, Vishnu once revealed to a sage that he and Shiva were not separate beings but one and the same. To affirm this unity, Vishnu

△ **18th century copper statue of Harihara**

manifested himself in a dual form. In this composite aspect, Vishnu, often identified with *Prakriti Tattva*, the cosmic principle of nature, takes the place traditionally held by Parvati in depictions like Ardhanarishvara. Thus, in the Harihara form, the "feminine" half bears Vishnu's emblems: the *shankha* (conch) and *chakra* (disc-like weapon), symbolizing his divine qualities and power. TA Gopinatha Rao, a pioneering Indian archaeologist and epigraphist, notes, in *Elements of Hindu Iconography*, this image is not just an artistic innovation but a theological statement, one that emphasizes the indivisibility of Vishnu and Shiva. Neither exists without the other; each reflects and contains the other. It is a visual and philosophical reminder that they are a seamless fusion of form, function, and faith.

Visual depiction

In classic depictions of Harihara, Shiva's third eye is partially visible on the right side of the forehead, and behind the image there should be a halo. The left side, representing Vishnu, features two arms – one holding a *chakra*, *shankha*, or *gada* (club) to signify his divine attributes, the other in a graceful *Kataka* gesture near the thigh – closely associated with the goddess Parvati, symbolizing offering and receiving. An earring adorns the left ear, complemented by ornate hand ornaments. Precious stones embellish Vishnu's side, while both legs remain straight. Garuda stands to the left, and Nandi to the right, writes Rao.

In the early centuries of the Common Era, the Kushan king Huvishka introduced gold coins that depicted Harihara with two heads and wielding the weapons of both deities. By the time of the Gupta Empire, artistic representations of Harihara had become more refined and localized, especially around Mathura. These sculptures often featured a single head crowned with dual symbolism: Vishnu's elegant *kiritamukuta*, studded with gems, and Shiva's rugged, matted locks – the *jatamukuta*. In some examples where only the head survives, this duality is emphasized with striking detail. Subtle variations, like the slightly protruding left eye, hint at the artists' careful efforts to distinguish divine characteristics while maintaining the unity of the figure.

Resolving differences

This iconographic form also suggests the belief that divine power was fluid, transferable, and could be shared across communities and traditions. It also reflects the ancient practice of merging deities – a conscious effort to ease tensions between different denominations. In fact, it is possible that the worship of Harihara emerged after tensions between Shiva and Vishnu devotees had eased, reflecting a compromise that both deities were essential in the creation, protection, and destruction of the universe.

◁ **Bebe Nanaki, elder sister of Guru Nanak, embroidered this wall hanging depicting Harihara** in the 15th–16th century. Shiva is on the left with matted hair and the Ganga flowing from his head, while Vishnu is on the right, wearing a crown and holding a conch.

Epigraphic evidence points to a temple dedicated to Shankaranarayana, another name for Harihara, in early medieval Madhya Pradesh. A similar syncretism appears later in the figure of Krishna Shankara and its belief system gained prominence around the 9th century, likely emerging as tensions between the Shaivas and the Vaishnavas began to ease. According to the *Skanda Purana*, these groups once clashed over religious dominance. Later on, composite deities like Shankaranarayana symbolized a compromise and move toward unity.

Power dynamics

Historians of iconography often interpret composite deities as symbols of cosmic unity, male and female as inseparable forces. So the placement of Vishnu on the "female" side of Harihara may allude to the myth of the churning of the ocean, where Vishnu took the form of Mohini to enchant the Asuras. As religious studies scholar Ellen Goldberg in *The Lord Who is Half Woman* points out, Shiva frequently embodies the dominant, masculine role, whether paired with Vishnu or Parvati. In traditional iconography, the left side, often deemed "female", is associated with fragility or weakness, reinforcing Shiva's perceived superiority in the composition. This suggests a layered theological, philosophical, and social commentary on gender and power dynamics.

Harihara embodies the idea that divine reality is one, even as it takes on multiple forms. The image unites Vishnu and Shiva to depict the interconnection of opposed forces inside the ultimate reality, Brahman. Vishnu, shown on the left, takes on the symbolic role of *prakriti*, or dynamic matter, typically represented by Shakti. In this way, Harihara parallels the concept of Ardhanarishvara, blending opposites to express unity.

▷ **A striking 9th-century sandstone sculpture** titled "God Harihara (Half-Vishnu, Half-Shiva)" from Madhya Pradesh, India. The Vishnu or Hari half is adorned with a tall crown and elaborate jewellery. He holds a conch shell or *shankha*, in his front right hand, while his rear right hand carries a discus or *chakra*.

◁ **A sculpture of Sharabha slaying Narasimha** at the Munneswaram Temple in Sri Lanka. A small figure of Narasimha is seen beneath Sharabha's forelegs. The Shaivic association is evident from the crescent Moon and Ganga on his head, as well as the snake and fire in his hands.

SHARABHA

PART LION, PART BIRD

A formidable sphinx-like creature, Sharabha has a powerful body, a long, piercing nose, razor-sharp claws, and a flowing horse-like mane and tail. With mighty wings and often eight legs, this fierce beast eclipses lions and elephants in strength and ferocity, and can soar across valleys with a single, thunderous bound.

Whenever evil threatens to take over the world, Vishnu takes on a physical form to kill the Asuras and restore balance. One such incarnation is the lion-headed Narasimha, who emerges to destroy the tyrant Asura Hiranyakashipu. After fulfilling his mission, however, Narasimha's rage was uncontrollable. According to Shaiva traditions, it is Shiva, who, disguised as the formidable beast Sharabha – part lion, part bird – subdues Narasimha, reestablishing harmony in the universe. In this form, Shiva is also knownas Sharabheshvara or Sharabheshvaramurti. This version of the story, found in later Shaiva scriptures, aims to assert Shiva's supremacy over Vishnu.

When gods collide

In the myths, Sharabha ripped Narasimha apart, wrapping himself in his victim's skin and hanging the severed lion head around his neck. The original Narasimha tale depicted a conflict between gods and anti-gods, whereas the Sharabha myth is the source of inter-cult hostility and serves no religious purpose. Puranic literature emphasizes the overt antagonism between devotees of Vishnu and Shiva. Shaivite and Vaishnavite traditions offer competing accounts of the Narasimha episode. Shaivite texts claim that Shiva, as Sharabha, subdued Narasimha, asserting his supremacy. Vaishnavite sources reject this version, stating that Vishnu transformed into the powerful two-headed bird Gandabherunda and defeated Sharabha instead.

While some texts describe Shiva taking on various avatars, his transformations differ significantly from those of Vishnu, both in purpose and nature. Shiva's incarnations often emerged in response to the Vaishnava doctrine of avatars. One of the most debated of these is Shiva's transformation into Sharabha. Far from a coherent figure, Sharabha is often described as a monstrous hybrid – part lion, part bird, part beast – comparable to a chimera. Historians and mythologists note that the textual descriptions are inconsistent and symbolically empty.

In the eyes of the beholder

The images of Sharabha also challenge usual expectations of beauty and piety. They evoke the paradox of how can something that appears grotesque also be revered as sacred? The power of Sharabha's visuals is rooted in the intense dynamic between devotee and deity. What appears "repulsive" to some is, for others, a profound expression of spiritual truth, power, and transcendence. According to the *Shiva Purana*, Shiva's fearsome appearance reflects a deeper spiritual purpose, where, in this form, he absorbs the sins of his devotees.

△ **A wall carving at the Dakshin Kashi Shiva Temple in Maharashtra** depicts Sharabha lifting elephants in its powerful paws.

TRIPUNDRA AND TRIDENT

Tripundra marks the soul, the trident guards the path, igniting peace, a deep awakening, and eternal purpose. Together they are symbols not just of Shiva, the god, but also of the faith of a devotee.

The three horizontal stripes of sacred ash on the forehead, known as the tripundra, mirror the three prongs of Shiva's trident, the trishula. Together they reinforce the concepts of divine power, balance, and cosmic order. The tripundra is rich with layered, symbolic meaning, much of it expressed through the power of threes. It represents the three *gunas* – *sattva* (purity), *rajas* (activity), and *tamas* (inertia) – that shape human behaviour. The trishula, Shiva's sacred trident, is a symbol of cosmic balance. Its three prongs represent creation, preservation, and destruction – the eternal cycle that governs all life. They also reflect the flow of time: past, present, and future – reminding us that Shiva exists beyond it all. On a deeper level, the trishula speaks to our own being – body, mind, and soul – the three layers of human existence that must align for true transformation.

Sacred ashes

According to Hindu mythology, Shiva adorned his brow with ashes from the three seemingly invincible Asura cities of Tripura, marking his triumph like a victorious warrior. Since then, the tripundra has become a powerful symbol of devotion to him. Ashes hold deep significance in Shiva's realm – not only worn as sacred markings, but also used in creative ways, such as coating his body to form a radiant, ethereal sheen. Rich in meaning, these ashes are as varied in purpose as they are in name. The tripundra reflects the three sacred fires used in Vedic rituals and spiritually symbolizes the destruction of ego, ignorance, and attachment. Its lines evoke Shiva's triple power – *Iccha Shakti* (will), *Jnana Shakti* (knowledge), and *Kriya Shakti* (action) – which govern the universe. The ashes used to apply the tripundra come from sacred sources – a sanctified fire, a funeral pyre, or cow dung. Perhaps the most revered, is the ash from the Manikarnika Ghat in Varanasi, Shiva's legendary cremation site and favourite dancing ground.

Tripundra carries deep spiritual meaning, with interpretations that vary by context. When made with *vibhuti*, the Sanskrit term for sacred ash, it is seen as both purifying and symbolic of life's impermanence. This aligns closely with Hindu ascetic ideals, which emphasize detachment from material life and the pursuit of spiritual liberation.

Devotees often apply the tripundra before meditation or religious ceremonies to deepen focus and strengthen their connection to Shiva. Ancient Hindu texts like the *Bhasmajabala Upanishad* and *Kalagni Rudra Upanishad* link it to universal truths and liberation.

The trishula in ritual and worship

Three lines of ash, three prongs of power – the tripundra and trident reflect Shiva's path to burn illusion, balance existence, and transcend the self.

The trishula holds profound symbolic meaning. It symbolizes the flow of time – past, present, and future – as well as the three dimensions of human existence: body, mind, and soul. It serves as a powerful reminder of balance, transcendence, and the interconnectedness of all things. According to mythology, the trishula was forged from the blazing energy of Surya, the Sun god, by the celestial architect Vishvakarma.

It plays a prominent role in temple rituals, religious processions, and devotional practices. Many Shiva temples display a trishula at the entrance or beside the idol, signifying the deity's presence and authority. Devotees may also offer small tridents during worship, seeking guidance, courage, and spiritual clarity. It is also believed to purify the mind and spirit, dispelling negativity and ignorance – making it a central element in certain cleansing and transformative rituals.

◁ **A mural featuring Shiva's trident,** showcasing devotional and decorative elements typical of regional temple motifs, in a small shrine at Mehrangarh Fort, Jodhpur, Rajasthan.

HARIHARAPITAMAHASURYA

A DIVINE CONFLUENCE OF FOUR FORMS

The radiant form of Surya, the Sun god, embodies the divine convergence of the Trimurti – Brahma the creator, Vishnu the preserver, and Shiva the destroyer – manifesting as Hariharapitamahasurya, a unified force of cosmic balance and power. Three faces crown his head, one reflecting Brahma's tranquil wisdom, the second Vishnu's serene radiance, and the third Shiva's fierce asceticism, each fixed in an eternal gaze that sees across time and burns with ancient knowledge. In one hand, he holds the discus that slices illusion; in another, a trident that anchors truth; in yet another, the water pot of the creator; and in his final palm, the sun itself – small, round, and alive. His presence is overwhelming – a body wrought of light and wrapped in the golden radiance of dharma itself.

Iconographically, this form may be shown with four heads and multiple arms, each bearing symbols associated with the deities it unites: Vishnu's chakra or discus and shankha or conch, Shiva's trishula or trident and naga or snake, Brahma's *kamandalu* – small, elliptical vessel, traditionally used by Hindu ascetics to store water – and Vedic book, and Surya's radiant solar beams. The *Vishnudharmottara Purana* and *Skanda Purana* refer to such syncretic forms, while the *Nilamata Purana* affirms the equal importance of these deities, promoting a non-hierarchical view of divinity. Pitamaha, or "paternal grandfather," is a reverent epithet for Brahma, the creator and source of all life and knowledge. With four faces representing the Vedas, and symbols of purity and wisdom in hand, Brahma joins Vishnu and Shiva in the cosmic trinity known as the Trimurti, embodying creation, preservation, and transformation.

Surya is an important Vedic deity in this unity. He is the jewel of the sky – life-giving and tireless. Described as a bird soaring through the heavens, Surya generates light, drives away darkness and disease, and infuses all beings with vitality.

Cultic syncretism

One of the best-known sculptures of Hariharapitamahasurya is in the Puratan Shivalaya Temple at Ambernath, Maharashtra. The deity has a single visible face and four hands, two of which hold the chakra and dhvaja or flag. Another striking image, dated to the 11th century, comes from the Dewas district of Madhya Pradesh. The figure stands with one body and four heads – the front being Shiva's – flanked by worshippers and a seated Ganesha.

These works exemplify the spirit of cultic syncretism, expressing theological unity through sculptural innovation. This composite form is not rooted in a specific mythology but instead reflects a philosophical reconciliation of rival sects – Vaishnavism, Shaivism, Brahmanism, and the worship of the Sun. As noted in the *Bhavishya Purana*, it stands as a symbol of the oneness of the divine.

Ultimately, Hariharapitamahasurya is more than a syncretic icon – it is a radiant vision of divine interconnectedness, a testament to the fluid boundaries between sects, and a celebration of spiritual unity at the heart of Hindu philosophy.

◁ **A sculpture of Hariharapitamahsurya from the 11th–12th century Duladeo Temple** in Khajuraho, Madhya Pradesh. It depicts a composite deity seated in a yogic posture, with Shiva on the right, Vishnu on the left, Surya at the front, and Brahma at the back, though not visible. The figure holds symbolic attributes of each god – a serpent for Shiva, a mace for Vishnu, a *kamandalu*, or an oblong water pot, for Brahma, and twin chakras for Surya.

THE ANICONIC SHIVA

Shiva's true presence is not just in a statue, but in an aniconic form – the lingam. It stands at the centre, deep within the temple's innermost chambers – raw, eternal, and commanding absolute devotion. For the devotee, this unyielding symbol is Shiva himself made manifest for all humankind.

The worship of the lingam lies at the heart of Shaiva theology, offering countless ways to contemplate this representation of Shiva. Boundless Shaiva myths introduce the concept of the lingam, often presenting diverse and sometimes contradictory explanations.

It is understood as a phallus, combined with the yoni or vulva, which forms the base of the image, with the lingam rising from its centre. This union symbolizes the creative force that generates and sustains the life of the universe. On a metaphysical level, the lingam is also an abstract emblem – the formless one, a unique visualization of the infinite.

It is neither entirely human nor non-human; it exists somewhere in between. As a form, it is tangible, yet it raises the question of what it embodies in the worshipper's mind. The lingam is full of mystique and complex interpretations, yet its power is rarely questioned or doubted by devotees.

Early history of lingam worship

The worship of the lingam has a long history, rooted in ancient civilizations. As German Indologist and linguist Heinrich Zimmer notes in his seminal work *Myths and Symbols in Indian*

Art and Civilization, the lingam form of Shiva may be traced back to the worship of primitive stone symbols as early as the Neolithic period. In fact, the discovery of lingam-like stone objects at Mohenjo-daro, an ancient city of the Indus Valley Civilization, suggests that the lingam may have been a significant element of worship in that era. The *Rig Veda*, the oldest Sanskrit text composed between 1500 BCE and 1000 BCE, also offers some evidence of phallus worship. It alludes to certain non-Vedic peoples, who are described as Shishnadevah, meaning "penis worshippers". This might refer to people who used phallic symbols or stones as cult objects in their rituals. An alternative meaning of Shishnadevah is "having the phallus as their god". In the *Rig Veda*, Indra, an important Vedic deity, was asked to keep them at bay and away from the sacrifice, and he is said to have overcome them during an attack on an indigenous stronghold with a hundred gates. By inference, this may be a reference to the Indus cities, which had an abundance of gateways, further suggesting that this cult may have been popular in the Indus region.

Despite the presence of lingam worship, many scholars emphasize that it was originally unconnected to Shiva. Indian historians such as RG Bhandarkar, JN Banerjea, and JN Farquhar believe that lingam worship originated from the aboriginal peoples of India, and that the association of the lingam with the worship of Rudra–Shiva was initially foreign to Rudra's early followers. Even the earliest writings on Hinduism by foreign scholars reflect this view. English Indologist HH Wilson, writing in the 18th century, notes that Shaiva worshippers were most prevalent in northern India, judging by the number of

> The lingam is seen as nishkala–sakala, that is a subtle form that exists between the formless state of Brahman and rupa, the anthropomorphic form.

shrines dedicated to the lingam. However, he claims that devotees rarely visited these shrines, as the lingam was considered a rude and unattractive emblem. It is possible that the phallic cult was independent until it merged with Rudra worship much later.

The link to Shiva

It is in the early Upanishads that make up the concluding sections of the Vedas and composed between 800 BCE to 300 BCE, that philosophical ideas around the lingam begin to emerge, with connections drawn between this abstract concept and Shiva. Brahman, the universal spirit as expounded in the Upanishads, is *alinga*, that is formless and featureless. Shiva is also *nishkala*, that is without attributes, and is understood to manifest from Brahman. In this context, the lingam closely reflects the concept of Shiva's formlessness. The lingam is seen as *nishkala–sakala*, that is a subtle form that exists between the formless state of Brahman and *rupa*, the anthropomorphic form.

The term "lingam" as signifying the phallus in connection with Shiva, as Rudra, was not recorded until the time of the epic literature, that is 600 BCE to 300 BCE. In the *Mahabharata*, there is a clear reference to the worship of the Shiva lingam as a phallus. Sage Upamanyu, while recounting the glories of Shiva to Krishna, says: "Mahadeva was the only god whose organ of generation (linga) is worshipped by men . . . all beings of Maheshvara bear the marks of the male or female organ of generation on their bodies." As Indian historian RG Bhandarkar notes, the reference here is to the lingam in *arghya*, a symbolic ritual object, and not merely to the male organ itself.

The Puranic exposition of the lingam

The connection between the phallus and the lingam is further elaborated in Sanskrit scriptural texts composed between the 3rd and 10th centuries, known as the Puranas. In one episode, Shiva dishonoured Sage Bhrigu, who, angrily, cursed him to be worshipped in the form of a lingam. In another story, Brahma asked Rudra to create mortal beings, but Rudra refused, unwilling to be the source of suffering. Instead, he stood still, his erect organ pointing upwards, a sign that he had not shed his seed, which remained consumed or transubstantiated within the body. A third tale links the origin of the lingam to Sati's death. After she immolated herself and Vishnu dismembered her body, Shiva found Sati reborn as yoni and united with her as the lingam. Through this union, Sati, in the form of yoni, drew Shiva out of ascetic seclusion and into the world, making him accessible through the form of the lingam.

The Puranas not only establish the connection between the phallus and the lingam, but also make it clear that it was actively worshipped. For instance, the Daruvana episode points directly to phallus worship, as by the end of the story, the sages were diligently engaged in phallic worship, into which Shiva had initiated them. It also signals that lingam worship was a new development in the region, just as, in Daksha's myth (*See pp84–85*), the worship of Shiva himself was an unfamiliar experience. It is telling that Shiva must force his way into the barred world of Brahmanism through destruction, otherwise, he would have to suffer the fate of

◁ **A medieval period ekamukhalingam,** or one-faced lingam, from Bihar in eastern India. It combines the phallic and anthropomorphic forms of Shiva. The figure features a third eye and what appear to be matted locks, characteristic of the deity.

an interloper and outcast for eternity. In another episode, the sages curse Shiva's lingam to fall to the Earth. It burns everything in its path like fire, until the sages appeal to Brahma for help. Brahma tells them that as long as the lingam remains unstilled, nothing auspicious can occur in the universe. Only by propitiating Devi, so that she takes the form of the yoni, can the lingam be calmed. When Parvati receives the lingam, calmness descends, and thus, the worship of the lingam is established.

A theological diversion

However, these texts also create an early dichotomy of meaning for the lingam – the sexual organ of Shiva and as a pillar representing rooted stability and renunciation. One of the most significant myths illustrating this is the Lingodbhava, in which Shiva emerges from a pillar of light while Vishnu and Brahma search in vain for its base and top, symbolizing the impossibility of comprehending Shiva's origin or end. The lingam is thus often associated with this infinite pillar, rather than with the phallus. For those uncomfortable with the antiquity and Vedic roots of its phallic symbolism, this interpretation offered a kind of theological refuge. But the cult of the pillar also has great antiquity, as seen in the *Skambha Sukta*, a Vedic hymn dedicated to Skambha, wherein it portrays Skambha as the central pillar upon which all the worlds are established. It goes beyond a simple description of a physical pillar, exploring profound philosophical ideas, including the nature of the individual soul, the Supreme Being, and the path to liberation. This concept provided an alternative for those unwilling to accept the lingam solely as a phallic symbol.

Even though there is ample evidence of Shiva's connection with the phallus in history, mythology, paintings, inscriptions, and sculptures, many scholars argue that the lingam is actually a pillar of light, fire, or a tree symbol, or an abstract representation of the Godhead.

One of the greatest modern Indian thinkers, Swami Vivekananda, refuted the idea that the lingam represents a phallus and instead described it as a symbol of the eternal Brahman. He maintained that the worship of the lingam originated from a hymn in the *Atharva Veda*

△ **A c.1700 painting from Himachal Pradesh,** in the classic Pahari style, depicting two women worshipping the lingam. Their bowed heads and offerings of flowers and incense clearly illustrate the act of devotion.

praising the Yupa stambha, a sacrificial pillar used in Vedic rituals, particularly in animal sacrifices. American scholar David Frawley, who has written extensively on Vedic traditions, argues that the lingam represents universal consciousness rather than a physical form. RS Rajaram, a researcher exploring the scientific and historical aspects of Hindu traditions, also supports the idea that the lingam symbolizes cosmic balance.

Devotion to the lingam

The lingam is worshipped in various ways, though only some rituals emphasize its phallic aspects. In most Shaiva temples, milk is poured over the lingam, symbolically inverting the production of semen from the convex-topped pillar. Devotees also chant the *Lingashtakam* during Shiva puja, especially in the auspicious Hindu month of Shravan, to seek blessings and spiritual elevation. The *Lingashtakam* is a revered Sanskrit hymn dedicated to Lord Shiva, praising the divine lingam. This eight-verse composition is believed to have been written by Adi Shankaracharya, a great philosopher and devotee of Shiva. Each verse glorifies different aspects of the Shiva lingam, highlighting its purity, power, and ability to destroy sins and grant liberation.

△ *(1)* **A *svayambhu* lingam from Gangotri, Uttarakhand.** This naturally shaped stone, resembling a Lingam, likely became an object of devotion over time. The addition of Tripundra markings and a nearby trident affirms its deep connection to Shiva.

(2) **A *manusha* lingam sculpted from sand.** In this, the lingam is accompanied by an outlined shape suggestive of the yoni.

(3) **The Svayambhu Lingam at Doleshwar Mahadev Temple in Bhaktapur, Nepal.** This temple represents the head of Shiva, who evaded the Pandava brothers in bull form after the *Mahabharata* War, with the body believed to reside in Kedarnath.

FORMS OF THE ICON

The icons of most Hindu deities are often anthropomorphically complex, but Shiva's emblem, the lingam, stands out for its striking simplicity, However, it hides a fascinating evolution beneath its minimalist surface.

The story of the lingam iconography begins with anthropomorphized phalluses of the 2nd century BCE found in different parts of the subcontinent. Most prominent of these are the Gudimallam Lingam in the southern state of Andhra Pradesh and the colossal lingam in Aghapur in the northern state of Rajasthan. These are depicted as a phallus, that is the male sex organ, with a complete and faithful anatomical likeness.

However, the early lingams, with their close resemblance to the phallus, were perhaps considered unsavoury and inappropriate. As a result, during the Gupta period, that is the mid-3rd to mid-6th centuries, a shift in iconography occurred. The overt realism of the lingam was subdued, giving way to a more stylized and normative design – a simple cylindrical form with a rounded top, emerging from an oval or horizontal base. This abstraction, in turn, also came to symbolize Shiva's formlessness.

Outer form and inner essence

There are many taxonomies associated with the lingam. On a philosophical level, it is classified into two types – the exterior and the interior lingam. The exterior lingam is tangible, while the interior lingam is an abstract concept, believed to reside within the outer form, like the soul within the human body. Those devoted to external rituals and sacrifices find fulfillment in worshipping the tangible lingam, as they are unable to visualize the inner one. The inner lingam is imperceptible to the limited-minded, who take external reality to be absolute and deny the existence of anything beyond it. The unstained, unchanging lingam is revealed only to those who possess true knowledge.

Manifest forms

On the sculptural level, there are many kinds of lingams, but the most important distinction is between those that are *svayambhu*, that is,

"self-manifest", and those that are fashioned and consecrated by humans. In the lingams that are *svayambhu*, the powerful presence of Shiva is discovered, sometimes even revealed, in the earth. These lingams are spontaneous, perhaps even miraculous, appearances of Shiva. Then there is a third type, a mix of the first two. These are *parthiva*, or earthen, lingams — crude and simple. In these, human creation and divine revealing are present together. Shiva appears in response to the simple, focused adoration of a devotee who makes and honours a single lingam of earth. With a prayer called *avahana*, meaning "invitation", Shiva is beckoned to be present in this simple earthen lump. At the end of the self-worship, such a lingam may be thrown away in a sacred river or any body of water. Its use as a temporary focus of God's presence has gone.

As Indian historian Roshen Dalal notes in her comprehensive work on religious terminology, *The Penguin Dictionary of Religion in India*, even the Agamas, scriptures that explain external methods of divine worship, describe different types of lingams. The list may vary, but essentially there are six types: *svayambhu*, or self-created; *daivika*, made by the gods; *arshaka*, made by the rishis; *ganapatya*, made by the Ganas; *manusha*, made by human hands; and *bana*, ellipsoid shaped stones found in the waters of the Narmada river that resemble lingams. One must, however, understand that the prevalence and immense popularity of the aniconic image does not mean there were no anthropomorphic representations of Shiva. There are about 25 known anthropomorphic sculptures of the deity.

NUMISMATIC EVIDENCE

The earliest evidence of the lingam on ancient Indian coins is seen on an uninscribed cast coin of unknown provenance. It features a symbol identified as a lingam placed on a square pedestal. A tree within a railing to its left could represent the *sthala vriksha*, or sacred tree, often associated with Shiva's emblem. Another coin discovered at Taxila, an ancient archaeological site in present-day Pakistan, bears a more abstract representation. In contrast, coins from Ujjain, an ancient sacred city in Madhya Pradesh, depict a much more realistic form, but without the base beneath it. These examples suggest that the worship of Shiva through the phallic emblem was established and widespread in India from before the Christian Era.

△ *(4)* **A lingam placed on a rock in Kanyakumari, Tamil Nadu.** It may be a naturally shaped stone venerated for its resemblance to the lingam, or a *khandit*, or broken, one no longer used for formal worship.

(5) **The 1.5-metres (5-foot) ancient lingam at Kedareshwar Cave Temple in Maharashtra.** The lingam is perpetually always surrounded by waist-deep water. Once encircled by four pillars symbolizing the four Hindu ages, only one remains — its fall is prophesied to bring an end to the world.

(6) **The black stone lingam at Chaurasi Temple in Chamba, Himachal Pradesh.** It features anthropomorphic elements, such as eyes, alongside the traditional form. To emphasize its connection to Shiva, the lingam is adorned with the tripundra, a third eye, and a large serpent.

Revered by devotees as a powerful symbol of Shiva, the lingam serves as a timeless focal point for worship, meditation, and spiritual connection. In the holy city of Rishikesh, nestled in the Himalayan foothills, along the River Ganga, a sadhu offers prayers beside a Shiva lingam.

GUDIMALLAM LINGAM

THE EARLIEST ICON OF SHAIVA TRADITION

In a temple in the tranquil village of Gudimallam, Andhra Pradesh, stands a striking relic – five feet tall, thick, and unmistakably phallic. Carved with shocking realism, Shiva's figure emerges, and the structure, divided by a deep incision, reveals an anatomical likeness that is both divine and unsettling. This is the Gudimallam Lingam, possibly the earliest Hindu icon, heralding the later Shaivite imagery.

The naturalistic figure of Shiva resembles a vigorous hunter. In his right hand, he holds the legs of a ram, upside-down, while in his left, he grips a battle axe. A hatchet rests on his left shoulder. His matted hair is styled in a *jatabhari*, with all the ropes tied atop his head like a headband, interwoven with strands of flowers and wound around his head like a turban. A thin, muslin-like *ardhoruka*, or a short dhoti, is wrapped around his waist, hanging down in the middle, yet it leaves his sexual organ exposed. Though portrayed as a hunter, he is adorned with jewellery – a necklace, earrings, bracelets, and armlets. With slanted eyes and high cheekbones, the figure reflects Dravidian features rather than Aryan ones.

Dating the icon
The Gudimallam Lingam is carved from a single, dark brown, polished igneous stone, likely sourced locally from the Tirupati Hills, in Chittoor district of Andhra Pradesh. It once stood in the open, beneath a tree, as depicted in reliefs from Mathura and Kanchipuram, but was later enshrined in the Parasurameswara Swami Temple, where it is still worshipped today.

As contemporary inscriptions are silent on its time of creation, scholars differ, placing it anywhere between the 3rd–2nd centuries BCE and the 4th century CE. In composition, however, it is related to the reliefs of Yaksha – a class of nature spirits – carved on the uprights of railings around Buddhist sacred enclosures, and like them can be dated to around the 2nd century BCE.

What sets it apart
Unlike other Lingodbhavamurtis, where only a part of Shiva is visible, the Gudimallam Lingam is the only lingam where Shiva is carved entirely within the lingam itself. It represents a complete, fully integrated form of the deity. It is also the oldest known sculpture in South India, predating all monuments and sculptures from the region, which largely date from the 7th century onwards.

Beyond its distinctive iconography, the Gudimallam Lingam is also recognized for its incredible technical mastery, in the way it exhibits an impressive level of muscular tension.

▷ **In the Gudimallam Lingam**, Shiva stands atop a pot-bellied dwarf, possibly representing a rival cult he subdues. The composition could also symbolize his triumph over *avidya*, or ignorance.

JYOTIRLINGAS
ILLUMINATING THE INNER CONSCIOUSNESS

They mean the pillar of light or lingams of light. These 12 sacred places across India is where Shiva appeared as an incandescent, infinite column. Collectively called Jyotirlingas, where *jyotir* means "light", they span the length of the country – from Kedarnath in the high Himalayas to Rameswaram at the tip of southern India, from Grishneshwara in Maharashtra to the holy city of Ujjain in the heart of India, Madhya Pradesh. These sacred shrines dedicated to Shiva are a wonderful example of the interleaving of cultic myth and sacred geography.

The earliest textual reference to these lingas as a group, comes from the *Shiva Purana* in around the 12th century, notes American scholar of religious studies Diana L Eck in her book *India: A Sacred Geography*. There is also mention in the works of ancient India's greatest playwright and poet Kalidasa's epic poem *Raghuvamsha*.

The never-ending pillar of light
The myth of Lingavirbhava or Lingodbhava establishes the story behind the Jyotirlingas. Brahma, the creator, and Vishnu, the preserver, were in an argument over their supremacy. Each proclaimed themselves the greatest god. As the skirmish took on an alarming, almost apocalyptic nature, the rest of the deities approached Shiva who had stayed away from this argument. Shiva decided to end the rivalry once and for all, and pierced the three worlds, appearing as a huge, inestimable pillar of light, the *jyotirlinga*.

Brahma and Vishnu were dumbfounded. United in their stupefaction, mingled with some fear, they decided to see the beginning and the end of this monumental edifice, not realizing its infinite nature. So, Vishnu as the mighty boar in his Varaha avatara dove underground in search of the pillar's end. Brahma transformed into a gander and flew upwards.

They returned thousands of years later, exhausted and flabbergasted, for they could not comprehend something greater than themselves. Vishnu admitted defeat, but Brahma took recourse to travesty and claimed he had reached the pinnacle, producing a Ketaki flower as proof.

At this mockery Shiva appeared from an aperture of the pillar. The two gods bowed to him with complete humility, recognizing the ultimate truth. However, angered by Brahma's dishonesty, Shiva cursed him – the creator could never be revered, whereas Vishnu would be eternally worshipped for his honesty.

While there is no reference to the structure of the phallus as the lingam in this myth, it does endorse the theory behind the worship of Shiva by his emblem, the pillar-like structure. Since it is called *jyotir*, *jyoti* being the shining spiritual light of the inner consciousness, the "light" in Shaiva theology bridges the gap between knowledge and action and brings about absolute bliss, that is *ananda*.

▷ *(clockwise from top left)* **Intricately carved relief panels on the outer pillars of the Somnath Temple in Gujarat.** They depict deities and celestial beings from Hindu mythology, scenes from the *Mahabharata* and *Ramayana*, and Shaiva icons such as Nataraja; **A statue of Nandi,** Shiva's sacred bull, at the Tryambakeshwar Temple in Maharashtra; **The five-tiered *shikhara*, or spire, of the Grishneshwar Temple** in Maharashtra. The temple reflects an early South Indian architectural style, with friezes in rust, pink, and yellow depicting Hindu deities; **The verandah and the orange spire** of the Mahakaleshwar Temple in Madhya Pradesh; **Kedarnath Temple in Uttarakhand,** set against the snow-clad Garhwal Himalayas. Built from massive interlocked grey stone slabs, the temple stands on a raised plinth and is designed to endure the region's harsh mountain weather; **The 1,220-metre-long (4,000-feet) corridor of Ramanathaswamy Temple** in Tamil Nadu. One of the longest temple corridors in the world, it is lined with thousands of pillars and sculptures.

LEGACY AND RITUAL

ANCIENT VOLCANOES
Some believe that India once had 12 active volcanoes, but the gods nullified them and installed 12 Jyotirlingas on those spots so that no one would accidentally or deliberately activate them again. This is why these sites are sources of powerful energies.

ADI SHANKARACHARYA
While the concept of Jyotirlingas existed before Adi Shankaracharya's time, he is credited with schematizing the concept and encouraging pilgrimage to these sites, emphasizing their spiritual significance and importance in Hinduism. His contribution is well-documented in texts, such as the *Shankara Vijaya*, which mentions his visits to all the Jyotirlingas.

BHASMA ARTI
An important ritual takes place every morning at the Mahakaleshwar Temple in Ujjain, when priests gently apply a layer of ash to the lingam in what is popularly known as the Bhasma Arti, or the offering of ashes. Ash plays a prominent role in Shiva worship (*See pp288–89*), symbolizing the transience of life.

Centres of enlightenment

Jyotirlingas are considered *svayambhu*, or self-born, and are scattered across India, each region bringing its own distinctive cultural mythology to the larger Shiva ethos. Every Jyotirlinga gives space to a specific form of Shiva, with an associated story that tells of the god's appearance to assist a devotee and staying on to protect all who would follow. In fact, it is while exploring this concept that a dynamic relationship between local traditions and an emerging pan-Indian consciousness becomes apparent. What is crucial to understand, however, is that these are not famous temple sites built by rich patrons, kings, and nobles, but are cultic centres not necessarily known for their art and architecture, where ordinary devotees through their devotion witness the presence of Shiva. It is believed that they possess spiritual energy and power and symbolize the infinite, eternal, and omnipresent nature of Shiva.

The 12 Jyotirlingas

Starting as rocky outcroppings or simple stones, they grew popular over time and are now the lingas of Shiva. Devotees believe that visiting these shrines can bring spiritual enlightenment, blessings, and liberation.

The temples include: Somnath and Nageshwara in Gujarat, Kedarnath in the high Himalayas, Mallikarjuna

◁ **Priests at the Mahakaleshwar Temple in Ujjain** perform the Bhasma Arti at dawn. As one priest offers the *bhasma*, or ashes, to the lingam, others chant sacred mantras. By the end of the ritual, the lingam is entirely cloaked in ash and the sanctum resonates with solemn devotion. For Shiva, linked with cremation grounds, ashes are both his adornment and his very essence.

in Andhra Pradesh, the Mahakaleshwar Temple in Ujjain, Omkareshwar along the River Narmada, Vaidyanath in Jharkhand, Rameshwaram in Tamil Nadu, Kashi Vishwanath in the holy city of Kashi (formerly known as Benaras, now present day Varanasi), and Bhimashankar, Ghrishneshwara, and Tryambakeshwar in Maharashtra. Each is connected to a specific form of Shiva with an accompanying myth – sometimes it is Shiva appearing to save his ardent devotee from evil or illness and sometimes to help them walk the path of self-realization.

The oldest and perhaps the most revered is Somnath, in the western state of Gujarat. The name means "lord of the Moon", one of Shiva's names, and alludes to the myth of Chandra, the Moon god, and his wives.

High in the Garhwal Himalayas is Kedarnath, a famous Shiva shrine with a connection to the *Mahabharata*, for it is believed that this is where Shiva appeared as a lingam to the Pandavas. The lingam is a shapeless mass of rock appearing somewhat as a pyramid and is believed to be the hump of a bull or a buffalo. Another myth associated with this place is from the *Shiva Purana*, when Nara and Narayana requested Shiva to visit the Shiva lingam they had installed. Shiva accepted their request and visited it every day. When Shiva asked them to choose a boon, they requested him to stay there in his form and accept the devotion of his devotees.

One of the seven sacred cities in Hinduism is Ujjain, in the state of Madhya Pradesh, also considered the centre of India. Some even believe that it is the centre of the universe as it is located where the Tropic of Cancer and the zero meridian of longitude intersect. The Jyotirlinga, in the Mahakaleshwar Temple, is called Mahakaal and considered the *nabhi*, or navel, of the Earth. It is also considered one of the seven *mukti-sthalas*, or places of salvation, and shares a deep connection to the cycle of life and death. A popular myth associated with this place tells of Shiva emerging in his Mahakaal form to protect his devotees and staying on to protect all those who follow him. Another popular Jyotirlinga is in Varanasi or Kashi (*See pp250–51*) at the Kashi Vishwanath Temple and it is believed that Shiva himself installed the lingam there.

Omkareshwar means "lord of Omkara", and the temple is located in Khandwa, Madhya Pradesh, on an island called Mandhata or Shivpuri along the River Narmada. The story, according to the *Shiva Purana*, tells of the Mountain Vindhya that had grown arrogant of its might. When Sage Narada told it that the Mount Meru was loftier, Vindhya created a lingam and began a penance. When a propitiated Shiva told him to ask for a boon, Vindhya asked for the intellect to achieve its object. Shiva fulfilled his desire. With enlightenment, Vindhya realized the petty nature of his desire and abstained from it. The Bhimashankar Jyotirlinga in the midst of a lush forest in the western state of Maharashtra is also a place where Shiva is seen as the destroyer of ego, pride, and evil, much like the Nageshwara Temple in Dwaraka, Gujarat.

On the other hand, the Vaidyanath or Baidyanath Jyotirlinga in Deogarh, Jharkhand, *vaidya* meaning "physician", is called so because it is believed that Shiva cured Ravana in this location. The *Ramayana* connection is apparent in the Jyotirlinga at Rameshwaram, located on the southern tip of India on Pamban Island. Literally translating to "Rama's lord", Rameshwaram is where Rama worshipped Shiva before crossing the ocean to rescue Sita and destroy Ravana. The Tryambakeshwar Jyotirlinga, on the banks of the River Gomati in Nashik, Maharashtra is known for its three-faced linga, while the Mallikarjuna Jyotirlinga, situated on a mountain in Andhra Pradesh features both Shiva and Parvati, their presence is linked to Karttikeya, their son. The Ghrishneshwara Jyotirlinga, also in Maharashtra, is close to the Ellora caves, a UNESCO World Heritage Site, and is connected to a myth where Shiva revived a devotee's son and stayed on for the welfare of the people.

Neither have I **ears,** tongue, nor **nostrils,** nor **eyes**

Nirvana Shatakam, Adi Shankaracharya

2 | SHIVA
THE FIERCE ONE

With Brahma as the creator and Vishnu as the preserver, there arose a need for a divine force of disintegration, as all creation is subject to decay.

THE GOD WHO DESTROYS

Shiva's most remarkable and earliest feature is his wrath. Over time, this aspect has been elaborated and deepened, shaped by many myths and philosophy. What once appeared as a pure destructive force has, over time, been reinterpreted as carrying a transformative, even positive, purpose.

In early Sanskrit texts, such as the Vedas, composed between 1500 BCE and 500 BCE, Shiva's defining trait is his unrelenting anger, his *raudra*, a fierce and primal rage. Known as Rudra, the "livid god", his roar is like thunder, striking fear even in those who hear it from afar. His wrath is so immense that it brings disease and death in its wake. There is no clear cause for his fury in these texts – it is simply an inherent part of his nature. Rudra seems to carry his anger heedlessly. The few triggers for his rage include his resentment for being worshipped alongside other deities and his irritation with praise he deems insufficient or faulty.

Anger as the catalyst for ascension

Shiva's entry into the divine realm is that of an outsider, a *persona non grata*. This is evident in the Vedic texts, where his share of sacrificial offerings were cast aside, at the crossroads, well outside conventional sacred spaces. In later texts, such as the Puranas, composed from the 4th century onwards, his anger becomes the force through which his status ascends.

The myth of Daksha's yagna *(See pp84–85)*, almost serves as a justification for Shiva's integration into the Brahmanical pantheon – albeit in the form of Veerbhadra *(See pp86–89)*. This myth marks his rise to legitimate divine status, also reflecting the broader transition from a religion dominated by Vedic and upper-class supremacy to one that began to acknowledge Shiva, the phallic deity, and other deified heroes worshipped by people in the outlying regions.

Patterns of Shiva's wrath

As Shiva's mythology evolved in the Puranas, his role as the angry destructor became more established. Unlike in the Vedas, this concept was no longer unfounded. With Brahma as the creator and Vishnu as the preserver, there arose a need for a divine force of disintegration, as all creation is subject to decay.

So, Shiva's anger became justified through his battles with Asuras and it often culminated in decapitation – a favoured form of retribution. This can be seen in his interactions with Brahma, Daksha, Ganesha, Jalandhara, and Andhaka. The ultimate horror, yet morbid fascination, of a chopped head rolling on the ground is not just macabre and an effective punishment for the recalcitrant, but also something one could never forget. This drama, dealt out in Shiva's own inimitable way, heightens his presence as a god of wrath, leaving devotees and storytellers alike both fascinated and in awe.

At times, Shiva's ferocity also extended to those who are not Asuras. In such cases, the cause is usually tied to two of his deepest concerns – his fierce determination to preserve the sanctity of his meditation, and his unwavering love for Parvati. Both Kama's story *(See pp80–81)* and that of Ganesha *(See pp176–77)* bear witness to this.

Over time, profound philosophical meaning was accorded to Shiva's destructive aspects, transforming what seemed like a negative force into one full of purpose. His acts of destruction came to be seen not as mere annihilation, but as the necessary prelude to regeneration and transformation.

THE INTERPLAY OF GOOD AND EVIL

The benevolent and the malevolent, both inhabit the Hindu divine pantheon. As Indian sociologist Ashis Nandy observes in *Time Warps: The Insistent Politics of Silent and Evasive Pasts*, there exists an intricate, personalized, and ambivalent relationship between gods and Asuras. The two are dialectically interrelated as neither can exist, or even be imagined, without the other. Shiva, as the slayer of Asuras, epitomizes this idea as his battles with Asuras reveal not merely conflict, but the dialectical interdependence of good and evil within the cosmic order.

RUDRA

THE HOWL IN THE STORM

He is the lone, gory hunter, associated with rough storms. He is mighty and must be dreaded for his wilful anger, and pointed shafts, for he will spare no one – cattle or humans. Praise his glory, praise his power, for he is the benefactor of disbursing herbs and medicines known only to him. This is Rudra, the god feared, the god appeased, most beseechingly, through flattery. Yet over time, he will transmogrify and, like barnacles, add to his persona many an auspicious characteristic without entirely giving up the wildness of the original.

Rudra is howling. Rudra is tawny. Rudra is copper-coloured, blue-necked, young, fierce, strong, unassailable, wise, and associated with a feared aspect of nature, the wind, thunder, and lightning. The divinities of the stormy winds, the Maruts, accompany him and he is said to be their father. Puranic texts mention plural Rudras who helped Indra, the lord of the Devas, in his battles. They were the sons of Rudra and numbered either 11 or 33. He seemed to embody those aspects that threatened the peace of the people. He is a hunter who camouflages himself, clothed in an animal skin, and is brown, with a black belly and a red back. He carries different weapons, such as the bow and pointed shafts, which he hurls at people and cattle. He adorns himself with the horns of animals. To beguile his prey, he assumes many forms, endlessly changing his appearance. In the *Mahabharata*, Shiva or Rudra emerges as a tribal hunter when he bestows on Arjuna the most powerful weapon (*See pp32–33*). Rudra's very name is frightening and must not be mentioned directly. He is so feared that sometimes, seers do not even want to take his name, but call him *asau devam* or "that god". There is almost a cringing

admiration for Rudra, as worshippers try to curry his favour. However, it is best to be shrewd and keep out of his way.

In his name

Chief of all born art thou in glory, Rudra,
armed with the thunder, mightiest of the
mighty. Transport us over trouble to well-being:
repel thou from us all assaults of mischief.
Let us not anger thee with worship, Rudra,
Ill praise, Strong God! or mingled invocation.

Hymn 33, Verses 3–4, *Rig Veda*, from *The Hymns of the Rig Veda* by Ralph TH Griffith

The practice of theonymy, or study of divine names, is key to develop an understanding of the functions and societal views of certain gods, particularly Shiva who originated with the theonym Rudra. It later became an epithet, exceeding the original theonym by the post-Vedic period. The name Rudra, in the Epics and the Puranas, is a synonym for Shiva, the two often used interchangeably.

In the earliest accepted text, the *Rig Veda*, Shiva is only known as Rudra. However, some scholars do not think he is a Vedic god. Vedic scholar and Indologist RN Dandekar in his *Vedic Mythological Tracts* notes that there were two distinct Rudras – a celestial god in the *Rig Veda* and an Earthly god in the post-Rig Vedic period. However, there is no doubt that one can see the forerunner of present-day Shiva in the earliest Rudra. His name has many derivations. It comes from the root *rud*, or to howl and roar, reminiscent of his role as a storm god. It is derivable from *ru*, or to cry, and *dru*, or to move. In fact, the Puranas make frequent references to the cry of the Rudras. It is said that the noun has been derived from the adjective *raudra*, that is to be violent and savage. Seeing these, it is almost as if the name Rudra is given with great nervousness.

The cause of anger

To Rudra bring these songs, whose bow
is firm and strong, the self-dependent
God with swiftly-flying shafts, The Wise,
the Conqueror whom none may overcome,
armed with sharp-pointed weapons: may
he hear our call.

Hymn 46, Verse 1, *Rig Veda*, from *The Hymns of the Rig Veda* by Ralph TH Griffith

It is clear that the god concept that we understand today owes much to the Rig Vedic antecedents, for there are some traits in the *Rig Veda* that have a bearing on how Rudra is perceived later. The composers of the hymns painted a picture of a destructive, capricious, and frightening god. Yet, he has knowledge of medicines. He is the protector and healer of animals and humans. This resonates with the later epithet "Vaidyanathan"; he gives the disease and the cure.

He seems infuriated if praised along with other deities, that is *sahuti*, or mingled invocation. It does seem that *dushtuti*, or faulty praise, angers him too. Another reason could be because he seems to be standing at the margins, both metaphorically and physically. What comes out

strongly is his association with the relegated, which brings him closer to those who were castigated in the Vedic literature, who live in the forests and in the mountains.

His outsider status is further endorsed as he is not offered the same sacrifices as the other gods – He is worshipped by offerings at the crossroads and never with a share in the Vedic sacrifices. Historian Upinder Singh notes offerings to him consisted of a ball of food thrown on the ground, similar to propitiating spirits.

Successors of Rudra

O Lord! Thou Resident of the Mountain! Thou the Primeval Hunter! Go not hither and thither, but reside within me alone. For in the forest of my mind there are many beasts of prey like envy, infatuation and the rest. Killing them, Thou shalt satisfy Thy fondness for the hunt.

Verse 43, *Shivanandalahari*, from *Sivanandalahari*

Over time, Rudra evolved, and gradually became linked with Shiva, one of Hinduism's principal deities, emphasizing his role as a force of cosmic dissolution and renewal. Later myths tell of Shiva manifesting in frightening forms such as, Bhairava (*See pp108–09*) and Veerbhadra (*See pp86–89*), a nod to this early form of Shiva.

However, there was no one unilinear historical development from a single Rudra to Shiva, but a more complex development of several distinct parallel traditions. The raw materials that fed into the scriptures emanated from the collective practices of many communities including the pastoral and the forest dwellers. Deities changed with the transition from pastoral to settled agriculture. New deities confronted a broader cultural complex and deities from their original locus were Brahmanized.

The results were products of mutual exchanges and borrowings, a mutual osmosis of the Brahmanical and the non-Brahmanical as they

# THE THIRD EYE

Shiva's third eye burns like an eternal fire, piercing through darkness and illusion. It annihilates, to expose raw truth beneath all existence. Both terrifying and sacred, it represents the ultimate transformative force.

Shiva is often described with epithets such as *Trinetra*, *Triaksha*, and *Tryambaka* – for he bears an extraordinary mark upon his being: the third eye. Among all male deities in Hinduism, he alone is portrayed with three eyes, with the third one depicted as a vertical eye on his forehead. While goddesses such as Kali and Durga are also sometimes shown with three eyes, especially in esoteric Tantric and Shakta traditions, they too belong to the Shaivic world and, therefore often have similar attributes to proclaim their affinity.

Stories of its origin

There are several accounts of the origin of Shiva's third eye, many of which are intertwined with his consort Parvati. Once, when Shiva and Parvati were sporting on the slopes of the Himalayas, she playfully closed his eyes with her two palms. The whole universe was at once submerged in cosmic darkness and all activity came to a halt. Sacrifices stopped and Devas became quiescent. To save the world from this deadly predicament, Shiva willed a third eye in between his eyebrows, sending forth light, fire, and heat to dispel the darkness. So fiery was the glance of the third eye that it caused Parvati's palms, placed over the left and right eye, to sweat.

Indian mythologist and author Devdutt Pattanaik, known for his modern retellings of Hindu myths and epics, in *Devlok with Devdutt Pattanaik* highlights another story. When Parvati appeared before Shiva, he was so struck by her beauty that he realized two eyes were not enough to behold her loveliness, so a third eye emerged, allowing him to fully experience her beauty.

The eye of wisdom

The third eye is a metaphor for inner vision, intuition, and spiritual awakening. As the eye of knowledge and wisdom, it stands for Shiva's omniscience. Unlike the two sensory eyes, the third eye perceives truth beyond what one can "see". It is the gateway to higher consciousness. Even today, the metaphor of the third eye is used, in a colloquial fashion, to describe an epiphany, or a moment of complete clarity, often providing the right direction.

The left and right eyes represent a gaze that distinguishes between proper and improper comportment. The third eye is indifferent to such categories, as it is the human mind that has manufactured them. The eye of wisdom, representing the transcendental gaze, looks at all rules as artificial.

It also symbolizes destruction, burning away illusion, ego, and toxic energies, not out of vengeance, but to purify and renew. It signifies the destruction of desire as well.

In yogic thought and practice, there are seven chakras, or energy centres, in the body. The third eye corresponds in position to the sixth chakra, that is, the Ajna chakra, located between the eyebrows. This fiery chakra is so hot that it is often smeared with cooling sandalwood paste or turmeric. In Hindu practices, the tilak, a traditional mark applied to the forehead using sandalwood or vermilion, is placed precisely where the third eye is believed to exist.

Perils

The third eye is not to be taken lightly as it can have deathly consequences. The most famous instance of its destructive power is when Shiva opens it to incinerate Kamadeva, the god of desire (*See pp80–81*). This myth symbolizes the annihilation of desire and distraction and the triumph of asceticism over passion and worldly temptations.

For the sake of his followers, Shiva keeps his third eye shut. Only on the day that he wishes to destroy the illusions, that are the bedrocks of the world, will he open it and allow an unbridled spectacle of fiery apocalyptic destruction.

◁ **The 1890 illustration, Madan-Bhasma (Shiva Turns Madana (Kama) to Ashes),** depicts an event from Hindu mythology when an angry Shiva opens his third eye and reduces Kama, the god of love, to ashes for breaking his *samadhi*.

FROM THE SHIVA PURANA Triumph of spirituality over desire

DESTROYER OF KAMA

Kamadeva, the deity of love, had a difficult task. He had to rouse Shiva from his deep meditation or *samadhi* so that he may unite with Parvati.

Kama was a popular god, prancing with Vasanta throughout the spring season, accompanied by his beautiful wife Rati, the goddess of love. He rode a parrot and his entourage had musicians and celestial beings such as Apsaras and Gandharvas. Kamadeva never imagined that his life could ever be in danger, or that he would cross paths with someone who could destroy him. For all his life, he believed in the notion that everyone desired to fall in love, experience love, and die in love.

Until he encountered Shiva, for whom love was a distraction, something to transcend.

Kama accepted the challenge of disrupting Shiva's meditation. He approached the place where he sat and filled it with a bouquet of heavenly scents. He transformed the harsh, snow-capped mountains into a beautiful wonderland brimming with flowers, bees, butterflies, parrots, pollen, and nectar. Gandharvas sang love-filled melodies and Chakravaka birds displayed tender gestures.

The deer frolicked in pairs and peacocks danced in abandon. Every creature's intention was to stir Shiva's senses while he remained in *samadhi*. But they failed to captivate Shiva who remained deep in meditation, oblivious to the temptations around him.

In desperation, Kama raised his bow made of sugarcane, pulled the bowstring strung with buzzing bees, and shot five flower-tipped arrows straight at Shiva. Infuriated at the disruption, Shiva opened his third eye and, in a flash, set Kama ablaze, reducing him to ashes. After destroying the god of love, Shiva resumed his meditation.

Later, Parvati pleaded with Shiva, who, out of compassion, and at his beloved's behest, resurrected Kama – not in his physical form, but as *Ananga*, the bodiless one – permitting love to exist in its formless state.

In Hindu philosophy, *Kama*, which means "love" or "desire", is one of life's three components, alongside Artha and Dharma. This particular myth is a powerful symbol of the triumph of spiritual discipline over desire, reaffirming Shiva's status as the supreme ascetic.

In Kannur, Kerala, during the flaming rite of Fire Theyyam, the dancer becomes more than mortal, and a living embodiment of Shiva, lord of destruction and rebirth. The fire is not mere spectacle; it is Agni, the god of fire and Shiva's purifier and witness. As the dancer moves through flames, their steps mirror Shiva's cosmic dance, the Tandava, shaking the worlds, channelling rage, release, and divine ecstasy. Smoke coils like serpents, an echo of Shiva's own adornment. Here, devotion burns hotter than pain, and the ritual becomes a bridge: between earth and sky, man and god.

▷ **Sati argues with her father**, the king Daksha seated on a throne in this colour lithograph, dated 1895, titled "The Great Sacrifice of Daksha". The great gods Brahma and Vishnu can be seen standing in the background, with a sadhu in the foreground who seems to symbolize Shiva.

FROM THE SHIVA PURANA Overcoming ego and connecting with the divine

DAKSHA'S FOLLY

Daksha loathed Shiva, his daughter Sati's husband. He felt Shiva was a blot on decent, civilized society and often ridiculed him because he went about dressed as a beggar. Daksha just could not understand the god. The king believed he was worth the condemnation as Shiva did not know about rituals, their practice, or the importance of sacrifice. Instead, Shiva with his beliefs further confused the hapless, beleaguered worshipper.

Daksha often made acerbic remarks and would comment that where people daubed sandalwood paste on their bodies, Shiva chose to smear ash from dead bodies. He wandered in nudity in the terrible abodes of ghosts, such as crematories, surrounded by spirits and hosts of goblins, his hair scattered and adorned with garlands made of corpses and human bones. He is Shiva, Daksha would say, auspicious, only in name.

Puffed with pride because of his own proficiencies, such as Brahma Vidya or the knowledge of the absolute, Daksha decided to hold the Brihaspatisava, an acclaimed sacrifice. He decided not to invite Shiva and Sati to the sacrifice, but his daughter insisted on attending it. There, she, before everyone, contended with him about the merits of her husband. She told her father, respectfully, that his intellect was confused by *arthavada* in the Vedas. With his intellect wrongly concentrated on the body as the soul and having forgotten the real nature of the soul, Daksha was inept. Those who considered sacrifices and other religious acts as real knowledge, she told him, and those who followed Daksha in his censure of Shiva, would remain in the endless cycle of births and deaths.

The bickering was endless. Until, Sati, unable to bear the insult directed at her beloved Shiva and furious over her father's refusal to recognize Shiva as a great god, walked into the holy fire, removing herself from this world.

When Shiva heard of the tragic turn of events, he turned into the fierce Veerbhadra, contaminated the sanctity of the yagna, and decapitated Daksha. He later brought Daksha back to life, on Vishnu's entreaties, albeit with a goat's head.

DAKSHA'S FOLLY | 85

> # VEERBHADRA
>
> ## PERSONIFICATION OF SHIVA'S WRATH

"I am not a god, nor an Aditya; nor am I come hither for enjoyment, nor curious to behold the chiefs of the divinities: know that I am come to destroy the sacrifice of Daksha, and that I am called Veerbhadra, the issue of the wrath of Rudra. . . . Take refuge, king of kings, with him who is the lord of Uma. For better is the anger of Rudra than the blessings of other gods."

Veerbhadra at Daksha's yagna in
Vishnu Purana, from *The Vishnu Purana*
by HH Wilson

When there is good reason for extreme anger, Shiva metamorphoses into "beings" that are not just furious but rapaciously furious. One such emanation from him is Veerbhadra – a conglomeration of rage, repugnance, vengeance, and punishment.

The backdrop to Veerbhadra's formation is Daksha's triumphant yagna, or sacred fire ritual. Daksha, Shiva's father-in-law and Sati's father, invited every soul except Sati and Shiva. Out of unbearable pathetic humiliation, she immolated herself. Shiva's wrath was immeasurable – not only due to the contempt shown to him and Sati, and Sati's tragic demise, but also because the ritual opposed his brand of religiosity. Uprooting a strand of hair from his matted locks, Shiva dashed it off a mountain, from which Veerbhadra, dark and immense, arose as a personification of his righteous outrage. Veerbhadra, eager to act, awaited Shiva's command. Told to destroy Daksha's yagna, ominous signs followed: a rough wind scattered gravel and sand, blood rained from the heavens, darkness enveloped the quarters, and meteors fell to Earth.

The debacle
As Veerbhadra approached, amidst the great din of his entourage, Daksha and the Devas, frightened, sought refuge in Vishnu. Vishnu remained unmoved. Everything was fruitless, he told them, for not only was Daksha disrespectful to Shiva, he had failed to understand true dharma.

Veerbhadra led an army of ghosts, Ganas, and Pramathas – all inauspicious and wild creatures who go about destroying the precincts. Everything holy became unholy. Urine, sputum, blood, and vomit filled the pots and pans. Screams, shouts, and cackles replaced melodious hymns. Dogs

VEERBHADRA | 87

◁ **An early 19th-century watercolour painting of Veerbhadra, likely from Patna, Bihar.**
The dark-skinned figure wears tattered clothes. His ferocity is evident in his large fangs, wild hair, and open third eye. In his 12 pairs of hands, he wields numerous weapons such as a noose, discus, trident, axe, bow, sword, mace, and dagger.

△ **This mid-19th-century Pahari painting depicts Shiva and Sati**, with Nandi and the Ganas, in their mountain abode as they watch the Devas and other celestial beings making their way to Daksha's fateful sacrifice.

howled and ghosts screeched. The entire sacrificial order was disrupted. The attending Devas, including the mighty Indra, lay wounded or stunned. When Veerbhadra found Daksha crouching in hiding, he struck him down with one swift blow. Finally, Vishnu intervened and sought Shiva's mercy. Daksha's head was restored, replaced with that of a goat. Daksha, humbled, became a devoted follower of Shiva. Once Veerbhadra had successfully destroyed the sacrifice and humiliated all the Devas present, he joined the ranks of other deities such as Nandi (See pp200–01) and Bhringi (See pp196–97) as a close attendant of Shiva. In this way, the tale of Veerbhadra remains a timeless reminder of the eternal dance between destruction and creation within the cosmic order.

Symbolism

Beyond the mythological narrative, Veerbhadra carries profound symbolism. He leads Shiva's army to destroy Daksha's yagna, demonstrating the terrifying aspect of divine justice. He represents the uncontrolled power of anger and vengeance but also serves as a protector of righteousness. As Shiva's manifestation of wrath, he represents the inherent power within individuals to overcome the destructive and prideful ego – depicted by Daksha – offering profound insights into the human experience. Veerbhadra, with his imposing presence and divine purpose, remains a potent symbol of the transformative power that lies within the pursuit of higher consciousness.

It may be said that in this cosmic drama, Shiva embodies the higher self, Sati symbolizes the heart, and Daksha personifies the ego. The story unfolds as the higher self annihilates the ego for the sake of the heart, portraying a deeper spiritual lesson of compassion, forgiveness, and the pursuit of inner harmony.

Imagery

There are two types of Shaiva icons – the *saumya*, depicting Shiva performing acts of *anugraha*, or grace, and the *ugra*, portraying Shiva in acts of *samhara*, or destruction. Veerbhadra belongs to the latter category.

In his iconic portrayal, his stance is dynamic and forceful, capturing the essence of his swift and relentless nature. His counterpart, the Goddess Bhadrakali, is sometimes shown by his side. The dark complexion of Veerbhadra symbolizes the intensity of his rage and determination, while his eyes radiate a fiery glow, signifying the divine energy and awareness that fuel his actions.

Veerbhadra, with his imposing presence and divine purpose, remains a potent symbol of the transformative power that lies within the pursuit of higher consciousness.

Swami Harshananda, a renowned Indian scholar of Hinduism and spirituality, notes in his work *Hindu Gods and Goddesses* that Veerbhadra is depicted with three eyes and four arms, holding weapons like a bow, arrow, sword, trident, and mace, while wearing a garland of skulls. His multiple arms are symmetrical, showcasing a harmonious balance in his divine form. The weaponry he brandishes symbolizes the cosmic arsenal at his disposal, reflecting his role as the divine enforcer of justice and cosmic order. The choice of weapons in Veerbhadra's hands holds significance. The sword represents discernment and the cutting of ignorance, while the trident symbolizes the trinity and his authority over the three *gunas* – *sattva*, or harmony; *rajas*, or activity; and *tamas*, or inertia – which are fundamental qualities that influence all aspects of nature and human experience. The bow and arrows denote precision and focused energy, highlighting Veerbhadra's ability to target and eliminate obstacles with precision. These symbolic weapons collectively underscore his role as a cosmic warrior, embodying the divine will to maintain equilibrium.

Veerbhadra's crown of skulls is also a powerful visual element, representing the transcendence of the cycle of birth and death. The skulls signify the ephemeral nature of mortal existence, emphasizing the eternal and immortal aspect of the divine. This imagery reinforces the overarching theme of cosmic balance and the inevitability of cosmic forces that surpass the limitations of worldly existence. In his hand, he holds the head identified either as Brahma or as Daksha. It appears like he is the alter ego of the serene Shiva who meditates in his mountainous abode Kailasha. The overall iconography of Veerbhadra serves as a visual narrative, conveying righteousness.

Cultural reverence and worship

Veerbhadra holds a significant place in Hindu mythology, particularly within the Virashaiva movement, a devotional movement that emerged in Karnataka in the 12th century. In this region, people worship Veerbhadra as a powerful and protective deity. Temples dedicated to him, such as those in Perambalur in Tamil Nadu, Lepakshi in Andhra Pradesh, and the town of Veerbhadra near Rishikesh in Uttar Pradesh, serve as pilgrimage sites where his divine energy is venerated. He is also worshipped in Maharashtra. In fact, there are famous sculptures of him in Ajanta and Ellora – ancient rock-cut cave complexes in Maharashtra – where he is represented with eight hands.

▽ **An artist performing the Veerbhadra folk dance during Gudi Padwa** – the New Year festival in parts of western India – at the Vithoba Temple in Goa, dressed in royal costume, wielding swords, and embodying the fierce deity with painted face and long hair.

COSMIC RENEWAL

Shiva represents the cosmic force of dissolution, making way for renewal and transformation. His role is not one of mere annihilation, but of restoring balance by bringing to an end that which has fulfilled its purpose. Shiva ends each cosmic cycle, embodying the eternal rhythm of birth, life, and death.

> . . . he is Sadashiva, the eternal, formless consciousness that remains after all dissolution.

Anything Shiva does or takes part in becomes a major earthly and cosmic event. Even his grief has a physically forceful and riveting dance form, the Rudra Tandava. Devastated and enraged by the death of his wife, Sati, he performed the dance of galactic fury and destruction, shattering mountains, dissolving worlds, and threatening cataclysmic and violent annihilation. The moment marks one of the most emotionally intense episodes in Shiva's lore.

Prima facie it appears to be a reaction to extreme grief, but since it is the mighty Shiva – it is a world-affecting act that reflects the cycle of destruction and renewal. It marks the transition from personal loss to universal transformation, from emotions to cosmic action.

Symbol of the cosmos

The transition reveals the deeper philosophical dimensions of Shiva's actions. According to Shaiva philosophy, the universe is an expression of Shiva's dance. It represents the rhythmic energy of the universe and the eternal cycle of birth, life, death, and rebirth. His dance is a metaphor for the five cosmic functions – *srishti*, or creation, that is the birth of new forms; *sthtiti*, or preservation, that is sustaining life and order; *samhara*, or destruction, that is the dissolution for renewal; *tirobhava*, or concealment, that is hiding the truth; and finally *anugraha*, or grace, that is liberation and divine blessing. At a practical level, it means that all living creatures die and are reborn, and each birth gives rise to a different form. The philosophical insight also applies to the inner landscape of thought, emotion, and consciousness. All thoughts and dreams rise and fall, and awareness brings repose and calmness. Shiva's dance then becomes both a cosmic performance and an inward meditative truth.

Cosmic dissolution

Shiva dances everywhere – in temple grounds, on the Himalayas, and even in the crematoriums. When Shiva dances in cremation grounds, he smears ash on his body, and the dance stands for the principle of destruction.

The principle is *mahapralaya*, or the "Great Dissolution", that is the dissolution of the universe. The process is described in the *Shiva Purana* and Shiva plays a central role in this cosmic drama as he is the force that initiates *mahapralaya*. It takes place at the end of a *kalpa*, or cosmic age, which spans 4.32 billion years. When *mahapralaya* strikes, the entire world, including its creator Brahma, comes to an end. It is not just destruction, but a return to primordial unity, where all forms dissolve into the formless ultimate reality, called Brahman.

Mahapralaya is also a spiritual metaphor. Souls who attain moksha, or liberation, remain unaffected as they merge with the eternal Brahman.

Shiva's role is transformative, clearing the way for renewal. After dissolution, creation begins anew, often with Shiva and Shakti initiating the process. Through *mahapralaya*, Shiva emphasizes that

COSMIC RENEWAL | 91

◁ **This painting by contemporary Indian artist Muskan Agrawal** captures Shiva's formless dance, symbolizing his essence as both everything and nothing. It illustrates how his cosmic dance sustains the universe.

all things are temporary, and through the cycle of dissolution and creation, new beginnings emerge. This understanding highlights the Hindu philosophy that destruction should not be feared as it is an essential force in the ongoing cycle of life, death, and rebirth. It teaches acceptance of impermanence, the duality of existence, and the interconnectedness of all life.

In the deepest sense, Shiva is not just the destroyer – he is Sadashiva, the eternal, formless consciousness that remains after all dissolution. He is *Avimukta*, or never absent, even during *mahapralaya*, as he is the eternal witness.

STAGES OF DISSOLUTION

"*Pralaya*" is a Sanskrit term that refers to the dissolution or end of objects, beings, or even the universe itself. In Hindu philosophy, there are several kinds of dissolution, each occurring at different levels of existence. *Nitya Pralaya* refers to the death of individual beings. *Naimittika Pralaya* takes place at the end of Brahma's day, marking a temporary dissolution of the universe. *Prakritika Pralaya* occurs at the end of Brahma's lifespan and involves the complete dissolution of the physical universe. Finally, *Atyantika Pralaya* is the dissolution of the individual self through liberation, as the soul merges with Brahman.

THE COSMIC DANCE

Tandava refers to the cosmic dance of Shiva in Hindu tradition, and symbolizes the cycle of creation, preservation, and destruction. Beyond form, it embodies Shiva as the universe's pulsating force, a profound expression of the energy that drives existence.

A distinctive feature of Hinduism is its aesthetic vision of the divine, embodied in Shiva as the cosmic dancer who sets the universe in motion. He performs all types of dances throughout the long span of his celestial existence. However, in the specific image of Nataraja (See pp98–101), which became famous during the Chola period, the dance encapsulates everything at once – birth and death, joy and sorrow, all come together in a moment of becoming. The universe itself is seen as an expression of Shiva's dance, which is why he is depicted dancing in a crematorium, smeared with ashes. This image signifies the simultaneous presence of creation and destruction.

He dances every evening to relieve the sufferings of creatures and to entertain the gods who gather in Kailasha (See pp202–03) in full strength. He is thus called Sabhapati, "the lord of the congregation". More privately, Shiva is believed to entertain Parvati with his dancing in beautiful, bucolic scenes, often captured in paintings. The moods of his dance range from graceful to ecstatic and ultimately to the dance of death – the Tandava.

The wrathful dance

The Rudra Tandava is fierce, intense, and almost frightening. This form represents the frenzied throes of extreme grief and wrath and is the dance of destruction. Shiva performed this dance after Sati's death and signifies impending destruction. The positive aspect here is that this very destruction, although inevitable, leads to transformation. So, Shiva's dance is a catharsis, destroying evil and ignorance.

Depending on the context, Shiva's wrathful dance takes on multiple connotations. When Shiva dances on Asura Apasmara, his dance signifies the subjugation of ego and conceit, which must be checked as they block the path to knowledge. After the annihilation of the Tripurasura, Shiva's dance becomes one of victory, expressing his might. In this form, he adopts the Alidha pose, symbolizing the warrior, representing omnipotence. This is his dance of supreme power.

When Kali killed Asura Raktabija, her dance was uncontrollable. Shiva danced to placate her and exhausted her. Eventually, he lifted his leg in a vertical, phallic pose, known as *urdhva*, which Kali was unable to replicate. This could be due to her modesty, or perhaps because she could not match Shiva's power. In depictions of Urdhva Tandava, Kali is sometimes shown as minuscule compared to Shiva, emphasizing his supremacy.

Parvati's dance

Complementing the Tandava is Parvati's Lasya. Following Shiva's fierce Tandava after slaying Tripurasura, Parvati performs the Shringara Lasya

THE DANCE OF JOY

The Ananda Tandava is the blissful, joyous dance of the soul within oneself. This dance symbolizes joy, harmony, and the purest state of being. The beauty of this form was so profound that Saint Appar, in the Tevaram, a collection of Tamil Shaiva hymns, expressed the belief that even a rebirth on Earth would be worthwhile if it granted one the chance to witness this divine dance, as Indian art historian Vidya Dehejia notes in *Indian Art*.

△ **A modern sculpture** of Shiva in the powerful Tandava posture, carved in black stone, from Mysore, Karnataka.

◁ **A 19th-century gouache painting** depicting Shiva, shown in white, dancing to calm Kali after her uncontrollable frenzy following the slaying of the Asura Raktabija. In the background are Kali's companions and Shiva's attendants, the Ganas.

— a dance of joy, beauty, and conjugal love. Her movements embody feminine energy and peace, making this dance the tender counterpart to Shiva's masculine intensity. Together, Tandava and Lasya form a cosmic duality, balancing aggression with gentleness, and destruction with creation.

Symbolism in the Nataraja image

The Nataraja form exudes *arul*, or grace, expressed through the *abhaya* gesture, and the hand pointing to the raised foot assures the ocean of bliss, describes Indian art historian C Sivaramamurti in *Nataraja in Art, Thought, and Literature*.

◁ **An ornate Indian plate** with Shiva, as Nataraja, in the centre.

All poets and hymnographers have beseeched Shiva as Nataraja to dance in their hearts. In the *Shivananda Lahari*, a devotional hymn composed by philosopher Adi Shankara (*See pp270–71*), the poet pleads with Shiva not to hurt his feet on the rocky slopes of the Himalayas, but instead to dance within the devotee's heart. He also writes that the dance of Shiva was a bliss-conferring sight that only Parvati witnessed. She, in turn, passed the vision on to everyone else.

Nataraja became the patron deity of the monarchs of the Chola Dynasty in southern India, which reigned from the 9th to the 13th century. By the late 10th century, it had become an emblem of their dynasty. During this period, sculptures of Nataraja were increasingly frequent in temples sponsored by the Chola queen Sembiyan Mahadevi in the deltaic region of the River Kaveri. Art historian Padma Kaimal explains in "Shiva Nataraja: Shifting Meanings of an Icon" that Nataraja's visual form may even have encouraged Chola patronage and strengthened the alliance between the kings and the priestly community that maintained the temple at Chidambaram. After all, the dance symbolizes victory over ignorance, and by extension, political triumph. From the Chola period onwards, inscriptions and temples began highlighting the central role of Tandava as a way to honour Shiva and invoke divine blessings. Kaimal maintains that sculptural representations of Nataraja have signified various meanings to viewers over time, shifting with different audiences. While some are drawn to Shiva's cosmic elegance, others interpret him through an anthropological lens, seeing him as reminiscent of a tribal shaman or medicine man involved in fertility rites.

The Nataraja image is not only a profound spiritual metaphor but also a masterful expression of Indian art, embodying balance, movement, and transcendence.

ASURA APASMARA

Shiva is often depicted dancing, or sometimes standing, atop the prostrate body of a dwarf Asura. This figure is Apasmara Purusha, also known as Muyalaka or Muyalakan. He symbolizes *avidya*, or spiritual ignorance, and *ahamkara*, or ego, the inner obstacles that bind the soul to worldly bondage. His conquest represents the attainment of true wisdom and liberation from the material world. It is likely that Apasmara began as a simple pedestal figure. To be beneath Shiva's foot is a highly coveted position, for his immense power makes any connection with him a great honour. It must be emphasized that Shiva does not kill Apasmara, but eternally subdues him, signifying that ignorance must be kept in check – not destroyed – to preserve cosmic balance.

◁ **A 17th-century** carving of Shiva in Urdhva Tandava from Meenakshi–Sundareswarar Temple in Madurai, Tamil Nadu.

Within the shadowy interior of Elephanta Island's ancient cave temple, Shiva manifests in stone as Nataraja, the cosmic dancer whose Tandava puts the universe in motion. Carved between the mid-5th to 6th centuries CE, this UNESCO World Heritage Site in Maharashtra is a sublime expression of divine rhythm and timeless balance. Shiva dances the cycles of birth, death, and rebirth here, and in the quiet of stone, his movement is eternal. In this photograph from 1903, two worshippers kneel before the towering form, where stone breathes with centuries of devotion, and silence echoes with the presence of the divine.

▷ **This dynamic copper-alloy sculpture,** c. 950–1000 CE from Tamil Nadu, India, depicts Shiva as Nataraja, the Lord of Dance, whose movements symbolize the cosmic cycles of creation, preservation, and destruction.

NATARAJA

LORD OF THE COSMIC DANCE

At once dynamic and still, fierce and compassionate, Nataraja, the form of Shiva as the lord of dance, captures the entire cycle of creation, preservation, and destruction in a single, unified expression. Among the most powerful and iconic symbols of Indian art and spirituality, Nataraja is a cosmic statement of destruction and creation, rhythm and stillness, transcendence is inherently held together in a moment of eternal dance. As the noted English author Aldous Huxley once wrote, this is the Leela, the divine play of Nataraja.

Nataraja means "king of dance" and the image is not merely artistic – it is deeply tied to Indian classical thought, especially the *Natya Shastra*, the ancient treatise on performance arts, dating from around the 2nd century BCE to 2nd century CE and written by the sage Bharata, which aligns with the iconography of Nataraja.

The eternal dance

Shiva, as Nataraja, has the long hair of the yogi and it streams out as though flying wildly, as he dances. Entwined within his hair is a skull and a New Moon – the symbol of death and rebirth at the same moment, a cosmic rhythm without beginning or end. Encircling him is a ring of fire, the *Jwala Prabha*, a blazing halo that represents the cosmos itself. Each flame along its edge is both a spark of creation and a reminder of eventual dissolution. Held in his upper left hand is a single flame: not a threat, but a symbol of the inevitable destruction that purifies the universe, making way for its rebirth. As mythologist Joseph Campbell observed, this flame burns away the illusion of time and opens the mind to eternity.

A defining feature of Indian sculpture is the language of gesture, mudras, through which deep symbolic meaning is conveyed. Each of Nataraja's four hands speak to a cosmic truth. His front right hand, in the Abhaya Mudra or the gesture of fearlessness, offers protection and reassurance. His other right hand positioned behind the front arm holds the *damaru*, a small hourglass-shaped drum made from two human skulls. This is the drum of time – its rhythmic beat, the pulse of the universe, echoing the heartbeat and the cosmic sound of *shabda*, the primal Word from which all creation emerges.

While one hand calls things into life, the other, the upper left, holds the flame that will return them to ash. In this balance of opposites, Shiva's dance becomes a profound meditation on the nature of reality. His front left hand gestures toward his raised foot in the *gajahasta*, or "elephant trunk" pose. This foot, lifted and poised in motion, symbolizes transcendence – a state beyond the ordinary mind. Meanwhile, his other foot presses down on Apasmarapurusha, a symbol of ignorance and ego, held beneath him as a reminder that enlightenment requires the conquest of illusion.

Apasmarapurusha

The small, dwarfish figure, Apasmarapurusha, is sometimes also called Mujalaka. While he may appear demonic, he is not an enemy in the traditional sense. Some interpretations, particularly from Tamil traditions, suggest that this figure could represent a devotee who throws himself under the feet of the god in an act of surrender and devotion.

Most commonly, however, Apasmarapurusha is understood as the embodiment of *maya* or illusion, ignorance, and spiritual forgetfulness. According to Swami Harshananda, a monk of the Ramakrishna Order who wrote over 200 works on spirituality, Hinduism, and Vedanta philosophy, Apasmarapurusha is not an evil Asura but a symbol of the inner darkness that causes us to lose balance, clarity, and consciousness.

He represents that subtle yet persistent force that keeps us trapped in delusion, forgetting our true nature and the eternal reality beyond appearances. Shiva's act of crushing this figure underfoot is deeply symbolic. It is not an act of violence, but of liberation – the subjugation of ignorance by divine wisdom. In the cosmic dance, Apasmarapurusha must be subdued for enlightenment to arise. Only when forgetfulness is held beneath us can we awaken to truth.

In Chola Art

While depictions of a dancing Shiva existed in India as early as the 6th century CE, the form we now recognize as Nataraja, with its distinctive symbolism and posture, did not emerge in full until around the 10th century. Earlier representations vary significantly: Shiva might appear with up to 16 arms, his leg raised, but not crossing in front of the body, and often dancing on a platform rather than atop the dwarf Apasmara, the embodiment of ignorance. These earlier images, though powerful in their own right, lack the visual philosophy that the Nataraja embodies.

It was in the 10th century that the image of Nataraja took on its definitive form – both in stone and, most famously, in bronze. As academic and art historian Vidya Dehejia notes, this was the period when the iconic representation of Shiva as the cosmic dancer became established in Indian art.

It was under the Chola dynasty, a Tamil imperial dynasty that ruled from the 9th century CE to 13th Century CE, dominating South India, Sri Lanka, and parts of Southeast Asia, that the form reached its artistic and symbolic pinnacle, with bronze sculptures that continue to captivate the world. These Chola bronzes became the standard, and the image of Nataraja has been reproduced ever since – in metal, stone, and a variety of other materials – right up to the present day. While there are variations across regions and periods, the most widely recognized form shows Shiva in the Tandava pose – the powerful, rhythmic dance of destruction. But this destruction is not mere chaos – it is a sacred dissolution, making way for renewal and transformation.

Symbolism

The Nataraja image captures the dynamic rhythm of the cosmos – a dance that brings the universe into being through the creative, benevolent energy of Shiva. This dance is not merely physical – it is metaphysical, symbolizing bliss, balance, and the eternal cycle of creation and destruction. As Huxley observed, the image reflects the universe – space, time, matter, energy, and even the psychological realm. Its symbolism is profound and layered.

Though Shiva is worshipped across India, Nataraja is especially venerated in the South, with the grand Thillai Nataraja Temple at Chidambaram, Tamil Nadu, being the most important shrine. The temple's origins trace back to the 6th century CE, though its present structure was completed in the 10th century under Chola patronage. What sets Chidambaram apart from other temples is its focus on Shiva in anthropomorphic form. Here, the deity is not enshrined in a lingam, as is traditional, but as a freestanding bronze image of Nataraja. This figure, arms flung wide, hair flying, one foot raised, has become an emblem not only of Hindu art, but of cosmic rhythm and divine grace.

The image is not merely symbolic. It is considered a living presence. Daily rituals – bathing, clothing, offerings, music, and dance – are performed for the idol as they would be for a monarch. It is awakened in the morning, fed, honoured, and laid to rest at night. For devotees, this is not a representation of Shiva – it is Shiva.

▽ **This exquisite rock-cut relief** from Cave 1 at the Badami Caves in Karnataka, built by the early Chalukyans, is considered one of the earliest depictions of Shiva as Nataraja. Here, the god with 18 arms in motion dances surrounded by musicians and Ganesha.

▷ **In this vibrant mural** from the Chidambaram Temple in Tamil Nadu, Shiva is depicted as Nataraja, the cosmic dancer, performing the Ananda Tandava. Radiating energy and grace, he embodies the eternal rhythm of the universe. The figure beneath his foot symbolizes ignorance, which the dance triumphs over.

DRUM OF CREATION

One of Shiva's most potent and iconic symbols, the *damaru* embodies the primal sound — Nada — that underlies all creation, and with each beat, invokes the rhythm of the cosmos.

One of the earliest and most vivid iconographic depictions of Shiva with the *damaru* appear in his form as Nataraja dating back to 9th–10th century South India. In this form, as the Lord of Dance, he holds the *damaru* high in one hand, creating the rhythm of the cosmos.

This beat is no ordinary sound. According to legend, Shiva played the *damaru* at the dawn of creation, producing the primordial vibration — Nada Brahma — from which the universe unfolded. It was not a mere instrument, but the heartbeat of existence itself. In Shiva's ecstatic Tandava, the *damaru's* rhythm marks the cycle of creation or srishthi, and destruction or *pralaya*.

In *Understanding Shiva*, DK Hari and DK Hema Hari explore the significance of Shiva in Indian tradition, and note that the *damaru's* rhythm does more than create *tala* or tempo; it evokes *layam* — a deep sense of unity, where the listener melts into the music. Its sacred beat draws all things back into the stillness of Shiva. Traditionally made from wood, metal, or strung with leather drumheads, the *damaru* is, in some esoteric traditions, even crafted from the tops of two human skulls joined together — symbolizing the ceaseless cycle of death and rebirth. Shaking it sets the *damaru* in motion, making the beads or knots on its strings strike the drumheads to produce a rhythmic beat.

Symbolism

In Hindu mythology, the rhythmic beats of the *damaru* are intimately linked to the origins of sound and language. According to tradition, these beats gave rise to the Sanskrit alphabet, making the *damaru* not just an instrument of sound, but a symbol of speech, language, and the transmission of knowledge.

The *damaru* is not always associated with sound. In some depictions, it hangs from Shiva's trident, motionless, in a quiet reminder of its profound symbolic weight.

In Tantric rituals, the *damaru* represents the union of opposites — male and female, life and death, sound and silence — embodying the essential dualities that shape the cosmos. In yogic traditions, it is used to invoke divine energy, awaken spiritual awareness, and deepen meditative focus.

Sound, in Indian philosophy, is associated with *akasa* or ether, the first and most subtle of the five elements. Ether is the primal field through which the divine first manifests, and from which the other elements — air, fire, water, and earth — emerge. In this sense, sound and ether together represent the first fertile moment of creation, the pure, generative force of the absolute in its most potent form.

So, the *damaru* is far more than a ritual object — it is a spiritual metronome, echoing the pulse of creation, dissolution, and the eternal rhythm of the universe. It is said to echo the primordial vibration of "Aum," the sound from which the universe emerged. In this way, the *damaru* becomes a symbol of divine resonance — the interplay of sound, vibration, and cosmic energy that sustains universal harmony.

> ... There He sounded the *damaru*, producing sweet noise; there He created a great manifold, beautiful, and delightful scene ...

NADATANUMANISAM SANKARAM

A SPIRITUAL UNION OF SOUND AND DIVINITY

I bow repeatedly with my head and mind before Shiva, whose form is cosmic sound. He is the essence of Samaveda, the best of Vedas, the cause of bliss. He delights in the art of the seven great notes, *sa ri ga ma pa dha* and *ni*, which emerge from his five faces, beginning with Sadyojata. He crushes death. He is the protector of Tyagaraja, whose heart is immaculate.

From *Nadatanumanisam Sankaram*

The great saint Tyagaraja, a pioneer of Carnatic music, wrote *Nadatanumanisam Sankaram*, a revered *krithi* or devotional song, which is set in the Chittaranjani *raga* or melody and *Adi tala* or rhythm. It honours Shiva as the embodiment of Nada – the divine sound or cosmic resonance. The word, *Nadatanumanisam* appears to be a Sanskrit compound, rooted in spiritual and philosophical traditions, though not widely cited in mainstream texts or temple references. *Nada* is a Sanskrit word for sacred sound or tone of divine origin. *Stanu* is another name for Shiva, meaning "the immovable" or "eternal pillar". *Manis* may stem from *mani*, which translates to jewel or radiant gem.

A devotee's soul

The connection between Tyagaraja and Shiva is rich with layers of devotion, symbolism, and musical mysticism. Though Tyagaraja was unwavering in his devotion to Rama, his name, intriguingly, means "king of renunciation" – a title often attributed to Shiva, the great ascetic. More than a composer, Tyagaraja was a seeker – one who understood music not merely as art, but as Nada Yoga, the spiritual path of inner sound. His compositions are infused with this understanding, where melody becomes meditation and rhythm becomes prayer.

In this profoundly philosophical *krithi*, Tyagaraja speaks of Shiva as the embodiment of Nada – the eternal, all-pervading cosmic vibration from which all creation flows. This vision reveals a deep reverence for Shiva – not just as a deity, but as the source of music itself, the primal sound that underlies the universe. His very name invokes profound stillness, detachment, and universal resonance.

So while Tyagaraja the devotee sang primarily to Rama, Tyagaraja the mystic recognized and honoured Shiva's essence, especially as the divine wellspring of sound, rhythm, and transcendence.

Chanting the infinite

Nada – the subtle, primordial sound – is more than just an auditory phenomenon. In ancient Indian philosophy, particularly in Shaiva Tantric philosophy, it is understood as the very pulse of consciousness. It is the "State of Power" the yogi experiences when turning inward, plunging beyond thought, form, and ego. This sound is often equated with "Aum" – the ancient sound said to carry the essence of creation in Hindu thought – all creation, sustenance, and dissolution.

In Shaiva philosophy, Shiva is recognized as the source of this Nada, the original stir of existence. The universe is nothing but the vibrational play of his consciousness, eternally unfolding and dissolving. Practices such as mantra chanting, deep listening, and bhakti or devotional surrender are not merely spiritual exercises – they are methods of attuning the self to this cosmic vibration. At elevated states of devotion and awareness, one does not just chant the divine name – one becomes the vibration, merging with that sacred frequency where the personal dissolves into the universal.

△ **Carnatic musicians perform devotional hymns** as they walk down a street in south India's Chennai to mark the beginning of the month of Margazhi, auspicious for the devotees of both Vishnu and Shiva.

THE TIMELESS LORD

In Hindu thought, time is linked to both birth and death, and it is Shiva, as the lord of time, who holds the supreme power over this cycle. He is not merely a deity who exists within time but is often portrayed as time itself, and its ultimate conqueror.

The passage of time is a fundamental aspect of reality. It is fitting, then, that Shiva – who embodies many elemental forces of life – is closely associated with time. However, this association holds a duality – Shiva is both the master of time and beyond its grasp. He governs its flow, yet transcends its limits.

Master and conquerer

Shiva holds dominion over all three *kaals*, or times – *bhoot*, or the past, *vartamaan*, or the present, and *bhavishya*, or the future. In him, all three are united, for he does not move through time, rather time moves through him, and he alone has the power to alter its course.

In Hindu philosophy, time is viewed as a cyclical and eternal flow, marked by vast epochs known as *kalpas*. This concept of time reflects the endless cycle of creation, preservation, and destruction, each phase continuously giving rise to the next. At the heart of this cosmic rhythm is Shiva as the destroyer in Hindu trinity (See pp40–45). Time is the force that brings all things to an end. Since he rules over time, he is, by extension, the ruler of destruction itself. He dismantles the old, not as an act of negation, but as a vital step in the process of renewal and rebirth.

Beyond the bounds of time

While Shiva governs the flow of time, he, at the same time, transcends its limitations. This is because time can not bind him, as he is beyond it; he is both its origin and its end. Also, there is nothing that exists beyond Shiva, not even time. He existed before time began, and he will endure beyond its end. The *Yajur Veda*, one of the four Vedas composed between 1200 BCE and 800 BCE, reveres Shiva as "he who was before all things", affirming his existence prior to the emergence of time. His epithet Sadashiva or "the one who always was and always will be" reflects this eternal nature.

Shiva as Adi Yogi, or the primordial yogi and master of meditation best represents this transcendence over time. In this form, he is eternally still, immersed in deep meditation, symbolizing his unchanging essence and detachment from the progression of time. He is the silent observer who witnesses time unfold, yet remains untouched and unaffected by its flow.

Mahakaal

When Shiva is associated with time, he is personified as Mahakaal. In this context, the word *kaal* means not just time, but specifically the "time of death". Also known as Mahamrityunjaya, the conqueror of death, Mahakaal is Shiva as the devourer and keeper of time, embodying the very cycle of life and death.

In this fierce form, he is the most ruthless, deadly, and uncompromising, mirroring the nature of time, which spares no one. People worship Shiva's manifestation as Mahakaal for *moksha*, or liberation from the cycle of birth and death. He brings an end not only to the physical body, but also to *maya*, or illusion, ego, and attachment. Mahakaal represents the ultimate end, the final destination where all dualities and boundaries dissolve. What remains is the timeless realm into which everything returns.

◁ **An early 18th-century painting from the Rajput kingdom of Mewar, Rajasthan,** features Shiva as Mahakaal performing a fierce dance. Surrounding deities, including the many-headed Brahma, Nandishvara, and the elephant-headed Ganesha, pay obeisance with folded hands.

A fearsome icon

In iconography, Mahakaal is depicted with multiple arms, red eyes, and surrounded by cremation imagery, signifying his role as the lord of death and ruler of cremation grounds. One of the most prominent sculptures of Mahakaal is in the Elephanta Caves, a collection of Shaiva cave temples in Maharashtra. Here, in one hand, he holds a human figure; in another, a sacrificial sword or axe; and in the third, a basin of blood. With two of his hands, he draws a veil that extinguishes the Sun. For devotees, this terrifying form symbolizes the destruction of ignorance and negative forces, guiding them towards enlightenment. The most famous Mahakaal temples belong to the 10th–11th centuries and are located in Madhya Pradesh with the Mahakaleshwar Temple in Ujjain being one of them.

IN BUDDHISM

Mahakaal also appears in Vajrayana Buddhism, a Tantric tradition of Buddhism practised primarily in Tibet. Here, he is Dharmapala, a wrathful manifestation of Avalokiteshvara, the bodhisattva of compassion. He serves as a fierce guardian who removes obstacles and protects practitioners on their spiritual path. Much like Shaivites, Buddhists also revere Mahakaal as a powerful force of transformation and transcendence.

▷ **A restored sculpture of Bhairava from the 13th century,** originally found at Candi Singosari in East Java. In this terrifying representation, the god is shown standing on a pile of human skulls with a dog behind him, and holding, among other things, a cleaver and a bowl made of a skull. He also wears a garland and crown of skulls.

KAAL BHAIRAVA

THE LORD OF TIME

The hostile, contaminating presence on the outskirts of civilization and the phallic god of prehistory are fused into a single ritualized archetype – Kaal Bhairava. Embodying a primal, anti-traditional, and ritually impure identity, he is the horrific, the frightful, and the terrifying. His eyes bulge, fangs jut from his mouth, his matted ascetic locks rise into a wild headdress, and a garland of skulls coils around his lower body. Sometimes he stands nude; at other times, a hissing serpent hangs in place of a loincloth, or he is draped in elephant skin. On occasion, he wears the wooden sandals of an ascetic. But the most striking feature is the cranium of a human skull he uses as a begging bowl.

Despite his fearsome appearance, Kaal Bhairava is revered as a powerful protector, particularly against evil spirits, negative energies, and black magic. He is the embodiment of *kaal*, or time itself, possessing the power to control, transcend, and ultimately destroy it. In this form, Shiva reminds the world of the impermanence of life and the destructive nature of time, and compels worshippers to confront their own fears.

The sin

The half-skull Kaal Bhairava carries is a sign of truly cosmic criminality, and he was condemned to expiate his crime. Once, overcome by pride, Brahma insulted Shiva. Out of the fire of Shiva's anger, Kaal Bhairava was born. Instantly, Kaal Bhairava rushed at Brahma and pinched off his fifth, or crowning, head. Brahma was the archetypal brahman priest, and thus Shiva was technically guilty of committing *brahmahatya*, or the sin of killing a brahman, by severing one of Brahma's heads. The severed head stuck fast to Bhairava's hand and he was condemned to wander as a begging ascetic, carrying the skull for hundreds of years. At last, Kaal Bhairava, went to the holy city of Varanasi and bathed in the waters of the Ganga, to wash away his sin. There, his sin was washed away. He left the head behind, and the place came to be known as Kapalamochana Tirtha, meaning "the skull-liberating ford".

Tantric dimensions

Sometimes regarded as an attendant of Shiva, Kaal Bhairava is a Tantric deity, especially prominent in North India and regions of Nepal. Therefore, he is also closely associated with the Chaunsatha Yoginis, as their great leader. As Vidya Dehejia observes in *Yogini Cult and Temples*, Sanskrit texts like Bhavabhuti's *Malatimadhava* and the Kashmiri collection *Kathasaritsagara* suggest that Yoginis would gather in cremation grounds, forming a circle to ritually offer a human victim to Shiva in his fierce form as Bhairava. Tantric sects such as the Kapalikas (*see pp280–83*) also emulate Shiva's extreme asceticism. Devotees of Bhairava, they roam as naked ascetics, carrying human skulls as begging bowls.

Transgression

Kaal Bhairava is often shown with a dog, considered his vehicle, symbolizing his deep connection to realms of transition and transformation. As a deity who dwells on the fringes of purity, in cremation grounds and places of transgression, Bhairava's bond with the dog reflects his own liminal, fearsome nature. Together, they represent a raw, boundary-defying force that challenges convention, existing in the spaces where the line between purity and impurity fades.

▽ A 16th-century Nepalese mask of Bhairava.

The Lakhey dancer, dressed in a fearsome demon mask, storms through Kathmandu's streets in Nepal, accompanied by pounding drums to represent the Lakhey, a powerful yet protective demon, who is said to guard the city from evil. This sacred ceremony, rooted in Newar tradition, and frequently associated with Shiva's Bhairava avatar, is believed to protect children and ward off evil. Performed during festivals, the dance blends mythology, music, and motion to create a powerful display of divine guardianship and cultural pride.

FROM THE MARKANDEYA PURANA Defying death through faith

MARKANDEYA'S DEVOTION

Mrikanda, a revered sage, and his wife Manasvini lived a life of piety. They served the poor, honoured cows, and worshipped God. They also longed for a child and no matter how much they tried, they remained childless. Saddened, Mrikanda performed severe penance and prayed to Shiva for a child.

Pleased with his devotion, Shiva appeared before him, but offered him a choice: Did they want a son who lived a long life but lacked virtue, or a virtuous son who would live for only 16 years.

Mrikanda asked for a virtuous son and when Manasvini gave birth, they named him Markandeya. He mastered the scriptures early and grew up kind and intelligent. But, as his 16th birthday approached, his parents grew anxious. They knew his time would soon come to an end.

When Markandeya learnt of his fate, he consoled his parents and vowed to seek Shiva's protection. He went to the seashore and shaped a lingam out of wet sand. He adorned it with fresh flowers, and worshipped Shiva with deep devotion.

On the appointed day, when Yama, the god of death, approached to claim him, Markandeya pleaded for time to complete his rituals. Driven by fear or faith, he clung to the lingam, refusing to let go. Yama, firm in his duty, refused to compromise. "No one escapes me when their time has come," he said and threw his noose around Markandeya. The noose caught him but tightened around the lingam as well. In that instant, Shiva burst forth from the lingam to protect his devotee and in a blaze of divine fury, struck down Yama. Shiva later revived the god of death, as the world cannot exist without death, but declared: "Markandeya, your unwavering faith has made you immortal".

It is believed that Markandeya still lives in the Himalayas, eternally young. He went on to become a great rishi and composed the *Markandeya Purana*. After this incident, Shiva became known as Mrityunjaya or "the conqueror of death", and Markandeya, Dirghayus or "the long-lived."

▷ **Markandeya clings to the Shiva lingam** demonstrating unwavering devotion and faith in his god, in this statue from Brihadeeswara Temple in Thanjavur, Tamil Nadu.

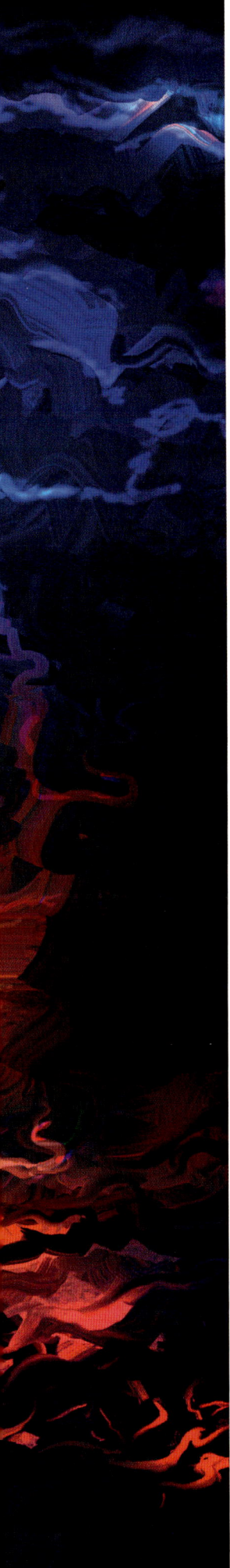

DIVINE JUSTICE

One of Shiva's most profound qualities is his unwavering commitment to justice. Yet, his righteous fury at adharma is often tempered by boundless compassion. The two forces appear like natural concomitants, intertwined in mythology, philosophy, and devotional practice.

Many believers call Shiva *karma phaladata*, or the dispenser of the fruits of karma. This is because in his story, he ensures that every action – good or bad – receives its due consequence, making him the ultimate upholder of dharma.

Shiva annihilates ignorance and adharma, not out of wrath but to restore cosmic balance and to guide beings towards the right path. His destruction – dramatic and at times macabre – is always purposeful and regenerative. The spectacle is meant to be remembered in all its frightening glory and lifelong lessons.

The saviour

Shiva's role as the saviour of the cosmic balance is evident in many mythological episodes. Acting like a true saviour time and time again, he is called upon to save the universe. One of the acts that epitomizes his self-sacrifice and divine grace is the Samudramanthan (*See pp124–25*). When the deadly poison, Halahala, threatened all existence, Shiva drank the venom, without thinking of his own safety.

In another episode, Ganga, proud of her powers as a river, refused to leave the comforts of heaven. She warned of disastrous consequences if she descended to Earth. Once again, Shiva was asked to step in and avert catastrophe. He took Ganga into his tangled hair, and she nearly lost herself. Eventually, she flowed out in gentle streams, merging her power with Shiva's. Together, they sanctified the Earth and its people.

Indignant yet kind

Just as there is a deep theology behind Shiva's role as a saviour, there is a philosophy that shapes his anger and fury. Often, Shiva is associated with an excruciating, boundless fury, though more often than not, this fury has a reason – to deliver divine justice.

At the same time, even though he embodies wrath in his stand against adharma, his heart remains bound by compassion. Shiva goes about destroying evil but is quick and always ready to forgive, empathetic to the foibles of the Asuras and the lack of their understanding. No wonder he is *Ashutosh*, the one who is easily pleased. He is often portrayed as forgiving even the most fearsome beings if their devotion is sincere. This theme recurs in various Shaiva myths.

The one related to Sati is an ideal example. When Sati died at her father Daksha's yagna, or sacrificial ritual, (*See pp84–85*), Shiva manifested as the fierce Veerbhadra (*See pp86–89*) and defiled and destroyed everything. The worst outcome was Daksha's beheading. However, true to his nature, Shiva felt compassion for Prasuti, Daksha's wife, who was weeping in a corner, and moved by her sorrow, restored Daksha and replaced his fallen head with that of a goat.

In the famous Lingodbhava episode, when Brahma resorted to deceit, Shiva created Bhairava from his brow. On Shiva's command, Bhairava seized Brahma's fifth head – guilty

▷ **A 19th-century portrait of Ravana,** who was trapped by Shiva beneath a mountain.

of lying – and prepared to cut it off. Brahma begged for mercy, and again, Shiva's compassion ruled. He forgave Brahma, declaring that even though he would not be honoured with temples or festivals, he would be the presiding deity in domestic rites. Shiva's combined wrath and compassion can also be seen in his encounter with several Asuras. As Andhaka lay dying, he repented and chanted Shiva's name. Shiva revealed Andhaka's true parentage and forgave him, making him a chief of the Ganas. Similarly, despite Gajasura's faults, Shiva granted him a place of honour in the divine realm, displaying his ability to forgive and transform rather than punish. When Ravana tried to uproot Shiva's abode, Mount Kailasha, to demonstrate his power, Shiva pressed the mountain down with his toe, trapping Ravana (See pp30–31). The 10-headed Rakshasa composed a hymn, called *Shiva Tandava Stotram*, in repentance. Shiva relented and forgave him once Ravana realized his folly and showed humility and devotion.

At times, Parvati shows no mercy, as with the devout follower Bhringi (See pp196–97), whom she cursed. Left nearly lifeless, without flesh or blood to support him, Bhringi collapsed on the ground, barely breathing. Shiva intervened, believing he had been punished sufficiently and suffered enough humiliation. He gave

◁ **A c. 1800 painting depicting the Ganga** descending from Shiva's locks, displaying how Shiva tamed the river's uncontrollable force to save the world.

He forgives when it leads to growth, redemption, or cosmic balance. But when a sin threatens the very fabric of trust and dharma, even Shiva must withhold grace. His anger desecrates and his compassion rectifies, but not totally.

Bhringi a third leg to support his otherwise disintegrating body. This act exemplifies Shiva's deep consideration, love, and empathy for his devoted followers.

Compassion with boundaries

Shiva's forgiveness is neither unconditional, nor sentimental. It is transformative, balanced by dharma and cosmic consequences. He forgives when it leads to growth, redemption, or cosmic balance. But when a sin threatens the very fabric of trust and dharma, even Shiva must withhold grace. His anger desecrates and his compassion rectifies but not totally.

When Kama, the god of love and desire (See pp80–81), shot his arrows at Shiva's heart to stir love, he instead shattered Shiva's yogic trance. In a flash of fury, Shiva opened his third eye, incinerating Kama into ashes. With her own personal loss, Kama's wife Rati was devastated. Once again, her grief moved Shiva, who promised her that Kama would live on as *ananga*, that is a bodiless force of desire. This act symbolizes Shiva's transcendence over lust and physical desire, aligning with yogic ideals of inner completeness. It shows his compassion, but not his repentance. The punishment is still very clear with the transformation of Kama's very being.

▷ **A 12th-century statue of Shiva** as Lingodbhava, the cosmic pillar of light.

118 | SHIVA, THE FIERCE ONE

FROM THE SHIVA PURANA The destruction of the indestructible

TRIPURASURA SLAYED

The universe comprises *triloka*, or the three worlds — Earth, atmosphere, and sky. In ancient Vedic lore, after the gods slayed the Asura Tarakasura, his enraged sons — Tarakaksha, Vidyunmali, and Kamalaksha — sought revenge. Retreating to a remote cave, they performed intense austerities to please Brahma, the creator, and asked for immortality and freedom from aging.

Brahma, refused and said, "That cannot be granted. All born into this world must die. Age and decay are the natural consequences of birth and cannot be undone. Ask for any other boon."

So, the Asuras requested three invincible, fortified cities — Tripura — that only Shiva could destroy. Brahma granted their wish. The brothers took the architect Maya Danava's help to build three flying cities, indestructible except when they were aligned — a rare celestial moment. The Asuras ruled from Tripura with unchecked power, harassing gods and humans alike. The cities constantly drifted apart, so no one could defeat them. Only an arrow shot at the exact moment of alignment could destroy them — but no such bowman existed.

Responding to the pleas of the gods and humans, Shiva, the lord of wilderness and destruction, rose to the challenge. For this, Mount Meru became his bow, the serpent Vasuki the string, Earth his chariot, Sun and Moon its wheels, Brahma the charioteer, and the four Vedas the horses. Vishnu, meanwhile, disguised himself as a monk and subtly taught the Asuras renunciation. Their minds turned inwards, and they lost interest in conquest.

The cities aligned at that moment and Shiva let the arrow fly. Agni formed the arrow's blazing tip, and Vishnu's force shattered Tripura in a single, divine strike.

In victory, Shiva smeared the cities' ashes on his body, and drew three lines on his forehead — the tripundra, symbolizing the three worlds. He then danced in the fierce Alidha pose, triumphant as Tripurantaka, destroyer of Tripura.

◁ **Rasa United, a Delhi-based dance group,** performs the tale of Shiva's destruction of Tripura. The male dancers on the right embody the Asuras, in their final moments before alignment. At the centre, Guru Vanashree Rao, in black, portrays Shiva, drawing a bow and preparing to release the arrow.

FROM THE SHIVA PURANA When blind ambition met divine wrath

AN ASURA TRANSFORMED

Shiva sat on Kailasha, his sacred mountain abode, in meditation, when Parvati arrived in a playful mood, and covered his eyes with her hands. In an instant, the light in the universe went out, for Shiva's eyes are the Sun and the Moon. Life began to fade and living beings were consumed with fear.

Shiva opened his third eye so that the Sun would shine again. So fiery was the glance that Parvati's palms began to sweat. From the sweat that touched Shiva emerged an unbecoming physical being. One that was also blind, as he was born when both of Shiva's eyes were closed. The god told a horrified Parvati that the being was her son as he was born of their physical contact. He was given the name Andhaka, or one born from darkness.

Shiva gave the baby to the childless Asura Hiranyaksha as a boon for his penance. Andhaka eventually became lord of the Asuras. Discarded by the clan, he sought comfort in meditation. Brahma, the creator of the universe, pleased with him, granted him a boon that made him invincible, gave him the power of sight, and the ability to survive Shiva's wrath. The boon, however, came with a curse – he would die if he looked upon his mother with lustful eyes. Andhaka paid no heed to this as he thought he had no mother. He commanded his Asura army to become the ruler of the three worlds. Urged by his minister, he desired the beautiful Parvati, having heard of her beauty, and forgot his connection to Shiva.

He laid siege on Shiva's cave and the battle carried on for years until the god returned from his meditation and joined the battle. Shiva impaled Andhaka on his *shula*, the lance or spear, and kept him alive, impaled for a thousand years, draining him of blood until he became a bag of bones. Andhaka realized his mistake and apologized for all that he had done.

A benevolent Shiva forgave the Asura and made him a Gana, a divine guardian. In doing so, Andhaka's tale became a symbol of the conquest of ignorance and ego, and Shiva's acceptance of the Asura a representation of transformation rather than mere destruction.

▷ **A sculpture from the Ellora Caves,** Maharashtra, depicting Shiva slaying the Asura Andhaka at the entrance to the Kailasha Temple.

COILED AROUND HIS NECK

Vasuki has myriad roles. He is the adoring devotee, the string to Shiva's bow when he goes into battle, and the all-knowing messenger residing in the depths of the earth. A fundamental element in Shiva iconography, the ruler of the Nagas is a symbol of justice, time, and feminine energy.

From the moment Vasuki, the king of Sarpas, or the serpents, first witnessed the splendour of Shiva dancing, his reptilian heart carried but one wish, that he be allowed to go on a pilgrimage to Mount Kailasha, the god's abode. There, he desired to engage in severe penance so that he could uncover the true meaning behind this awe-inspiring galactic dance, notes ethnologist Wolf-Dieter Storl in his book, *Shiva: The Wild God of Power and Ecstasy*.

The Vasuki connection

Vasuki, who bore the mystical Nagamani jewel, has deep connections to Shiva, and Hindu mythology is replete with myths linking the two. In some, he is the devotee, striving to please his god, such as the popular Samudramanthan or the tale of the churning of the ocean (See pp124–25). In the myth, the serpent king played a prominent role when he allowed the Devas and the Asuras to wrap him around Mount Mandara and use him to churn the ocean and extract the nectar from the Ocean of Milk.

In one version, when the ocean emitted the deadly poison Kalakuta or Halahala, Shiva drank it to save the world, as did Vasuki and the other snakes in the water. Pleased with his sacrifice, Shiva accepted Vasuki and wrapped him around his neck, not just as a mark of honour but also to symbolize his mastery over destructive forces.

In another myth, Vasuki became the bowstring for Shiva's divine bow that the god used to destroy the three Asura cities, Tripura (See pp118–19). There are references to Vasuki in Vishnu's Varaha or boar avatar as well. When a flaming pillar of fire appeared in the universe, in the Lingodbhava myth, Varaha began digging into the earth in search of the pillar's starting point. At some unfathomable depth, he chanced upon Vasuki, who told him to give up on his quest. The blazing pillar, he told Varaha, is a manifestation of Shiva who has neither root nor crown.

Awakening of the senses

Vasuki also represents Kundalini, the dormant feminine spiritual energy, which some yogic practitioners believe resides in the base of the spine, coiled like a snake. It can be induced to unwind and rise by degrees to the brain and then enlightenment takes place, a symbol of the union of Shiva and Shakti. This is why Shiva's wearing of Vasuki translates to the full awakening and control of this energy. His control over the king of snakes reflects his transcendence over worldly desires.

Vasuki coiled around the god's neck three times, symbolizes the past, present, and future – the cycle of time, which Shiva as Mahakaal controls. Vasuski's head points toward the right shoulder, representing cosmic order and justice.

Symbolism

Snakes have a great affinity to Shiva as seen in countless depictions. His wearing the reptiles symbolizes compassion and dominion over even the most feared creatures. Snakes carry within them poison, but they are not affected by it and the same applies to Shiva. It's also why he is called Shiva Vishapaharana or the destroyer of poison.

▷ **Contemporary Indian artist Anag Kumar's depiction of Shiva** in meditation. His painting shows key elements from Shiva iconography, including the trident, third eye, crescent moon, and serpent around his neck, all rendered in striking silhouette.

◁ **Shiva drinks the Halahala poison** while a worried Parvati looks on. In the midst of the swirling waters of the ocean Devas and Asuras collapse in this work by artist and Carnatic vocalist S Rajam.

FROM THE BHAGAVATA PURANA Saving all creation by drinking deadly poison

CHURNING OF THE OCEAN

The two eternal rivals, the Asuras and the Devas, were temporarily united as they desired to own *Amrita*, the nectar of immortality. They had lost this sacred drink or elixir, probably referred to as *Soma* in the Vedic texts, and later *Amrita*, that gave them strength and vigour. It had sunk to the depths of the ocean floor along with innumerable other precious artifacts and holy treasures.

The Devas devised a daring scheme and turned to the Asuras for assistance. Many negotiations later, both decided to cooperate in the hopes of regaining the nectar.

Mount Meru and the great serpent Vasuki, residing in the netherworld, *Patala*, agreed to help. The snake king would be looped around the mountain and the Devas and Asuras would stand at either end and pull, turning Mount Meru into a gigantic churning stick. As soon as they began tugging, the mountain began to sink into the ocean as it had no solid foundation.

To support it, Vishnu assumed the form of Kurma, the heavenly tortoise, and used his broad, firm back as the foundation. With this, the great churning of the *Ksheersagar* or Ocean of Milk began.

The Asuras and Devas heaved and pulled and churned with all their might. But instead of *Amrita*, the first thing that rose from the ocean was Halahala, a deadly poison that threatened to destroy all life. Terrified, the Devas ran to Shiva, as he was the only one capable of containing the poison. In an act of the greatest sacrifice, Shiva, also known as Vishapaharana, the "Destroyer of Poison", devoured the poison.

Fearing that the poison would kill him, Parvati, Shiva's wife, placed her hands around his throat, preventing the poison from entering his stomach. Her quick action saved him and gave Shiva's neck a vivid blue hue. His worshippers lovingly gave him a new name – Neelakantha, the "Blue-throated one".

Shiva's act of swallowing the poison revealed his true nature. Although often regarded as the Destroyer, he destroys to protect and transform, not to cause chaos. In moments like these, Shiva appears as the saviour, protecting the world from impending disaster.

Every year, in the Hindu month of Shravan, millions of Shiva devotees, known as Kanwariyas, set out on pilgrimage to sacred Ganga sites such as Haridwar, Gaumukh, and Gangotri. They fetch the holy water from these sources and carry it for miles to offer at their local Shiva shrines or great Shaiva temples. The water is borne in a *kanwar*, a brightly decorated pole that can be simple or elaborate, small or towering. Called the Kanwar Yatra, this arduous journey – walking barefoot, with the most devout even crawling along the path – is rooted in Shaiva myths of Ganga, most famously the churning of the ocean, when her waters soothed Shiva's throat after he drank the deadly poison. In this image, Kanwariyas journey from Prayagraj to Varanasi to offer Ganga water at the Kashi Vishwanath Temple.

KUMBH MELA
AN EPIC PILGRIMAGE BEYOND TIME

As conch shells echo and incense thickens the air, millions of pilgrims immerse themselves in the holy waters, seeking not just cleansing but also liberation of the soul. This is the Kumbh Mela, the world's largest spiritual gathering that takes place every four years.

Origins of the mela
The word *kumbh* means "pitcher," and it refers to the mythical jar that held *amrita*, the nectar of immortality. According to the legend of the Samudramanthan, as the Devas and Asuras struggled for control of the jar, a few drops of the precious nectar spilt onto the Earth. These drops are believed to have fallen at four sacred sites, now known as *tirthas* or spiritual crossing points between the earthly and the divine. These are Prayagraj, which, sits at the confluence of three rivers: the Ganga, Yamuna, and the mythical Sarasvati. Then, there is Haridwar on the banks of the Ganga, Nashik located along the Godavari River, and Ujjain, near the banks of the Shipra River. These cities now host the Kumbh Mela in a 12-year cycle, rotating among them.

Rare and auspicious planetary alignments determine the timing of each Kumbh Mela, which is a time for spiritual cleansing and intellectual and religious exchange. The 8th century philosopher-saint Adi Shankaracharya encouraged sages, monks, and seekers to use this event to share wisdom and ideas.

Naga sadhus
The Kumbh Mela also offers a rare glimpse into the hidden world of India's reclusive spiritual ascetics. During this extraordinary gathering, hermits from the remote Himalayas descend in great numbers, particularly Shaivite ascetics known as Naga Sadhus or Naga Babas. These mysterious figures are instantly recognizable — nude or minimally clothed, their bodies covered in sacred ash, with matted hair, tridents in hand, and an intense presence that reflects years of renunciation and discipline.

With great ceremony, they lead the grand processions and are the first to take the holy dip in the sacred river — a symbolic act of purification and spiritual authority. The event also marks a powerful rite of passage for young sadhus, who undergo initiation rituals to become Naga Babas — warrior ascetics of Lord Shiva. Embracing a path of intense discipline, they renounce all material possessions and social conventions.

Spiritual rigours
Following the Naga Sadhus in the Kumbh Mela processions is a vibrant mix of spiritual seekers — sadhus, yoginis, faqirs, and gurus. Each comes with deep devotion, seeking a holy dip, to perform ritual ablutions, demonstrate yogic powers (siddhis), and offer or receive darshan (spiritual sight).

Among them are extraordinary ascetics known for extreme spiritual discipline. Some have kept an arm raised for years in devotion to Shiva, now gnarled and frozen in place. Others stand on one leg for life or sit on beds of nails, thorns, or coals — acts symbolizing their pursuit of liberation beyond physical limits. The 12-day Kumbh Mela is a profound expression of India's enduring spiritual traditions, drawing in millions in a powerful collective pilgrimage.

▷ *(clockwise from top)* **Priests perform evening prayers** holding lamps and chanting mantras in Haridwar; **Pilgrims gather in large numbers at Har Ki Pauri**, the famous Ghat or stairs on the banks of the Ganga in Haridwar; **Naga sadhus walk in a religious procession** of Atal Akhara, ahead of the Mahakumbh Mela in Prayagraj.

DECODING THE KUMBH

THE MYTH OF GARUDA'S FLIGHT
Clutching the precious pot of Amrita, Garuda, the divine eagle and mount of Lord Vishnu, soared across the heavens. Below him the Asuras gave chase, desperate to seize the elixir. During this flight, Garuda descended at four earthly spots. At each resting place, a single drop of the sacred nectar fell. These sites now draw millions in faith.

SACRED HINDU TEXTS
The festival is mentioned in sacred Hindu texts such as the *Bhagavata Purana*, *Vishnu Purana*, and the *Mahabharata*. These texts emphasize the transformative significance of ritual bathing during specific astrological periods, when divine energies are believed to be most accessible. The Kumbh is a living embodiment of devotion, and timeless spiritual tradition.

MAHAKUMBH MELA
The Kumbh Mela is held every four years, rotating among four sacred cities. Every twelfth year, the celebration becomes even more grand in scale, with the Mahakumbh Mela, drawing even larger crowds and deeper spiritual intensity. Pilgrims come not only to bathe in sacred rivers, but to cleanse their minds, hearts, and souls. The journey demands inner commitment, humility, and a sincere desire for purification and redemption from past sins.

MOON IN HIS EMBRACE

One of Shiva's most enduring and evocative epithets is Chandrashekhara, or "the one who wears the Moon on his crest". Its story begins with a curse but ends in cosmic balance.

The story goes that Chandra, the Moon God, married Daksha's 27 daughters, the nakshatras, but favoured Rohini, neglecting the others. Angered, Daksha cursed Chandra with a wasting disease, dimming his light and disturbing cosmic order. The gods intervened, and Daksha modified the curse – Chandra would wax and wane monthly. Weakened, Chandra sought refuge in Shiva's matted locks, regaining vitality. Shiva became known as Chandrashekhara, "the one who wears the Moon on his crest". Grateful, Chandra vowed to visit each wife every month, shining brightest with Rohini. The night he is alone is known as Amavasya.

A universal symbol

Across ancient cultures, the Moon symbolized transformation and eternity. Its phases reflected life's cycle – birth to rebirth – making it, as author Jules Cashford notes in *The Moon: Myth and Image*, a timeless, celestial being of endless renewal.

In early thought, people drew a connection between the curved horns of animals and the crescent shape of the waxing or waning Moon. This symbolic association led them to attribute the Moon's fertility and generative powers to horned animals. These animals, often used to plough and fertilize the earth, became incarnations of the Moon's life-giving essence. The symbolic relationship between the Moon, the horn, and fertility is believed to have existed for at least 20,000 years.

Shiva's dual nature

The Moon's presence on Shiva's brow also reflects a deeper metaphysical truth – the god's dual nature. In the epics and early iconography, Shiva possesses two forms – *ghora tanu*, the fierce and terrible body composed of fire, lightning, and the sun, and *saumya tanu*, the gentle and benign body made of water, stars, and the Moon. This duality manifests in Shiva's imagery – some depictions show him as fearsome and destructive, while others present him as peaceful and benevolent, bestowing grace upon his devotees.

Early images of Shiva often depict the crescent Moon directly on his forehead. In later representations, the Moon is typically seen on the right side of his tall, matted hair, coiled in a shape reminiscent of the lingam. As Art Historian TS Maxwell explains in *The Gods of Asia: Image, Text, and Meaning*, this crescent is not only a celestial ornament but also a vital marker of Shiva's cosmic role, as both destroyer and restorer, and fierce ascetic and nurturing lord.

> ... crescent is not only a celestial ornament but also a vital marker of Shiva's cosmic role, as both destroyer and restorer, fierce ascetic and nurturing lord.

▷ **An elaborate lithograph of Khandoba** depicted as a Maratha horseman, his wife seated alongside and his dog at the horse's heels, spearing an Asura.

KHANDOBA

THE VIRILE WARRIOR

In the heart of Maharashtra, Shiva assumes a fierce and majestic form, as a warrior god thundering across the land on a swift, battle-ready horse. In rural India, the horse and rider symbolize the great hero, and here, that hero is Khandoba. His sword burns with righteous fury; his trident hums with divine power. Crowned with a regal turban that proclaims his sovereignty, he appears as a royal protector. At his side are his two consorts, Mhalsa and Banai, while a loyal dog runs at his heels. Khandoba is an eternal force, riding with thunder to defend the faithful.

His story is told in the *Malhari Mahatmya*, a sacred text that recounts his heroic exploits. It describes his slaying of the Asuras Mani and Malla, who had terrorized the Earth after receiving powerful boons from Brahma, the creator. For this victory, he is also known as Malhari, meaning "enemy of Malla". At times, he is called Martand Bhairava, reinforcing his association with the dog as a companion.

A regional deity

A deity of the masses, Khandoba is the *kuladevata*, or family deity, for many Marathas and even some Muslims, reflecting the inclusive and syncretic nature of his worship. He is often regarded as a local manifestation of Shiva in Maharashtra, much like Mailara in Karnataka or Mallanna in Andhra Pradesh. He is also venerated as the god of shepherds, with the tree branch in his hands as a symbol of his sylvan roots.

The merging of two worlds

Khandoba's first wife, Mhalsa, comes from the Shaivite Lingayats (See pp262–63). His second wife, Banai, belongs to the shepherd community of the Dhangars in Karnataka. The contrasting complexions of the two wives – Mhalsa's fair and Banai's dark – reflect their differing backgrounds, but also prompt a philosophical dimension: the necessity of two poles of a duality, which merge into oneness at the centre, in the god himself. Mhalsa symbolizes permanence, settlement, and cultivated land (*kshetra*), while Banai embodies wildness, movement, and the forest (*vana*). Through these two consorts, Khandoba unites two essential ecological worlds – the agrarian societies rooted in settled life and the pastoral, hunting, and tribal communities of the forests and pastures.

In a cloud of gold

Khandoba's worship is deeply rooted in folk traditions. His primary offering is turmeric, symbolizing his non-Brahmanical and inclusive appeal. At his shrines, tribal priests and frenzied women priestesses lead the rituals. At the Jejuri Temple in west India's Maharashtra, Khandoba's most renowned shrine, devotees hurl turmeric into the air, covering the temple steps, idols, and each other in a golden cloud. This vibrant spectacle becomes a visual metaphor for divine blessings and collective joy. The temple is affectionately known as Sonyachi Jejuri, or literally "golden Jejuri", a name inspired by the dazzling turmeric showers, especially during festivals like Champa Shashti.

According to a local legend, Khandoba's second wife, dark-complexioned, once asked Shiva to make her fair. He granted her wish, turning her golden, hence the ritual use of turmeric by devotees. Fittingly, Maharashtra is also one of the highest producers of turmeric in India.

△ **An 18th-century metal icon of Khandoba**

◁ **In this 1830 painting from Tamil Nadu,** a graceful Mohini, adorned with elaborate jewellery, stands, as flames consume Bhasmasura. Clad only in a shawl draped over her lower abdomen, she holds a blooming rose in her right hand, while a parrot perches on a flower in her left hand.

FROM THE SHIVA PURANA Wielding power without wisdom

THE BOON THAT BECAME A CURSE

Shiva never played favourites and welcomed all disciples alike, whether Devas or Asuras. Among his most devoted followers were the Asuras and moved by their intense penance, Shiva often granted them powerful boons — acts of divine generosity born from innocence and grace. The Asuras, though disciplined in tapasya, were often unprepared for the power they received, turning their gifts into weapons of chaos.

One such Asura, Bhasma, according to a popular myth, undertook a relentless penance to win Shiva's favour. Moved by his devotion, Shiva appeared and offered him a boon of his choice. Bhasma asked for the ability to incinerate anyone with a single touch to the head. Though the request was unusual, Shiva, ever generous and unsuspecting, granted it, unaware of the destruction it would soon unleash.

To test his terrifying new power, the cunning Bhasmasura turned on Shiva, reaching out to touch his head. If Bhasmasura succeeded, Shiva would be reduced to ashes, and with his death, the world would plunge into chaos. Recognizing his grave mistake Shiva ran for his life, trident in hand — across mountains and valleys, through gushing rivers and still lakes, over plains where cattle grazed and farmers toiled, past quiet ashrams and dark, restless forests. Trailing him, relentless as ever, thundered Bhasmasura — never far behind.

Desperate and out of options, Shiva sought help from Vishnu, who devised a clever plan. He took the form of Mohini, a stunning enchantress. She appeared before Bhasmasura, standing between him and Shiva. Entranced, Bhasmasura forgot about Shiva, and instead begged Mohini to marry him. She agreed on one condition — he had to match her in a dance. Bhasmasura agreed. As Mohini danced, he mirrored her every move, completely enchanted. Then, with deceptive grace, Mohini placed her hand on her own head. Bhasmasura, blinded by desire, did the same and in an instant was reduced to ashes.

Vishnu's incarnation as Mohini is more than a tale of disguise — it is a lesson in how wisdom and strategy can triumph over brute strength and reckless ambition. Power, when misused, becomes a curse.

FLAME AND FURY

Many ancient deities woven into the fabric of the *Rig Veda* have long faded from the collective consciousness of the Hindu world. Yet, one stands resolute among them all – Agni, the god of fire. His flame never wanes. Instead, it has become an indelible part of Shiva's cosmic dance and being, forever blazing through the heart of the divine.

From time immemorial, fire has carried deep symbolism across cultures and religions. It is used to represent strong emotions, whether anger or erotic passion. Besides this, fire is a force of power that is a paradox as it proliferated and facilitated human survival and yet could lead to disastrous peril. Starting with the terrestrial, the hearth is at the centre of the home, just like the Sun is the celestial fire and is considered the heart of the heavens.

Sacred flames

Shiva and fire have had an intimate connection throughout Hindu mythic history and are almost always depicted as ruthless. They are linked not just in the mythology, but also religious traditions.

It is understood that fire, among many other symbolizations, denotes transformation as a natural concomitant. In Shaivic myths, for the greatest part, fire is a metaphor for transformation of a drastic kind. The old is destroyed with considerable haste and makes way for the new. This aligns with Shiva's primary role as the force of change. He is the god of destruction, and destruction is a tangible feature of fire.

Though everyone is aware that fire eliminates darkness, it also makes enlightenment possible. In fact, fire, in the form of what remains – its ashes – bursts with profound metaphoric truths.

In Hindu thought and practice, as German-American ethnologist and cultural anthropologist Wolf-Dieter Storl points out, Agni, the all-consuming fire god, is the ever famished, flaming mouth of the gods. Not only does Agni receive oblations in the yagna, fire itself is the door through which mortals enter the spirit world by their ultimate sacrifice to Agni at their cremation.

Where fire meets the divine

Numerous Shaivic tales and forms ignite with the fierce presence of fire and show that fire resides within Shiva. A well-known episode centres around Kamadeva, the god of love (*See pp80–81*). Once, when Shiva was deep in meditation, the Devas sent Kamadeva to awaken him. Shiva, opening his third eye, incinerated Kamadeva with a fiery blast, reducing him to ashes.

Another striking display of Shiva's fiery nature unfolds in the story of Karttikeya's birth. Shiva's seed – too hot for any being to contain – was dislodged. First Agni carried it, before passing it on to the river goddess Ganga. Another legend related to Karttikeya's birth, tells of how the young child came to be after a shower of fiery sparks sprayed out of Shiva's eyes and fell into a lake. Six boys were born of those sparks. Another story found, in the epic *Mahabharata*, described by Storl, says that since Parvati and Shiva were incapable of reproducing normally, they engendered a child by proxy, namely by fire and water, personified as Agni and Ganga. Shiva, taking on the ferocious Rudra form, slipped into Agni and filled

FLAME AND FURY | 137

◁ **A painting by Indian artist Ankita Biswas** depicting Shiva as Nataraja, dancing within a circle of flames, surrounded by awestruck devotees.

Shiva is the god of destruction, and destruction is a tangible feature of fire.

him with ardent desire, so that his seed might bring forth a long desired hero. At the same time, Parvati assumed the form of Svaha, one of Daksha's many beautiful daughters, whose name means "offering" or "oblation". Shiva, in his fierce form as Veerbhadra (*See pp86–89*), also doused Daksha's yagna as his furious hordes not only extinguished but severely contaminated and polluted the sacred fires.

The most popular episode, however, is the Lingodbhava episode. Shiva is fire himself and appeared as a humungous pillar of flame in an attempt to reveal himself as the omnipotent one whilst Brahma and Vishnu squabble. A nod to this myth appears later in the 12 sacred pilgrimage sites known as jyotirlingas, or the "lingas of light" (*See pp66–69*).

While the Lingodbhava myth is the most well-known fire-related story, it is Shiva as Nataraja (*See pp98–101*), the cosmic dancer, who stands as the most iconic and enduring symbol of fire.

In this image, worshippers embody Shiva and his companions as they head to celebrate Charak Puja, a Shaiva festival widely observed in West Bengal and Bangladesh. Across India, it is common to see devotees take on the roles of gods and goddesses, bringing myths alive on the streets. Stories are passed down through performance – sung, recited, and enacted – and that performative spirit continues to shape festivals and rituals today.

I am not the five great elements

Nirvana Shatakam, Adi Shankaracharya

3 | SHIVA
THE HOUSEHOLDER

. . . It is the balance between individual and society." With this revelation, Shiva also proclaims, "There shall be no worship, or yagna, without a man's wife being right by his side."

THE ASCETIC HOUSEHOLDER

Shiva, often celebrated as the great ascetic, also embodies the life of a householder, showing that renunciation and domesticity are not mutually exclusive. By embracing household life, he upholds the dictates of dharma, which stress marriage and procreation, and demonstrates the importance of family in the cosmic order.

The story of Shiva brings to the forefront a fundamental cultural quandary – the tension between engagement with the social world and the pursuit of spiritual liberation. While the social path emphasizes household responsibilities, familial duty, and the enjoyment of sensual pleasures, the ascetic path rejects worldly life, including sexuality and procreation, in the quest for spiritual salvation.

The paradox

Shiva is the deity who embodies both stages of life – he is the Maha Yogi, the great ascetic, and Shankara, the benevolent householder. Though an ascetic, he assumes the life of a householder to respond to worldly desires and restore balance to the world. Through this domestic role, Shiva integrates into Brahmanical theology, where only those who fulfill the responsibilities of father, mother, and child are regarded as complete individuals. Therefore, he reconciles two extremes within his own being.

This tension between renunciation and worldly engagement is a persistent theme in Shaiva mythology, though never fully resolved. In the myths, Shiva is often caught between solitude, as seen in his early portrayal as Rudra, and domestic life, including fatherhood. The conflict ultimately gives rise to a vision of reconciliation, interdependence, and harmony. This is reflected in symbolic forms such as the lingam–yoni, Ardhanarishvara (*See pp166–69*), Kalyanasundarmurti (*See pp152–53*), as well as in epithets such as Umapati, husband of Goddess Uma, and Girijapati, husband of Goddess Girija, which highlight the centrality of his consort in his life.

Parvati's influence

When it comes to Shiva as a householder, his primary consort is Parvati, who plays a crucial role in shaping his domestic identity. Although he was earlier married to Sati, their married life is scarcely developed in mythology, as the narrative largely focuses on Sati's death (See pp148–49), which drove Shiva into grief and asceticism. It is only through Parvati that Shiva's householder aspect is fully realized. She embodies the beauty, attraction, and values of married life – qualities that Shiva, the renouncer, had once forsaken in pursuit of asceticism. Her presence beside him accentuates his completeness, for through their union he is drawn into worldly life, extending his sphere of activity to the domestic and familial realm. Parvati brings order and structure to Shiva's life, guided by Brahmanical principles. Sculptures and Puranic literature depict them riding together on Shiva's mount Nandi, playing board games, enjoying aquatic sports, adorning each other with flowers, creating the *mundamala*, or the garland of skulls, and teasing one another like any loving couple.

The imperfect husband

Shiva is not portrayed as an ideal husband. Yet, female worshippers pray to the Shiva lingam, offer water and milk, observe fasts, and dedicate themselves to his service to win a husband who embodies Shiva's qualities. This raises the question: was he really such an ideal spouse? In the myths, he often loses patience with Parvati and speaks in harsh tones. On one occasion, while quarrelling over a trivial matter, he insulted her family, comparing her mind to the turbid clouds atop the Himalayas, her heart to the impenetrable hardness of mountain rocks, her temperament to the thickness of thickets, and her disposition to the crookedness of rivers – words that left her hurt and furious.

Yet there is another perspective. Quarrels, separation, and eventual reconciliation are intrinsic to many sexual and marital relationships, often intensifying passion and erotic energy. On a symbolic level, these quarrels may also represent a cultic tension between two powerful deities, whose marriage enforces unity despite their inherent differences. Shiva's imperfections as a husband, however, do not diminish the significance of his domestic role, rather, they underscore the complexities of marital life and the transformative interplay of love, conflict, and reconciliation within it.

Dialogue and discovery

Sitting on Mount Kailasha (See pp202–03), their celestial abode, Shiva and Parvati also engage in philosophical discussions, exploring the secrets of the cosmos. Shiva answers every question Parvati poses, and in doing so, he himself becomes more attuned to worldly matters, growing curious and thoughtful as he studies the world to provide answers.

Addressing the universe, he declares, "He who escapes from joy and sorrow, instead of living and dealing with them, is a fool and he shall forever fail to see the truth. And he who is only a part of pleasures and pains of life, is also a fool, he shall also never discover the truth. The truth lies in balance, in harmony, between body, mind and soul. It is the balance between individual and society." With this revelation, Shiva also proclaims, "There shall be no worship, or yagna, without a man's wife being right by his side."

COSMIC COMPANIONS

Shiva's divine consorts embody the many faces of existence – creation, destruction, love, and power. Each goddess he unites with reveals a new facet of cosmic truth, making their sacred relationships the heartbeat of the universe's eternal rhythm.

▽ **A Kalighat painting depicting a forlorn Shiva seated beside Sati's lifeless body** under a tree. Shiva is portrayed as a typical ascetic – clad only in a tiger skin, with snakes emerging from his matted hair – while Sati appears regal, with a crown on her head, reflecting her royal lineage as King Daksha's daughter.

Behold Shiva – whether standing tall or seated in serene stillness, his presence commands awe. His half-closed eyes reveal no emotion, yet a powerful aura of silent bliss surrounds him. Alone, and majestic in his solitude, he embodies *pratyahara*, the withdrawal of the senses from the outer world, turning inward to confront the truths of self and existence.

Worldly bonds move even this ascetic god, lost in deep inner stillness. Unlike many ascetics, Shiva does not renounce the pleasures of the body or the joy of family life. In fact, he is unique among Hindu deities as both a solitary yogi and a devoted householder – fully embracing both paths. He alone bridges the sacred divide between renunciation and relationship.

In the celestial realms, he appears with not one, but many divine consorts – each union rich with symbolism and cosmic delight. Each one of them is a powerful goddess in her own right, representing vital forces of life, creation, and transformation. Among them, Parvati, Sati, and Ganga stand out in legend and devotion, though many regional myths tell of other divine unions.

An extension of his self

Before meeting Sati, Shiva was the lone wanderer, untouched by desire, living in mountains and forests, indifferent to the world. Seeing Shiva's deep renunciation, Brahma, the creator and one of the Trinity, grew uneasy. He turned to Vishnu, the preserver, and said, "Shiva is the god of gods. If even he abandons the world, what hope is there for creation? Who will remain to uphold the joy of life, to take part in its unfolding?"

Vishnu remained calm and replied, "There is only one who can return him to the world – our Mother Goddess herself. She has already been born in the house of King Daksha. It is she who will bring Shiva back to life – not through command, but through the quiet power of love."

The first consort of Shiva, Sati, however, is not born merely as a mortal goddess – she was created for the salvation of the universe itself. Only she possessed the strength to absorb Shiva's blinding brilliance, the fierce intensity of his

ascetic power. Where Kama, the god of love, failed to stir even a flicker of desire in the meditating Shiva, it was Sati who succeeded – not by seduction, but by becoming an extension of his very self. She alone could draw him out of yogic stillness and turn his gaze towards the world.

Sati embodies the life of the householder, where energy is not repressed, but released in love, creativity, and connection. Through her, Shiva's immense spiritual force finds purpose in engagement, not withdrawal. Their marital bliss came to a tragic end with Sati's self-destruction at her father's *yagna,* or fire ceremony. The death of a beloved wife brought Shiva in touch with his feelings. It was all the more tragic as Shiva in his moment of heartbreak, responded by recoiling from the world.

Two halves of a whole

Withdrawn from the world, Shiva turned into the aloof ascetic once again, until the gods persuaded him to return to living through love. They pleaded with him to take a wife and rejoin the rhythms of creation. Waiting patiently was Parvati – ever devoted and ready. She was Sati reborn, still filled with the longing to be united with Shiva for all eternity.

Their union is not just a marriage, but a cosmic convergence. Together, they become the mother and father of the universe – Shiva and Shakti – two halves of the same divine force, each incomplete without the other, yet whole together. In each other's presence, they function at their fullest – creation and destruction, stillness and movement, asceticism and abundance in perfect balance.

Parvati, though often seen as Shiva's consort, is a goddess of immense power in her own right. She bears countless names – Durga, Gauri, Annapurna – each reflecting a different facet of her strength. Her deeds are legendary, her devotion unwavering, and her following vast. She is not only the gentle mother and devoted wife, but also a fierce protector, the slayer of Asuras, and the embodiment of Shakti, the primal energy that drives the universe.

However, Shiva's deep austerities, though awe-inspiring, often left Parvati feeling isolated and vulnerable. During his long retreats in the

△ **Wooden figurines of Shiva and Parvati** peering from a first-floor window of the Shiva Parvati Temple in Kathmandu Durbar Square, Nepal. Built in the 18th century, this three-storey wooden temple has intricate carvings and is the first temple visible upon entering the square.

△ **This Basohli painting, dated 1694–95 and attributed to Devidasa of Nurpur,** is part of a series illustrating the *Rasamanjari*, or Essence of the Experience of Delight, a 15th-century Sanskrit love poem by Bhanudatta Misra. In this scene, Parvati pleads with Shiva, who has just tricked her out of a necklace in a game of *chaupar*, a traditional cross-and-circle board game. The two are seated on a tiger-skin carpet.

mountains, his absence grew heavy, and she found herself yearning for his presence. One day, unable to hold it in, she confessed her fears. Shiva, ever the philosopher, responded gently:

"Why fear loneliness, O goddess? Fear arises only when we believe there is a second. But I am Brahman. I am all there is. There is no duality – no "other". What delusion, what sorrow can exist for one who knows that I reside in everything, including in you?"

It was a profound truth – one that resonated in her mind – but over time, even such cosmic wisdom felt distant to the heart. Parvati longed not just for union, but for creation. She yearned for a child – a son to complete their bond in a worldly, tangible way. She knew Shiva's disinterest in parenthood, so she prepared her plea carefully, drawing from dharma and tradition.

When Shiva finally returned from another long sojourn, she asked. "What of your *rinas*, your sacred debts? To the rishis, through wisdom; to the gods, through ritual; and to the ancestors, through begetting a son to perform the last rites. Even moksha, some say, requires a son". Unshaken, Shiva, responded with clarity and calm: "There are three worlds – the world of men, reached through sons; the world of ancestors, reached through fire offerings; and the world of the gods, reached only through meditation. Of these, meditation is the highest path. Praise that above all." Then, in a tone both affectionate and firm, he added: "For the householder, a son brings joy and performs rites for his father's rebirth. But I am Shiva – I know no death. Why perform rites for one who does not die? Where there is no illness, what need is there for medicine?" And finally, with a rare touch of sensual candor, he said: "Let us rejoice in the pleasures of love between man and woman – without burdening that joy with the weight of offspring." Parvati listened, torn between his detachment and her own longing. His words were unshakably rooted in truth, yet her heart beat with desire, for creation, for continuity, for the joy of nurturing life.

Despite Shiva's reluctance toward fatherhood, destiny compels him to embrace it. Parvati created Ganesha to fulfil her desire for a child and he went on to become the leader of the Ganas. Their second son, Karttikeya was born to defeat the Asura Taraka who was invincible to all but the child of the mighty divinities, Shiva and Parvati. Thus, even the ascetic god must yield to fate and to the pleas of his followers.

A matter of cosmic duty

Unlike the passionate relationship Shiva shares with Parvati, his connection to Ganga, the river goddess, is born of divine necessity and intimate proximity. When her fierce descent threatened to shatter the Earth, Shiva received her into his matted locks, tempering her wild force with calm restraint. He bore her on his head to control her power and protect the world, fulfilling a cosmic responsibility.

Ever since, she has flowed through his hair – an eternal consort not by marriage, but closeness, rooted in duty, not romance. Ganga rests against his crown, cool and fluid, while Parvati, his wedded wife, watches her with unease. Though Ganga is not his partner in the conventional sense, her presence is constant – she touches him always, moves with him, breathes with him – an inseparable witness to his stillness, fury, and transcendence.

In folklore and Sanskrit literature, Parvati often bristled with insecurity at Ganga's presence. She understood the necessity, but still felt hurt. This became a silent source of tension symbolizing the divide between duty and personal love. But, her dignity is later restored in a beautiful verse from the *Saundaryalahari*, attributed to Adi Shankaracharya. When Shiva bows to Parvati in her form as Tripurasundari, Ganga – resting on his head – flows down to touch

COSMIC COMPANIONS | 147

◁ **A Kalighat painting of the Goddess Ganga from c. 1890.** She is depicted with four arms, holding a water pot, and seated on her mount, the Makara, a mythical creature with the head of a crocodile. This iconography is typical of the goddess in Kalighat depictions.

Parvati's feet. Ganga is drawn to her feet, not out of devotion, but because of Shiva's own act of reverence, symbolically performing a ritual washing or *padam*, acknowledging Parvati's supremacy.

Another legend adds to Ganga's mystique. Though Shiva is *vairagi* or a renunciate, he is known for his rare but mesmerizing singing. Once, his song was so hauntingly beautiful that Vishnu, overcome with emotion, melted into water. Brahma, seeing this miracle, collected the divine essence in his *kamandalu*, or water pot, and thus Ganga was born.

These stories do more than mythologize a river. They weave Ganga into the very fabric of divine relationships, portraying her not just as water, but as emotion, tension, power, and grace – flowing endlessly between gods, between heaven and Earth.

Shiva's relationships with his wives define different parts of his journey. Sati's deep devotion ends in tragedy, leaving him in grief. Parvati brings healing and balance, becoming his true partner, while Ganga, unattainable and distant, symbolizes purity and flow. Each love leaves its imprint, like ash on his flesh, forming the god who is creation and destruction.

PRATYAHARA

Shiva's deep detachment drew gods and seekers alike – an embodiment of *vairagya*, the dispassion essential for *pratyahara*, or sensory withdrawal, as taught in Patanjali's *Yoga Sutras*. Unlike other deities, Shiva turned inward, mastering the art of stillness by letting go of all outward distraction. His every act – drinking poison, bearing the Ganga – was done without attachment. Nothing touched him, because he was free from desire. In this, Shiva reveals the path to *santulam*, or inner balance, and *atma-samyam*, the perfect restraint that leads to the highest meditative repose.

THE TRAGEDY OF SATI

Shiva's first wife, was born to restore cosmic balance. Only she could awaken him from his yogic trance. She became an inseparable part of Shiva, drawing him into the world through love and destiny.

▷ **A lithograph from Kolkata, created between 1878 and 1883,** shows a disheveled, grief-stricken Shiva wandering the wilderness with Sati's lifeless body slung over his shoulder – one arm hanging across his chest, the other draped over his trident. Her lifeless grey face appears over his right shoulder. Above, Vishnu gazes down from heaven, poised to cut Sati's body into pieces with his discus.

THE TRAGEDY OF SATI | 149

Shiva, the cosmic yogi, freely shared his knowledge and power with everyone. From time to time, after intervening to save the world from one catastrophe after another, he would retreat, leaving behind the noise of the world for the silence of deep meditation. Self-contained and self-sufficient, Shiva needed nothing beyond his inner stillness. Sometimes, clad only in a tiger skin, his body smeared with ash, he would wander through dreaded and forbidden places, embodying both renunciation and transcendence.

It fell to Sati, the daughter of king Daksha and an incarnation of the Great Goddess, to awaken Shiva – to draw him out of his fierce detachment and into the living rhythm of the world. Without Shiva's presence, creation lacked balance, its auspiciousness withering in his absence.

Sati's challenge

Her birth had one divine purpose: to lure the ascetic god into love, into marriage, and into the intimate, chaotic beauty of worldly life. Sati's love for Shiva consumed her. She prayed with fierce devotion, longing for a chance to meet him. Shiva, though deeply withdrawn in meditation, could sense the purity and intensity of her longing. After years of resistance, he appeared before her. In their meeting, Shiva remained blunt. Anyone who chose to walk beside him, he warned, would remain an outsider.

Sati accepted Shiva as he was, with no expectation of change. Moved by her unwavering love and clarity, Shiva embraced her – and thus began their union, one of the most profound in mythic tradition. Sati's parents, especially her father Daksha, opposed this union. To them, Shiva was the antithesis of a worthy husband – an ascetic draped in tiger skin, his matted locks coiled with serpents, his body smeared in ash. A wanderer with no home, no ambition, and no regard for social norms, yet Sati followed her heart and married Shiva, and their union became one of the most beautiful love stories ever told.

The understanding husband

Shortly after their marriage, Sati learnt that Daksha was hosting a grand *yagna*, a sacred Vedic ritual, inviting sages from across the world – but had excluded Shiva and Sati. Hurt, she urged Shiva to attend, but he refused to go uninvited. Sati insisted on going alone and Shiva, moved by her anguish, relented, revealing not weakness, but a husband's strength in understanding and respect.

He sent his Ganas to protect her, ensuring she had every comfort for the journey – a palanquin, a shade to protect her from the sun and rain, and things for her to eat and drink. At her father's home, she was met not with warmth, but with disdain. Daksha, proud and rigid, loathed Shiva. In a fit of anger and humiliation, she self immolated as she could not bear the insults being flung at her beloved Shiva.

Catastrophic grief

Shiva learnt of Sati's death through Narada. Overwhelmed with grief he flew into a rage and sent Veerbhadra, a fierce and powerful warrior deity born of his fury to destroy Daksha's sacrifice and avenge Sati's death. Clad in armour and wielding mighty weapons, Veerbhadra led the Ganas and destroyed Daksha's *yagna*, embodying righteous wrath and unstoppable force born of love and loss.

On seeing Sati's lifeless body, Shiva carried it in his arms and wandered the three worlds in frenzied despair. Blind with sorrow, Shiva wailed and raged. His mourning shook the cosmos – plants died, famine spread, and Brahma, the creator, and the other gods panicked. They realized that Sati's corpse would not decay as long as it was in contact with Shiva. Desperate they approached Vishnu, the preserver, for help who intervened and dismembered Sati's body with his *chakra*, or discus, as a way of calming Shiva.

In his pain, Shiva defies the patriarchal ideal of stoic manhood, showing that even the great god can grieve openly, fiercely, and without shame. He does not hold back his tears. In crying, in raging, Shiva reclaims vulnerability as an acceptable trait. But once his fury burnt out, a deep sorrow replaced his anger and Shiva retreated into silence and meditation.

△ **A stone sculpture of Veerbhadra** from the 16th–17th century.

▷ **A c.1920 print from the Ravi Varma Press, based on a painting by Raja Ravi Varma**, depicts Shiva as an ascetic, deep in meditation. Parvati approaches him in the guise of a tribal woman, seeking to win his attention.

FROM THE SHIVA PURANA AND THE SKANDA PURANA Longing, striving, becoming one

PARVATI'S SACRED TRIALS

Parvati knew that her path to Shiva would not be ordinary, but was not perturbed. For 3,000 years, she performed severe penance. She practised all deprivations, all mortifications of the body – clothing herself in sheer deer skin, sitting through countless eras immersed in meditation, surrounded by fire during the scorching summer, standing on one leg, neck-deep in water during the rains and harsh winters, and living on leaves and, sometimes, only air. Wild beasts did not harm her, nor did she fear them. Her mind dwelt on one thing only – her union with Shiva and the birth of their offspring who would free the worlds from the terror unleashed by the cursed Taraka (*See pp178–79*).

Even then, her devotion to Shiva was put to the test with exasperating regularity. The sages came and tried to dissuade her, saying, "The trident-bearing Shiva has an inauspicious body. He is free from shame and has no home or pedigree. He is naked and ill-featured. He associates with ghosts and goblins and the like."

Shiva came to test her as well, his curiosity kindled after listening to the Devas sing eulogies of her austerities. Appearing before her in the guise of a *brahmacharin*, a celibate spiritual man, Maheshvara said, "Look at you, you with eyes like the petals of the lotus – and where is that three-eyed creature Shiva? You are Moon-faced, he is five-faced. Shiva's birth and pedigree cannot be traced. His caste is not recognized. He has no learning or wisdom and has no knowledge of the enjoyments of a householder. His assistants are the ghosts, he holds poison in his throat. You wish to discard your fine garments in order to wear the hide; unmindful of the sunlight, you wish to seek the light of the glowworm."

His harsh words tested Parvati's resolve and commitment to the extreme. But she did not flinch and deemed it fit to remain silent, and looked up only as the "*brahmacharin*" walked away, perhaps with the trace of a smile playing on his lips.

Ultimately, Shiva, satisfied with her *tapas*, or austerity, graced her with his presence and asked her what boon he could grant her. She paid obeisance to him and said, "O Mahadeva, fulfil the desire of all the gods, fulfil the desire of the whole world, fulfil the desire of my heart and make me your wife." Her joy knew no bounds when Shiva acquiesced.

Perhaps, besides being pleased by her single-minded devotion to him, he too felt stirrings of love and desire just as she did.

▽ **An 1782 illustration of Parvati** by French naturalist and explorer Pierre Sonnerat.

KALYANASUNDARMURTI

THE ICON OF THE DIVINE WEDDING

▷ **The four-armed Shiva in the** centre holds a shy Parvati's hand in this carving of Kalyanasundara from the Ellora Cave complex in Dhumar Lena, Aurangabad, Maharashtra.

The dignified bridegroom Shiva, with matted locks piled high on his head to resemble a crown, stands in solemn grace. A shy Parvati tilts her head, much like a demure bride. Her companion, the Goddess Lakshmi, gently pushes her towards the groom. Parvati stands to Shiva's right, offering her hand in the *panigrahana* ritual – the symbolic "accepting of the hand" performed during a Hindu wedding. Sometimes, Vishnu is the priest officiating, but the four-headed Brahma, the god best versed in ritual lore, is more common. At times, Vishnu and his consorts are the givers, acting the parts of Parvati's parents. Surrounding them are other Devas, Rishis, Gandharvas, Matrikas, Yakshas, Siddhis, and a host of divinities, all gathered with arms folded in the *anjali* pose, a reverent hand gesture.

There is perhaps no other iconographic form as evocative in portraying a celestial wedding ceremony as the wedding of Shiva and Parvati. The composition is called Kalyanasundarmurti, meaning "the icon of the beautiful wedding". It is one of the most renowned heavenly pairings, uniting Shiva as pure consciousness and Parvati as divine energy. They represent the greatest and most powerful male and female principles, and their union signifies the alliance of two mighty cosmic forces. The marriage showcases divine love, as well as the supremacy of devotion and asceticism. Their wedding itself is a popular theme in Indian architecture, and Kalyanasundara scenes often appear in caves, carvings, and temple walls across India.

A Cosmic Union of Love and Power

One of the reasons Shiva and Parvati's wedding is so famed is due to the circumstances leading up to the celebration. Shiva was unwilling to enter matrimony after Sati's death, but Parvati, born as a reincarnation of Sati, achieved great spiritual merit through intense *tapas*, or austerity, thereby winning Shiva's admiration. It was a grand and auspicious wedding.

What makes this such a celebrated icon is perhaps its portrayal of divine love triumphing challenges. Parvati succeeds in her *tapas* despite severe challenges and gains Shiva (See pp150–51), and he, in turn, realizes the importance of conjugal love once again.

The wedding itself was held with great fanfare, for Parvati was the daughter of Himavat, the personification of the Himalayas. However, Shiva's entourage included bizarre and even impudent revellers – the numerous Ganas. Their strange appearance and outlandish behaviour caused both laughter and concern, even leading Parvati's mother Mena to faint in some versions of the tale. This story is often reenacted during the great festival of Mahashivaratri.

The Kalyanasundara icon is not a typical object of popular worship. Instead, it is used in the ceremonial celebrations of the divine wedding during annual temple festivals.

△ **The Shiv-Parvati vivah,** a vibrant print from the Ravi Varma Press (c. 1930), based on a painting by M.V. Dhurandhar, captures the divine wedding of Shiva and Parvati in a majestic procession – an artistic celebration of sacred union, regal splendour, and eternal devotion.

A CALL FOR SHIVA

THE SACRED SOUNDSCAPE OF SHIVA IN THE HIMALAYAS

Come Come Come … your throat colour has changed to blue
Your eyes are burning like fire
Your forehead is decorated by the crescent Moon
Your strong arms are ornamented by the sacred ash
My mind's very first dedication is to you "Hey Bhole Mahadeva"
you are welcome, please come.

Garhwali folk song invoking Shiva as Bhole baba

In the Garhwal hills of Uttarakhand, folklore breathes through music. The folk songs are not just entertainment – they are living expressions of the region's identity. They weave Shiva into the unique spiritual landscape, where the divine includes the malformed, the foreign – everyone held in Shiva's embrace.

Some songs, with their rhythmic beats, call on people to join the joyful *baraat* – the wedding procession of Shiva and Parvati. It is a celebration that blends devotion with festivity, inviting villagers and gods alike. Some other songs are an appeal, a request for Shiva to appear at a festival or a temple.

In this particular song, Shiva is invited to arrive and make his presence felt at the temple. The song describes his main attributes as an invocation, listing them one by one. They may sound somewhat intimidating, yet the epithet used is Bholenath – the Shiva who is guileless and innocent in his love for his devotees.

The folk songs call Shiva by many names. He is their raja, their Baba, their Lord, even husband of Gaura or Nanda Devi, the goddess of prosperity who holds the central position in Uttarakhand's spiritual life.

Divine landscape

Garhwal is a spiritual powerhouse nestled in the Himalayas and is known as Dev Bhoomi or the land of the gods. Here, mountains, rivers, and forests are not just scenery, but sacred beings. Temples aren't just places of worship – they're portals into myth, memory, and devotion spanning centuries.

From snow-capped peaks to lush valleys, Garhwal is home to numerous towns, but it is Kedarnath that stands out – a temple perched at 3,583 metres, one of the 12 Jyotirlingas, and a key pilgrimage site in the Char Dham route.

Shakti temples and myths

Sacred feminine energy also pulses through Garhwal's goddess temples here, which are associated with Shiva. Perched high in the Himalayas, the Kunjapuri Devi Temple holds deep spiritual significance. As one of the revered *Shakti Pithas*, it marks the sacred spot where the *kunj* or chest of Sati is believed to have fallen after Vishnu dismembered her body to end Shiva's grief. Chandrabadni Temple, where Sati's torso fell, contains no idol – only a powerful Shri Yantra, a sacred Hindu geometric symbol. Surkanda Devi Temple, near Dhanaulti, marks the place where Sati's head fell. From here, pilgrims can see majestic Himalayan peaks like Nanda Devi, and Hathi Parvat.

Shiva is not alone in Garhwali worship. Local guardian deities like Bhairavnath, protector of livestock and the community, are venerated through offerings of food and incense. Nanda Devi, the goddess of prosperity, holds a central place in the region's spiritual life. Her celestial marriage to Shiva is commemorated through the Raj Jat Yatra, a grand pilgrimage held every 12 years.

WHERE GODS WED
SHIVA BECOMES SUNDARESHWARA

In the ancient city of Madurai, Tamil Nadu, the presence of Goddess Meenakshi has been deeply felt for centuries. Revered as the goddess of love, strength, and fertility, she resides in the magnificent Meenakshi Amman Temple, also called the Meenakshi-Sundareshwara Temple, one of India's most iconic and expansive temple complexes. Its origins trace back to the 6th century, with layers of history added through centuries of devotion, renovation, and grandeur.

The birth of Meenakshi

According to legend, King Malayadhwaja Pandya and his queen, Kanchanamalai, longed for a child. To fulfill their wish, they performed a sacred yagna, invoking Shiva for a son. But instead of a male heir, a radiant three-year-old girl with three breasts emerged from the flames. The royal couple was bewildered until a divine voice reassured them to raise her like a son, crown her queen, and know that her third breast would vanish the moment she met her destined husband.

The child was named Meenakshi, meaning "carp-eyed", a symbol of grace and beauty. As she grew, she proved to be a formidable warrior and a wise ruler, expanding her kingdom and even conquering celestial realms. Legends say she reached Indralok, the abode of Indra, and set her sights on Mount Kailasha, Shiva's heavenly abode. At the moment she encountered Shiva, her third breast vanished – signaling destiny fulfilled. Meenakshi recognized him as her consort. She was, in truth, none other than Parvati in a divine earthly form. Shiva, once the wild ascetic, became Sundareshwara, the "Beautiful Lord". Together, they returned to Madurai, where the gods themselves gathered to witness their celestial wedding, an eternal union of power, love, and cosmic balance.

Tirukalyanam

Even today, Meenakshi and Shiva's celestial union is celebrated with grandeur during the Tirukalyanam – the sacred wedding festival – held in the spring month of Chaitra (April). It is the heart of Madurai's annual Chithirai Festival, drawing thousands of devotees. As part of the ritual, Meenakshi emerges in a towering temple chariot, a lifelike replica of her temple image, pulled through the streets by thick ropes and the sheer devotion of hundreds. This dramatic procession symbolizes her conquest of the earthly realm before her destined meeting with Shiva. Their divine wedding is then reenacted in a magnificent ceremony believed to be attended by all the gods. Even after the wedding, Meenakshi remains sovereign, with Shiva, now Sundareshwara, welcomed into her court, and not the other way around. This powerful imagery challenges and redefines conventional narratives of divine union. The entire event is not just a spectacle – it's etched into the very fabric of Tamil sacred history, richly preserved in temple sculpture and ancient texts like the Tamil *talapuranas* (regional sacred chronicles). As scholar Diana L. Eck notes in *India: A Sacred Geography*, the myth and ritual together create a living, breathing tradition where the divine wedding continues to shape Madurai's cultural and spiritual identity.

▷ *(clockwise from top left)* **The Meenakshi Amman Temple,** Madurai, South India; **An evening procession** carrying Shiva to the private chamber of Goddess Meenakshi; **The ceremonial wedding** of Meenakshi and Sundareshwara in Madurai.

WHERE GODS WED | 157

WEDDING TEMPLES ACROSS INDIA

TRIYUGINARAYAN
The Triyuginarayan Temple, in Uttarakhand's Rudraprayag district, is an ancient shrine dedicated to Lord Vishnu. Its name – Tri (three), Yug (ages), Narayan (Vishnu) – means "lord of the three ages". It is revered for being the mythical wedding site of Shiva and Parvati. Its most captivating feature is the eternal flame or Akhand Dhuni, believed to have burned since that sacred union.

EKAMBARESWARAR
According to legend, Parvati performed penance under a sacred mango tree at this temple to reunite with Shiva. With unwavering love, she sculpted a Shiva Lingam from the earth to pray. To test her resolve, Shiva sent fire and flood, but Parvati, undaunted, embraced the fragile Lingam, shielding it with her body. Touched by her devotion, Shiva appeared and married her here forever associating this temple in Kanchipuram, Tamil Nadu, with marital harmony.

THIRUMANANCHERI
A revered Shiva temple in Tamil Nadu, Thirumanancheri is most famous for being the divine site of the celestial wedding of Shiva and Parvati, making it a powerful pilgrimage for those seeking marital blessings. It is especially beloved among devotees hoping to remove delays in their marriage.

Like many Hindu festivals, Maha Shivaratri, celebrated as the marriage of Shiva and Parvati, blends solemn observances such as fasting, night-long vigils, and ritual offerings with vibrant public celebration. Grand processions fill towns and cities, where devotees dance, chant bhajans, shout slogans in Shiva's praise, and move large idols and tableaux of Shiva through the streets. Performers dressed as Shiva and Parvati bring these processions to life, as in this image from New Delhi where an artist embodies Shiva amidst the crowd.

SHIVA, THE HOUSEHOLDER

THE ETERNAL COUPLE

In the divine stillness of the cosmos, Shiva is not alone. Beside him, radiant and resolute, is Parvati, his eternal consort. Though the very embodiment of the sacred union, they also echo human relationships, one replete with passion, love, gentle teasing, and even arguments.

Shiva – the ascetic, the renouncer – dwells in the stillness of Mount Kailasha, withdrawing from the world not to escape it, but to understand it more deeply. From this place of solitude, he watches, waits, and intervenes only when the world teeters on the edge of chaos. Though his eyes are often turned inward, immersed in the boundless depths of inner reality, Shiva's third eye remains open – ever alert. It sees not the illusion, but the truth beneath it. And yet, it is not solitude alone that anchors Shiva in the vast dance of existence. It is Parvati – the goddess of life, devotion, and grace – who draws him back from the endless pull of detachment. Where Shiva retreats, Parvati reaches; where he dissolves, she restores. She is the rhythm to his stillness, the form to his formlessness, the voice that reminds him of the world's aching need for his presence. Without her, Shiva might remain forever in meditation. With her, he is engaged – not just as destroyer, but as protector, lover, and cosmic balance.

The silence in the storm

Shiva and Parvati together are Gauri-Shankar, Uma-Shankar, Shankar-Parvati – their names reverberate through the heavens, whispering the story of cosmic balance, devotion, and love that transcends time. They are gods, yes, but not immune to the human condition. Despite their divinity, their relationship often mirrors the very mortal love stories they watch over. They laugh, they banter, they tease each other with affection, but like any couple, they have their moments of friction. At times, Shiva's words, laced with mischief, strike too deep.

One night, as they lay side by side, spent from the fire of their passions, Shiva, in a mood of lazy arrogance, began to gloat about his fair skin, conveniently forgetting it was the ash of cremation grounds that gave him that whitish hue. Throwing an arm around Parvati, he murmured,

▽ **Shiva leans against his vahana**, Nandi, while talking to Parvati who holds a bowl, in this Pahari painting.

"Look how your dark, slender body coils around mine, like a black serpent wrapped around a white sandalwood tree. You are like the dark night, only faintly touched by the pale light of the moon. You offend my sight."

Parvati froze. She slipped out of his embrace, her pride flaring into fury. "I won your heart through relentless *tapas* – acts of self-denial and devotion – and this is my reward?" she snapped. "You call me black, yet you are known as Mahakaal, the Great Dark One. You speak of serpents, but it is you who wears poison around your throat. If anyone is crooked, it is not I."

Shiva's expression shifted – surprise, then sorrow, flickered across his face. His voice softened with regret: "I did not mean to wound you. It was jest, no more. I sought to flatter, not insult. Your mind is pure, clear as a crystal, yet those like me, whose dark skin is masked by white ash, often speak in riddles. What we say is not always what we feel. If my words have angered you, I will never jest again. Forgive me, O fierce and radiant goddess."

He folded his hands in reverence, bowing low before her. The sincerity in his voice melted the fire in her heart. In his humility, she found peace, and in his love, she released all hurt. For Shiva alone possesses the power to calm the storm within Parvati, to draw her back from the edge of wrath.

A mischievous game of wit

Parvati was rarely afforded the luxury of simply basking in Shiva's presence. For Shiva, the adored one of many, the devotee of his devotees, was never truly alone. His enthusiastic entourage of Ganas, led by the irrepressible Narada, the skeletal Bhringi, and the loyal Nandi, were a constant presence. The couple's favourite pastime? Chausara, the ancient game of dice. For Parvati, it was more than just a game; it was one of the rare moments she could engage Shiva in playful combat of minds. But every time they sat down to play, his followers crowded in, loudly cheering their lord, turning what could have been an intimate contest into a noisy spectacle. Parvati endured it all with outward patience and a wry, indulgent smile. But what tested her grace was the way they treated her – not with respect or sportsmanship, but with childish mockery. The moment her turn came, they would break into off-key love songs or erupt into laughter, deliberately distracting her so Shiva could win with ease. Worse still, when Parvati began to win, a fair and square triumph born of her sharp mind and uncanny ability to anticipate Shiva's moves, his loyal companions would grow restless. Murmurs of protest would rise, accusations followed, and they would sneer and mutter that she was using trickery, never once crediting her intelligence. Her success, in their eyes, was not wit but wile.

△ **A euphoric Shiva dances** as Parvati plays what seems to be a *kanjira* or Indian frame drum in this painting from the 1800s.

She is the rhythm to his stillness, the form to his formlessness, the voice that reminds him of the world's aching need for his presence.

Shiva, of course, sat serene, his eyes dancing with mischief. He smiled indulgently at her irritation, and sometimes, just to needle her further, would dare to laugh.

Once, with the quiet fire of triumph in her eyes, Parvati turned to Shiva, and emboldened by her win, said with a teasing smile, "Isn't it a little too obvious how partial your followers are, my lord? Perhaps it's time you surrendered something in honour of my victory. Remove that moon from your matted hair, for it now belongs to me."

Without protest, Shiva reached up and unfastened the crescent moon that crowned his locks. He handed it to her with an amused smile, even as Narada and the others looked on in dismay. Parvati, radiant in her conquest, fashioned the glowing moon into an earring and wore it proudly.

"Now," she said, her voice playful, but firm, "give me all your ornaments." Again, Shiva obliged, stripping himself of every divine embellishment and placing them in her hands, each act of surrender watched with disapproval, by his companions who shifted uncomfortably in the background.

Then, with an impish gleam, Parvati leaned in and whispered, "And now … remove your loincloth, my lord." A collective gasp shattered the moment. Shiva stiffened, his calm breaking for a beat. "What?" he asked sharply.

Parvati, undeterred, raised an eyebrow. "Why should it trouble you? Are you not the renouncer, the ascetic beyond shame? Did you not once walk the Daruvana naked, untouched by judgement, cloaked only in your purity?" A moment of silence hung in the air, heavy and expectant.

And in that moment, Shiva – Bholenath, the simple-hearted god who loved her without pride or pretence – began to comply, not out of obligation, but out of love. Parvati had long waited for a moment to gently chide Shiva for his earlier indiscretion, and now she'd done so, with a smile. But the hurt and confusion on his face instantly made her regret it. He was Bholenath, the innocent-hearted, the unworldly. Who else could she take such liberties with, if not him?

▷ **Parvati, playing the veena,** disrupts Shiva's deep meditation and angers him in this early 19th-century Pahari painting from Guler. Shiva's posture and flying hair reflect his ire at being interrupted.

Two become one

Her gentle chiding is almost unsurprising, for though Parvati admires the boundless devotion Shiva inspires, she is often baffled by how his followers treat her. It is almost as if she were somehow less divine. Once, during a blessing ceremony attended by sages and devotees, Parvati stood beside Shiva under the sweltering summer sun, quietly offering grace. When the sage Bhringi, Shiva's obstinate devotee approached, he bowed only to Shiva, ignoring Parvati entirely, as if her touch would defile him. A shocked murmur rippled through the crowd. Parvati's anger surged, but Shiva, though clearly embarrassed, said nothing and blessed Bhringi. In that moment, Parvati vowed to take a form no one could ignore. It took thousands of years, but the vow bore fruit. She merged with Shiva in the form of Ardhanarishvara – half man, half woman – his body split down the center, her divinity equal to his, and eternal (*See pp166–69*).

MORSEL OF LIFE

Goddess Annapurna, an incarnation of Parvati, is the divine embodiment of nourishment and abundance. Her name means "full of food", and she reminds the world that sustenance is sacred. In a powerful legend, she vanishes after Shiva calls food an illusion, plunging the world into famine. Only upon her return in Kashi is balance restored, as she generously feeds all beings – even the gods. Through this act, Annapurna reveals that food is not just survival, but a sacred gift, essential to life, humanity, and the spiritual order of the universe.

AND IT STARTED TO RAIN

A MELODY OF LOVE

Shivshankar lives in Kailasha
And the monsoon raindrops come down
Gauri sows her green-green mehndi
While Shiva sows his three-leafed bhang
And the raindrops keep coming down
Gauri's mehndi is flourishing
Shankar's bhang is also growing
Gauri's mehndi crop sways with the breeze
So does Shankar's bhang crop, now in full bloom
Gauri plucks the new leaves
Shankar cuts the bhang crop
Gauri grinds her green-green mehndi
And Shankar rubs the bhang in his palm
Gauri applies mehndi on her palms
Shankar quaffs the bhang
Gauri's mehndi turns a lovely red
While Shankar gets drunk!

A devotional song from Bundelkhand

Spanning southern Uttar Pradesh and northern Madhya Pradesh, the region of modern-day Bundelkhand is not merely a geographic region – it is a living tapestry of history and spirituality. At the heart of this region and its people is a deep and ancient devotion to Shiva. His presence permeates the region's folklore, architecture, and even its harsh, dramatic landscape.

In Bundelkhand, Shiva is not just worshipped, he is felt. He is lived through the region's stories, songs, seasonal rituals, and oral traditions. His most revered form may be Bhairava, wild and cosmic, but the region also cherishes a softer vision, often mirrored in its living cultural traditions and folk songs.

One that reflects a divine companionship, loving, egalitarian, playful, and deeply human. Many representations of a loving, embracing Uma–Maheshvara (Shiva–Parvati) depict their intimate moments – astride Nandi on a ride, deep in conversation, or playing Chausara, an ancient board game. Theirs is a mutual admiration and love, which is grounded in playful affection. Folk songs – like the one recounting the seasons as Shiva and Parvati cultivate bhang or cannabis seeds and mehndi or henna seeds together – often celebrate this intimate domesticity.

Music in the stones

In Bundelkhand, the rocks, rivers, and forests also seem to breathe with Shiva's energy, forming a sacred geography where the divine meets the temporal. It is fitting then that his presence is felt in the temples of Khajuraho and the forts at Orchha and Kalinjar. These are not just architectural marvels, but spiritual sentinels that stand witness to centuries of devotion.

Kalinjar, rising from the Banda district of Uttar Pradesh, derives its name from *Kaal*, time or death, and *Jar*, destruction, marking it as the place where Shiva is believed to have conquered death. Legend says that he meditated here to neutralize the effects of the lethal Halahala poison, which he had consumed during the churning of the ocean – becoming Neelkanth, the blue-throated one.

At the heart of the fort lies the rock-carved Neelkanth Temple, dedicated to this form of Shiva. The state of Madhya Pradesh also has the largest number of Chaunsatha Yogini temples, Tantric shrines where statues of 64 fiercely autonomous goddesses encircle the figure of Shiva as Bhairava. Set in remote hilltops, these sites express a mystical union of masculine and feminine forces, raw and transcendent. Another Neelkanth Temple, near Alipura, is carved directly into stone, surrounded by enigmatic sculptures that seem to emerge from the rock – silent, powerful, and otherworldly. In Panna, the so-called "Town of Temples," over 1,100 shrines, many dedicated to Shiva, transform the district into a spiritual mandala.

▷ **An early 19th-century Kangra painting depicts Shiva lifting a cup as Parvati serves him bhang. Their son Ganesha sits between Shiva's bull and Parvati's lion, while Karttikeya reaches up towards his peacock to offer it food.**

◁ **A miniature painting depicting a four-armed Ardhanarishvara.** The left half depicts Shiva, marked by a trident, *damaru*, serpent, third eye, *tripundra*, tiger skin, and a horn symbolizing the early crescent Moon. The right half shows Parvati, adorned with jewellery, draped in a saree, and holding a lotus and mace. Their mounts – the bull and the lion – stand beside them.

ARDHANARISHVARA

A SYMBOL OF ONENESS AND BALANCE

The composite form of the Ardhanarishvara is the embodiment of a divine concept, a visual representation of the unique balance of masculine and feminine energies, symbolizing that creation is incomplete without both aspects. Half-male and half-female, it depicts Shiva and Parvati, with physical differences, such as the coiffure, clothing, ornaments and attributes, distinguishing the two.

Shiva as the yogi has his hair matted as usual, holding the crescent Moon. Shiva's earring is a coiled serpent. The right side of the chest is that of a man and adorned with ornaments. His garment is a short dhoti made of tiger skin, covering the lower body up to the knees. There is also the *naga yajnopavita*, or the sacred thread of a snake. His entire right side is covered with ashes and a *sarpamekhala*, or the girdle of snakes.

The straighter line of Shiva's body contrasts with Parvati's left side: a single rounded breast and a voluptuous hip. Parvati's jawline is feminal, as against the manly outline given to Shiva. Her locks are arranged in an elegant fashion and her accoutrements are womanly. On her head is a *karanda mukuta*, or a fine knot of well-combed hair arranged in delicate curls. Half a tilak graces half her forehead, contiguous with the half eye of Shiva. On her left ear is a gold *kundela*, or earring. Her side of the torso is adorned with *haras*, or necklaces, of different lengths. The left leg is slightly bent and the left hand may be seen holding a flower, mirror, or lotus. Medieval texts note that Shiva occupies the dominant right side and Parvati the secondary left.

This is how Shiva and Parvati merge into one to allow worshippers to adore them as a single form. This androgynous form emphasizes the dual aspect of the godhead as explained by Indian art scholar Vidya Dehejia.

Transcending sexual polarities

This image may also be seen as an indicator of the bisexual creative principle where the godhead transcends sexual particularity, and, by extension, father and mother. The union is a symbol of effectively handling and surpassing one's conflicts of femininity and masculinity. The message here is that one who is close to godliness should be less concerned with the human-made division between the sexes.

This outstanding manifestation of human creation is mentioned in texts and depicted in images as early as the 1st century CE. The earliest image dates from the Kushan period, between the 1st and 3rd century CE in northern India. The oldest portrayal of them is a small stele of red sandstone from the Mathura area as described by Canadian author Ellen Goldberg.

Later, myths and legends were created to account for the creation of this deity and one such relates to Bhringi, a rishi or sage, who refused to worship Parvati. He took the form of a beetle and bored a hole through the composite body, still circumambulating only Shiva. The sage who was singularly devoted to

SHIVA, THE HOUSEHOLDER

△ **A circa 1050 bronze trident from the Chola Dynasty,** 10th–13th centuries, with an Ardhanarishvara figure on a pedestal. The facial features of the dual forms are unclear, but their attire distinguishes them: Shiva wears a tiger-skin up to his thighs, while Parvati's saree reaches her ankles. This three-armed iconography of Ardhanarishvara is characteristic of the Chola bronzes.

Shiva was eventually elevated, albeit after suffering bodily harm, to the retinue of Shiva's abode. Shiva became Ardhanarishvara, or half man, to dispel the ignorance of Bhringi.

Creative union

Historians like American Indologist Wendy Doniger O' Flaherty have asked whether this synthesis is a juxtaposition or a true fusion. The answer to this *samarasya*, or harmony, may lie in the Sanskrit text *Vishnudharmottara Purana*, in which this androgynous form is referred to as Gaurishvara, or lord of Gauri and symbolizes the identity in difference, or *abheda bhinna*, of *prakriti*, or nature, and *purusha*, or man.

On a philosophical plane, this is a creative union of the active and the passive principles that constitute creation – the male representing the passive *purusha* (Shiva) and the female, the active *prakriti* (Parvati).

Poetry and legend have tried to comprehend this iconographic image in their own ways. Folklore has it that the union was because Parvati was keen to keep an eye on Shiva, who had the nubile Ganga seated on his head. Shiva had two wives, Ganga and Parvati, the daughters of Parvat, the mountain. The story goes that the two quarrelled because one sat on Shiva's head and the other in his lap. Responding to Parvati's displeasure about keeping Ganga on his head, Shiva hugged her so tightly that they merged into one body and became Ardhanarishvara, as explained by Indian mythologist and writer Devdutt Pattanaik.

Dialectical relationship

Shiva and Parvati share the ultimate dialectical relationship and are incomplete without each other. It is only through Parvati, now inherent in him, that Shiva realizes his true nature. The Ardhanarishvara image symbolizes the fusion of the formless wholeness of Brahman, the supreme one, with the creative energy of existence, Parvati. The image indicates that Shiva is actually both: the eternal male and the eternal female. As half male and half female, he visibly reconciles the polarities of existence in his own being.

The idea of wholesome and holistic harmony is reflected in the physical manifestation as well. In the figure of the Ardhanarishvara, there seems to be an interchangeability and a flow between the male and female forms rather than a sharp demarcation between the two. Not only are Shiva and Parvati unmistakably shown to be the primordial pair, the image also ensures that Shiva is no longer assigned just a negative stature with the specific task of destruction, as was the case in the earliest depictions. However, since Shiva and Parvati have been fused into a single form, the Ardhanarishvara prevents a sexual union. They must separate to have sexual intercourse.

The image raises the question whether it is male with a female added. The name suggests that the male has absorbed the female and the myths indicate the same. Perhaps the form could be described more accurately as half male and half female, reiterating that the divine is both male and female.

Gender hierarchy

The image has also been used to promote the notion of women's equality. However, it is necessary to study the specific ways in which the male and female have been constructed and defined in Indian tradition to see if, in fact, the image is a positive emancipatory ideal for women, and for men for that matter, acccording to O'Flaherty. While the male and the female halves of the image are of equal physical stature, the name given to the icon – Ardhanarishvara – does not translate as "half woman–half man", but rather as "lord who is half woman". The epithet thus represents a masculine concept that incorporates a female partnership – Shiva's generative force, when he assumes the role of creator, requires a female presence. This immediately suggests a gender hierarchy because the male half of the icon is given the privileged title Ishvara, or god, lord, master, whereas the female half is simply designated as *nari*, or woman. The name then does not convey an equivalent status for both halves.

When Shiva and Parvati's younger son Karttikeya asks his elder brother Ganesha what happened to the other halves when father and mother became a single body, Ganesha replies that the one on Earth was born as everyman and the other everywoman, Dehejia explains. This vision, which comes from within the Hindu tradition cautions us to be circumspect with the use of such words as androgyny or hermaphrodite when speaking of Ardhanarishvara.

Ardhanarishvara unites the dualistic forces of the universe, the undifferentiated whole that both precedes and governs the cosmos of Indian concept of non-duality, or that reality is a unifed whole. The right half, Shiva, embodies consciousness and asceticism, while the left half, Parvati, represents creativity and nurturing energy. Ardhanarishvara challenges gender binaries and signifies unity, interdependence, and cosmic harmony.

Iconographically, the image is the symbol of sexual union, but is also representative of a situation in which union is physically impossible, according to O'Flaherty. Bhagiratha developed the theme of frustrated love for this form of Shiva: even though Shiva embraces Parvati forever, he burns with sorrow as he will never see the love in Parvati's eyes, says Dehejia.

The icon may also be seen as a symbol of syncretic ideology. Syncretism represents a blending of distinctly different or even opposite cultures to form an apparent or quasi-new entity or sub-culture. Ardhanarishvara may thus signify the coming together of two sects in one form to allay sectarian tendencies. With more or less equal status in the Ardhanarishvara form, both Shiva and Parvati would have to be worshipped at the same time. Ultimately, the message the image delivers is of Advaita, or oneness. The fusion of the masculine and feminine is a partial attainment en route to transcendence where all forms ultimately collapse.

▷ **An early 18th-century painting from the Bundi School of Rajasthan** of a cross-legged Ardhanarishvara seated on a tiger-skin carpet. The composition is unusual as neither side holds any weapons. Shiva, as the bearded ascetic, dominates the figure, with most attributes associated with him – a garland of skulls, *damaru*, trident, serpents, Ganga, and Nandi. The lotus-filled pond in the front symbolizes Lake Manasarovar.

On the ghats of River Yamuna in Uttar Pradesh lies Bateshwar, a temple town dotted with ancient Shaiva shrines. Once home to nearly a hundred temples, only around 40 still stand, some with ceilings that preserve delicate frescoes painted in vegetable pigments. Steeped in legend, Shiva is said to have once rested under a Banyan tree here – *Bat Ishwar*, the "Banyan Lord" – from which the town eventually took its name, honouring the presiding deity Vateshwarnath. In this image, a woman sits besides towering idols of Shiva (left) and Parvati (right) in one of the temples.

PROTECTOR AND GUIDE

Shiva is not just the conventional provider as father to Ganesha and Karttikeya. Though he remains very much the cosmic guardian, there are moments of deep attachment, love, pride, and joy, as he interacts with his sons.

△ **A 19th-century painting of the Shiva Parivar** depicts Shiva and his sons sewing a garland of skulls. Ganesha holds the red string, while Karttikeya in Parvati's lap, offers his father a skull. Behind them, Nandi lounges beneath a tree.

In all the myriad exploits of Shiva, one may tend to sideline his role as a father. After all, an inherent quality of Shiva is that of *vairagya*, or detachment. Yet he gets embroiled in family life as is illustrated enthusiastically in endless Kangra, Pahari, Kalighat, and Tanjore paintings labelled *Shiva Parivar*, or Shiva's family. Despite this, barring a couple of instances, he remains steadfast as the distant father.

That is not unusual, for since time immemorial, fathers were devoid of signs of nurturing. They were basically providers, while the emotional aspect was left to the mother. Shiva reflects the conventional role of fathers all over the world. His parenting therefore is not sentimental in the conventional sense – it can be defined as cosmic, symbolic and, at times, paradoxical.

A father's emotions

Subsequent illustrations are evidence of a pastoral harmony – the family members doing their own thing yet in happy, quiet togetherness. However, such was not always the case. Shiva's relationship with Ganesha begins in drastic conflict – Shiva unknowingly beheaded his own son. On realizing his mistake, Shiva revived Ganesha with an elephant's head. Taking on the role of a loving father in desperate haste, fearing Parvati's anger, he granted Ganesha the grand position of head of the Ganas, or attendants of Shiva.

In the earthly domain, Ganesha would then always be the first deity devotees paid obeisance to, allowing him to be above Shiva's own role as the great god of gods. He had witnessed young Ganesha's loyalty, courage, and resoluteness, and was impressed. Shiva's emotions of forgiveness and acceptance are on full display here.

In the *Skanda Purana*, one can see the rare tenderness of Shiva toward his other son Karttikeya. When he was born, Shiva held him in his lap and Karttikeya grabbed and pressed Vasuki, the serpent swirling around his father's neck. He then began counting his fingers in an incorrect order. Shiva laughed as he told Parvati of this. The Purana tells of how Shiva attained the greatest joy from the presence of his radiant son and was so moved with love that his speech faltered.

Sibling rivalry

A popular folk story, of a race between the two brothers, also appears in the *Skanda Purana*, with variants of it in the texts of the *Ganesha Purana* and the *Brahma Vaivarta Purana*.

In this myth, the sage Narada presented a divine fruit to Shiva and Parvati, saying it should be given to the worthiest of the two sons. Shiva, devoid of favouritism, declared that the fruit would go to the one who could circumnavigate the world three times and return to Kailasha first.

Karttikeya, in his eagerness to get the fruit and with it the approval of his rather aloof father, mounted his vahana, or vehicle, a peacock and set off across the globe. He raced through mountains, oceans, and skies, determined to win through sheer effort and velocity. Ganesha, because of his size and his tiny mouse vehicle, was unable to compete with a swiftly moving peacock that could move both in air and on ground.

After ruminating on this predicament, Ganesha chose a unique, pragmatic path. He beckoned his surprised parents and asked them to sit, before calmly walking around them three times, saying, "You are my world, circumambulating you is equivalent to circling the universe." Shiva and Parvati were moved by his sagacity and declared Ganesha the winner.

Karttikeya retreated to the Palani hills in Tamil Nadu where he becomes a symbol of penance and spiritual awakening and is worshipped as Murugan. It is believed that Shiva visits him on the day of the New Moon, never to forget his son.

Among Shiva's other sons is Ayyappan, the son of the union of Shiva and Vishnu's avatar Mohini, who represents the unity of Shaiva and Vaishnava traditions. Although not raised by Shiva directly, Ayyappan's birth is a divine collaboration, and his mission reflects Shiva's cosmic intent.

Andhaka and Jalandhara are the sons turned foes who embody darker aspects of human nature. Born from Shiva's sweat and rage, they become threats to the cosmic order. Shiva ultimately confronts and defeats them, symbolizing the necessity of destroying ignorance and ego – even within one's own lineage.

△ **An 8th-century brass sculpture of Karttikeya seated on a peacock.**

◁ **Shiva and Parvati are shown** with Ganesha and Nandi in this domestic scene, evoking intimacy and timeless connection, by Maharashtra-based artist Siddharth Shingade.

SHANKARA

THE FAMILY MAN

He is the hermit turned householder – benevolent, gentle, and compassionate. He is the protector, the father, an affable deity, who welcomes all. Shamkara, or Sankara, comes into existence when the hermit, the yogi, becomes the householder, a father, and a husband. Shankara is that synonym of Shiva that focuses on his benevolent form.

A combination of two words, Sankara signifies "the doer of good deed", where *sam* means "good", and *kara* translates to "doer". According to another interpretation, Shamkara means the source of samadhi or self-absorption. Here, *sam* means the state of sameness, equanimity or self-absorption, or samadhi, which arises when one transcends the state of *jiva*, or being, and enters pure consciousness, or Shiva. From this perspective, Shamkara means the cause of union, sameness or self-realization. Shankara is then the peaceful ascetic who has sunk deep into meditation, according to German anthropologist Wolf-Dieter Storl.

The auspicious one
This specific manifestation is often depicted as being benevolent, compassionate, and gentle. He is also the auspicious one and is worshipped as a personal deity. Here, Shiva, who represents the cosmic consciousness, becomes Shankara, more approachable and accessible. He is not so much the destroyer, as Shiva is always considered, but is seen as the preserver and protector. So, devotees turn to Shankara seeking his guidance and blessings.

Reconciling extremities
The distinctions may be subtle, but they highlight the complexities and nuances of Hindu mythology and the various ways in which one perceives and worships the divine. Shiva epitomizes balance because not only is he the Mahayogi, or the ascetic, he is also Shankara, the benevolent one. His *svabhava*, or inherent nature, is that of an ascetic, but he becomes the householder not just because of the desires of the world, but also to help its people. He does his *tapas*, or penance, but also performs his duty as a family man. So, Shiva as Shankara then reconciles the two extremes within his personality.

▷ **A dancing Ganesha** comes to life in this traditional Tala Pattachitra or palm leaf painting from Odisha, India. Etched with fine symmetry, Ganesha is shown with multiple arms, adorned in intricate jewellery, and framed within a decorative mandala that symbolizes balance and harmony.

FROM THE SHIVA PURANA The little boy who became a god

BIRTH OF GANESHA

One day, while Shiva was away, Parvati's friends Jaya and Vijaya complained about their lack of privacy as all the gatekeepers owed their allegiance to Shiva. Parvati faced something similar. Her husband's unannounced intrusions, especially when she was enjoying a bath, bothered her. But where would she find someone loyal only to her?

Then, Parvati had an idea. She had, for long, wanted a son. So, one morning, during her ablutions, she made a *lepa*, or a paste of scented unguents, and spread it over her body. When she was cleansed, she rubbed off the mixture and fashioned a little boy with great love and care, before breathing life into it. And so, Ganesha was born.

He was a beautiful little boy who never left his mother's side. Parvati would regale him with stories about his father and how he had saved the world from destruction.

One day Parvati stationed Ganesha at the entrance of her bath chamber to guard the door. She should have perhaps informed him about the tall man with matted locks, who would probably come seeking her, emanating a brilliant aura and bearing a trident in one hand. Alas, Ganesha knew little about Shiva. So when a stranger wearing animal skin and covered in ashes strode up, Ganesha blocked his way. Shiva was first amused but later became furious.

"Do you know who I am?" he thundered. "I am Shiva, Parvati's spouse, lord of the universe. I have free access to the entire cosmos, let alone my wife's chamber. Who are you to stop me?" Still blocking his way, Ganesha replied tartly, "Never mind who you are. I have never seen you before. Parvati is taking a bath and you cannot go inside."

Shiva instructed his followers to remove him from his station, but when the little boy defeated them, Shiva stepped in and hacked off Ganesha's head. Hearing the commotion, Parvati rushed out and seeing her beloved son on the ground, was overwrought with grief and then, fury. Shiva tried to placate her, pleading his innocence. Then, Parvati gave him an ultimatum: Restore her son or she would become Kali and destroy the universe. Aware that this was no empty threat, Shiva told the Ganas and the gods to bring back the head of the first living creature they saw.

Vishnu, the preserver, returned with the head of an elephant. Shiva placed it on Ganesha's shoulders and restored his life.

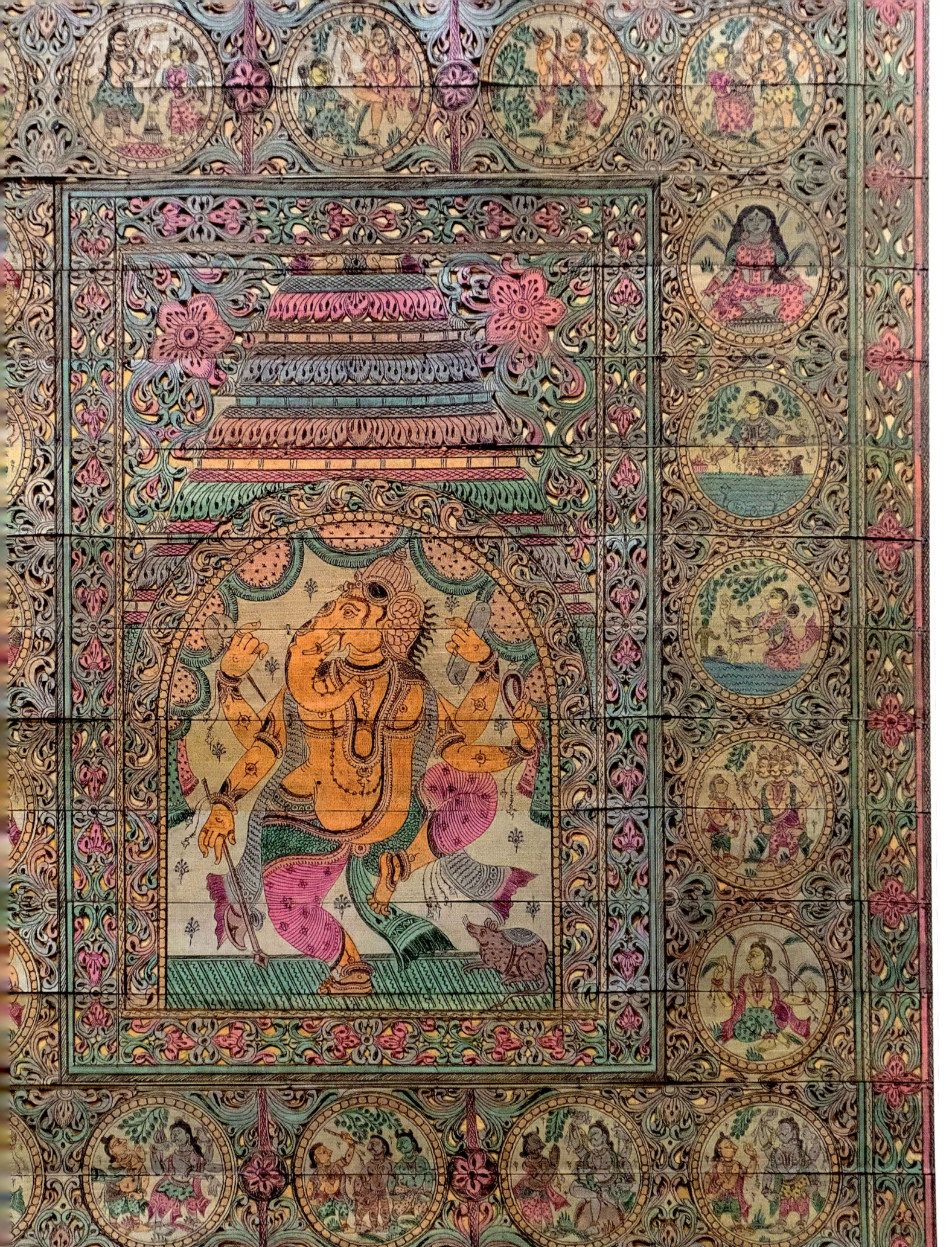

◁ **This c.1820 painting, in opaque** watercolour with gold on paper from the Mewar region of Rajasthan, captures the intimate, yet dramatic, moment of the conception of Karttikeya. Seen here are Shiva and Parvati in an intimate embrace, with Agni depicted in the lower right.

FROM THE SKANDA PURANA Manifesting a warrior to restore balance

KARTTIKEYA'S BIRTH

Taraka, a gleefully cruel Asura, had bedevilled the Devas after becoming indestructible because of the boons he received from an unsuspecting Brahma. The Devas huddled together to seek a solution to this insurmountable problem, and the first god who came to mind was Shiva. If he were to marry an equally powerful goddess like Parvati, their offspring would surely be capable of exterminating any fiend or foe in the universe, they thought.

A reluctant Shiva agreed to the marriage and the eager Devas awaited the birth of his son. However, the Devas grew concerned. Shiva and Parvati were making love and, not only was it extremely turbulent, it was also taking a very long time. What further disquieted the hapless Devas was the realization that since both Shiva and Parvati possessed such indestructible prowess, their child would inherit this unparalleled combined power.

What would be the fate of the Devas then? They had managed to get rid of one threat only to exist under the shadow of another. The Devas were convinced that they would be driven into forced retirement and eventual oblivion. So Indra, their king, interrupted the lovemaking. Shiva retained the semen, being an expert in yoga. Missing Parvati, the seed took a circuitous route via a series of carriers, including Vayu, the god of wind, and Agni, the god of fire. Agni swallowed it, but the seed's heat-energy was too great – even for fire. So, Agni bathed in Prayagraj, in the holy waters of Ganga, who then received the seed. She too could not bear it and cast the seed among a grove of sara plants, the reeds. There, a male child was born with six heads. The Krittikas, the Pleiades, fostered and nursed him, so he came to be called Karttikeya. He was also named Shanmukha, or six-faced, Skanda, Agnibhu, Gangeya, and Gangaputra, as all these forces played an important role in his birth.

Karttikeya grew into a handsome young man, with the peacock Paravani as his vahana, or vehicle, and a shining lance as his weapon. Known as Mahasenapati, the commander-in-chief of the divine army, he destroyed Taraka and kept the legions of Devas safe for a long time to come.

▽ **A chromolithograph** depicting Karttikeya seated on his mount, the peacock.

KUMARASAMBHAVA

LYRICS OF LOVE

> When they ritually grasped hands, the daughter of the Himalaya was overcome with shyness because of her love for Shiva. Her form became charming with passionate desire.
>
> Verse 8.1, Kalidasa's epic poem *Kumarasambhava*

Rich in *shringara rasa*, or romantic and erotic sentiment, with elements of *vira rasa*, or heroism and bhakti, or devotion, the *Kumarasambhava* is considered one of the greatest *kavya* or poems, in classical Sanskrit. Kalidasa, counted as one of the most brilliant classical writers of early India, composed this around the 5th century CE. The complete work consists of 16 cantos and is widely regarded as his finest work.

A cosmic love story

Kumarasambhava, or The Birth of Kumara, also known as Karttikeya, is an account of the courtship of Shiva and Parvati and most of the chapters contain rich and evocative descriptions about the love and romance between the two. Parvati, the daughter of Himavat, or the king of the mountains is portrayed as the embodiment of grace and devotion, and the poem details the austerities she performed as she wooed Shiva. It tells of the powerful Asura Tarakasura who was blessed with the boon that only the child of Shiva could vanquish him and the meeting of Shiva and Parvati was crucial. It then details their eventual passionate union, and the birth of a son, they named Kumara or Karttikeya, who being the god of war slew Tarakasura to establish peace and glory in all the worlds.

The poem also stands out for its majestic descriptions of the natural world. Kalidasa's portrayal of spring may have set the standard for nature metaphors in Indian classical literature. The Himalayas are the divine landscape of the poem, which begins with a grand description of the mountain range that is home to sages, celestial beings, and spiritual energy.

Divinity in love

The poem is also remarkable for its bold and sensuous portrayal of divine love, and its sensual and spiritual themes have inspired temple sculptures, especially those of the Khajuraho group of temples in central India's Madhya Pradesh.

Verse 8.5 titled "The First Embrace" is an ideal example:

> Her friends taught her, "Darling, curb your shyness and serve Shankara in private." But when her beloved stood before her, she got agitated, and forgot all about it.

However, it is also because of verses like these, in the eighth canto, in which Kalidasa describes the lovemaking of Shiva and Parvati, that have faced criticism. Mammata Bhatta, a Kashmiri scholar from the 11th century, in his Sanskrit text on poetics, *Kavyaprakasha*, claimed they were improper. Other orthodox critics believed that Parvati cursed Kalidasa for depicting divine intimacy too vividly.

Yet, there is no arguing that *Kumarasambhava* is a poetic masterpiece that blends romance and cosmic resolve with exquisite imagery.

▷ **In the "Ardhanarishwara" segment of Guru Vanashree Rao's dance-play** *Trayambakam*, Shiva is portrayed through the dynamic Chhau style, while Parvati moves with the lyrical grace of Kuchipudi – two distinct identities embodied in perfect union.

182 | SHIVA, THE HOUSEHOLDER

SOMASKANDA

THE THREE IN ONE

The infant Skanda stands poised between his parents, Shiva and Parvati, who sit at opposite ends of a shared dais. The child assumes the *araimandi pose* – a demanding foundational stance in Bharatanatyam – essential for grounding the dancer. Rich in symbolism, it stands for stability, strength, and unwavering dedication. It is as though he is preparing to perform for his divine parents, a silent offering of grace and discipline. Shiva and Parvati, seated in the relaxed *sukhasana*, radiate ease and contentment through their characteristic hand gestures. The composition exudes a serene familial charm, a tableau of tranquillity born of their intimate bond.

Originating during the Pallava period, 6th–8th centuries, this depiction, known as Somaskanda, emerged from efforts to integrate the worship of Shiva, Devi, and Skanda. The name is derived from the Sanskrit *Sa-Uma-Skanda*, meaning "with Uma (another name for Parvati) and their infant son Skanda".

Prominence in Tamil Nadu

As religious studies scholar Paul Younger notes in *The Home of Dancing Sivan*, this is probably the most common image of Shiva in Tamil Nadu and was extremely popular in the medieval temples of the region. It is the statue of Somaskanda that is carried in the festival processions of the Thillai Nataraja Temple, an important Shaiva temple of the 10th century. It is also remarkable how the profound significance of dance in this region has been incorporated into the image through the various mudras, such as *pataka hasta*, *kartarimukha hasta*, and *kapittha hasta*. The image was first perfected in bronze during the Chola period, 9th–13th centuries, but there are rare prototypes of this composite icon produced during the last phase of the Pallava rule in Tamil Nadu. In these, the two lower hands – which, during the Chola period, displayed mudras – now hold north Indian attributes such as the trident.

Paradoxes in the image

The image of Somaskanda presents two intriguing dichotomies. First, even though this is a formal family portrait, Ganesha, Shiva's other son, is absent. This stems from the fact that by the time this icon became popular, Ganesha had not yet been incorporated in Tamil Nadu where these images are found. Second, the term Murugan, the more favoured name for Skanda in this region, has not been used, perhaps because Murugan suggests a proto Indian god of the folk tradition. This is evident as his name does not appear in any Sanskrit texts and he has many temples independent of Shiva. As German Indologist Gunther-Dietz Sontheimer notes in "Sculptural Religion and Folk Religion in India: The Case of Rudra Siva and Khandoba", this shows the remarkable continuity between tribal folk religion, high scriptural religion, and interregional cults.

The family symbolism

In Somaskanda, the couple is regarded as the archetypal representatives of a content, fruitful marriage. This image brings to view the domestic aspect, representing the unity and harmony of the divine family. Shiva is shown with a serene expression, and the sculpture highlights his loving and nurturing side, family values, and the balance of masculine and feminine energies. It is indeed a beautiful representation of the divine family.

◁ **A bronze sculpture** of Somaskanda from Tamil Nadu belonging to the Vijayanagar period, c.1350–1450.

The mighty River Ganga cascades through the serene town of Gangotri in Uttarakhand, India. The Gangotri Glacier, a 20-kilometre trek away, marks the sacred source of one of the world's most revered rivers.

FROM THE VAYU PURANA When Shiva captured a river

THE DESCENT OF GANGA

The proud and arrogant goddess Ganga thrived on being a celestial river, as she frolicked among the gods with youthful abandonment. Little did she know that the tenacious Bhagiratha would change the course of her future. He wanted to immerse the ashes of his forefathers so that they could ascend to heaven. The only way that was possible was if he could submerge their ashes into Ganga's waters.

The determined king had been meditating for a long time, following the instructions of the great sage Kapila. Bhagiratha's ancestors had disturbed Kapila's deep *tapasya* or penance. The furious sage had cursed them and turned them to ash. Kapila Muni told Bhagiratha that only Ganga offered his ancestors a chance at attaining salvation or ending the cycle of rebirth.

Bhagiratha's zealous *tapasya* bore fruit and Ganga agreed to descend to the Earth. However, she warned Bhagiratha that she would not be able to control herself once she left her celestial residence, and would come to Earth with such force that it could destroy the world. Only Shiva, the gods agreed, could control Ganga's force, so they approached him as he meditated, waited for him to open his eyes, and then pleaded their case. Shiva decided to take Ganga by surprise and opened his *jata mukuta*, or crown of matted locks and spread them upon his broad shoulders. As Ganga descended, he captured her in his locks and suspended her slowly in order to prevent destruction due to her strong current. Ganga was furious and decided to go to the *patala*, or the underworld instead, while sweeping away Shiva. He, however, managed to control her, saved the world, and earned the name Gangadhar.

Aware of her plans, Shiva thought of keeping her in his dreadlocks, but remembered Bhagiratha's piteous condition. He had been praying for so long that there was a veritable network of visible veins on his person. Bhagiratha had earlier propitiated Shiva as well. The god knew he could not keep Ganga in his locks. So, he controlled his anger and released Ganga in such a way that the river had seven currents. Three flowed towards the east and three to the west.

Ganga was not so unhappy in the end. After all, she was the purest and most auspicious of rivers, was in close proximity to Shiva, and was the only river to flow across the heavens, the Earth, and the underworld. Shiva's intervention is not forgotten either, and Ganga, even today, is hailed with the chant: *Hara Hara Gange*!

△ **A chromolithograph from West Bengal's Calcutta Art Studio depicts the Dasa Mahavidyas** – *(from left to right)* Kali, standing on Shiva and holding a severed head; Tara, similar in form but bearing a knife, sword, fly-whisk, and lotus; Tripurasundari, resting on the supine body of Shiva, which lies upon a throne supported by male divinities; Bhuvaneshvari, adorned like a queen; Bhairavi, seated on a lotus and holding a manuscript; Chhinnamasta, decapitated and drinking her own blood; Dhumavati, aged and standing in a chariot; Bagalamukhi, seizing the tongue of an Asura; Matangi, dark-green and seated on a throne; and Kamala, seated on a lotus with elephants flanking her.

WILD AND UNTAMED

Kali – fierce and tempered by Shiva's calm beneath her feet – is one of the Dasa Mahavidyas, the ten Tantric goddesses. Like Shiva, she is both wrathful and liberating, embodying the balance of destruction, creation, power, and restraint.

One of the most extraordinary, indeed enthralling, divinities India has ever seen is Kali, a symbol of the dynamic aspect of primal energy, and the forbidding consort of Shiva as Mahakaal, or supreme power. Though, in her depictions, she appears less as a manifestation of the divine and more as a bloodthirsty, almost grotesque ogress, she is always Ma, or mother – both gentle and terrible.

To understand her is to witness her symbiotic relationship with Shiva, for they have many similarities. They both represent eternal time, devouring it. She is the Shakti, the active principle of the passive *purusha*, or Shiva.

Though often depicted with Shiva, she is not merely his consort, but is worshipped as an individual, a powerful goddess. However, when they are portrayed together, as in the iconic version of a bloodthirsty Kali dancing on the supine Shiva, they symbolize the balance of cosmic forces. Kali, with her energy and power to transform, is not only the goddess of time but of death and destruction. Shiva, on whom she is shown standing, is the calm and eternal aspect of reality. Theirs is the union of creation and destruction, a cycle that leads to renewal with silence giving way to action.

Benevolent, yet bloodthirsty

Dakshinakali, the benevolent form of Kali, is a seminal representation in Kali iconography depicting the goddess dancing on Shiva. According to the myth associated with this image, Kali immersed herself in a tempestuous dance of bloodshed with the massacre of the Asuras, resulting in an inebriation of destructive frenzy. She relished the blood and gore of her victims and left evidence of this trail of terror across the battlefield.

Yet this orgy of violence that destroyed the evil elements also endangered the world. So enthusiastically did she devour the Asuras that the gods turned to Shiva and begged him to stop the rampage.

Shiva, who proved to be a saviour countless times before in the cosmic world, intervened. He lay down in front of Kali, among the many corpses on the battlefield, allowing her to dance on his body so that she regained her senses. In her

ecstatic fury, however, she failed to see Shiva and continued on her rampage, until he cried out to get her attention and calmed her fury. It is here that she stuck out her tongue.

Shiva represents all-devouring time; Kali by dancing on Shiva represents mastery over the dark abysmal void that is above time, space, and causation. In this characteristic pose, suggest historians Donald and Jean Johnson, Kali affirms creation, which is the ultimate expression of the feminine principle of the universe, by conquering the god of destruction. Of course, Kali's iconography depicting her with her tongue out has many interpretations. Among them is one closely related to the myth in the *Devi Mahatmya*, part of the *Markandeya Purana*, wherein she did so to lap up the blood of the powerful Asura Raktabija, for every drop of his blood on the ground birthed many other Raktabijas.

The Dance of Kali and Shiva

A South Indian tradition tells of a dance contest between Shiva and Kali. After defeating the Asuras Shumbha and Nishumbha, Kali took up residence in a forest with her retinue of fierce companions and terrorized the entire area. A local devotee beseeched Shiva to rid the forests of this violent goddess. When Shiva appeared, she threatened him, claiming the area belonged to her, so the god challenged her to a dance contest and defeated her when she was unwilling to match his energetic Tandava dance, notes scholar of religion David Kinsley.

The temple of Chidambaram, a shrine dedicated to Urdhva Tandava Shiva, has a fascinating carving. There, it is believed, Shiva defeated Kali in the dance competition by raising his leg to his head. The Urdhva Tandava is the dance form in which Shiva performs this move. The carving depicts a dancing Kali on the ground beside the Urdhvatandavamurti stone carving. Placing one foot on the ground, Shiva raises his other foot to the sky, even as Kali hangs her head and draws in the dust with her toes, writes historian David Smith.

In the contest for the best dancer, Kali, representing blind unfettered absolute shakti, or energy, of the universe, is sure that she is the best

Though, in her depictions, she appears less as a manifestation of the divine and more as a bloodthirsty, almost grotesque ogress, she is always Ma, or mother – both gentle and terrible.

WILD AND UNTAMED

> In her association with Shiva, Kali's tendency to wildness and disorder persists. Although he is sometimes said to tame her or soften her, she incites Shiva into dangerous and destructive behaviour and vice versa.

dancer. As they danced, she was able to imitate Shiva's every move perfectly. But then one of Shiva's earrings falls, which he effortlessly catches with his foot and replaces on his ear in a single swoop without Kali even noticing it. That establishes him as the king of dancers once and for all, writes scholar Wolf-Dieter Storl.

The 10 Goddesses

Among the 10 goddesses of cosmic wisdom, Kali is the main one, the others differing forms that arise as per her command. Sati, Shiva's first wife, gave form to the Dasa Mahavidyas during Daksha's sacrifice. They are awakeners, anti-models, writes Kinsley, who make us understand that the world is not what we like to think it is.

In the original account given in the *Mahabhagavata Purana*, Sati took on the form of Kali before actually multiplying herself into the 10 Mahavidyas. Although Kali is not specifically named, Sati first turned into a dark, frightening naked four-armed goddess with dishevelled hair and a garland of skulls, and then created other forms from herself. In her association with Shiva, Kali's tendency to wildness and disorder persists.

Although he is sometimes said to tame her or soften her, she incites Shiva into dangerous and destructive behaviour and vice versa.

The Dasa Mahavidyas are all associated with Shiva but he is rarely depicted with them and, when he is, he is in a subordinate position. Even in the original myth of the Mahavidyas that features Sati, she stresses her decision to act independently of her husband and on her success in bending him to her will. Most of the goddesses are not submissive, and are rarely depicted with male consorts. When they are, such as in the case of Kali, Tara, and Tripurasundari, the goddesses dominate them. Kali and Tara stand on the supine Shiva while Tripurasundari is usually shown sitting on him.

Tara, like Kali, is black, with her left foot placed on a corpse or Shiva. She wears a tiger skin and her hair is tied in long braids. Bhairavi, with her ferocious appearance, resembles Shiva and is his female version. Tripurasundari is often seen seated on the supine form of Shiva, which in turn lies on a throne whose legs are Brahma, Vishnu, Shiva, and Rudra. According to *Vamakeshvara Tantra*, she dwells on the Himalayan peaks and sages worship her. Much like Shiva, she wears a tiger skin and a snake as a garland and her matted hair holds a trident and a drum, notes Kinsley.

◁ **In this 1920 watercolour painting** by Indian artist Jita Chitrakar, Kali appears dark-skinned, framed by an aureole, her blood-soaked tongue thrust out, and a garland of skulls hanging from her neck. She stands in a grotesque landscape, holding two severed heads that drip with blood, while a dog eagerly laps at one. Around her are her fierce companions, each clutching human skulls — one even drinks blood from the one he holds. Above them, four dark figures dance wildly, as if exulting in a sacrificial rite.

In the coastal village of Kulasekarapattinam in Tamil Nadu, Dussehra takes on a unique form. Known as Kulasai Dasara, it is centred around the historic Arulmigu Mutharamman Temple, dedicated to Sri Mutharamman, a fierce form of Kali. For 10 days, the village comes alive with colours as devotees arrive in elaborate costumes, painted bodies, and striking makeup to portray Kali and other mythical figures. They move as though possessed by divine power, offer prophecies, and receive alms from worshippers. In this image, a devotee is dressed as Kali, with her Shaiva connection evident from the third eye and the tripundra on her forehead.

THOSE CLOSEST TO SHIVA

Fierce, chaotic, and otherworldly, Shiva's attendants – the Ganas – throng the margins of the celestial world. Once local spirits or tribal deities perhaps, they were later absorbed into Shiva's retinue. They appear in many episodes of Shiva's mythic life – as guardians, tricksters, warriors, and devotees – always close to their lord and always part of his entourage.

Flocks, troops, multitudes – that is how Ganas are often imagined. But, in the Shaivic world, they are more than just a gathering; they are Shiva's chosen ones. Friends and protectors, attendants and emissaries, they move with him through myth and cosmos. Some beat the *damaru*, others play the vina; while warriors rise in his name.

Prior to their assimilation into the Shaiva tradition, the Ganas were likely a group of non-Aryan deities, and although they are revered as minor deities or inferior demi gods, they do not really perform any celestial marvel – their sole raison d'être is to exist in service of Shiva. They are completely devoted to him and reside with him on Mount Kailasha (See pp202–03).

The Ganas are typically portrayed as mischievous and playful beings – troublemakers who sometimes bring chaos. Therefore, there are different ways of viewing them. Scholar of Indian religions David Smith, in *The Dance of Siva*, calls these heavenly hosts howling ghosts. Cultural historian and Indologist Hans T Bakker, in *The Vakatakas*, notes that at times they carry moneybags and are referred to as Nidhis. In this way, they also function as guardians of wealth like Kubera, the god of riches. Occasionally, Ganas are also known as Pramathaganas, meaning "those with unpredictable ways". The root *matha* means "to churn", implying beings who stir or agitate the universe.

Laughter, music, and movement

Indian Art historian C Sivaramamurti, in *Nataraja in Art, Thought and Literature*, draws attention to the fact that the ill-shaped, impish, wild dwarves Pramathaganas – being in such close proximity to Shiva – can even take minor liberties with him. Moreover, they are privileged to witness the glory of Shiva's dance, even as higher celestial beings, such as those of the Trinity – Vishnu and Brahma – must wait in line to enter the arena.

Sometimes, sculptures give the impression that the Ganas possess an identity of their own, independent from Shiva. They are celebrated for their sense of humour, sometimes bordering on the obscene. In the *Shivatandava Stotra*, attributed to Ravana, the king of Lanka and a devout Shiva devotee, a verse describes the Pramathaganas as all having a comic appearance.

They are also known for their passion for music and dance. Legend says that Shiva used to dance every evening, performing the 108 *karanas*, or dance postures. The Ganas do not lag behind in imitating Shiva's dance. Filled with enthusiasm, they accurately depict all the emotions and the nine *rasas*, or emotional flavours, meticulously

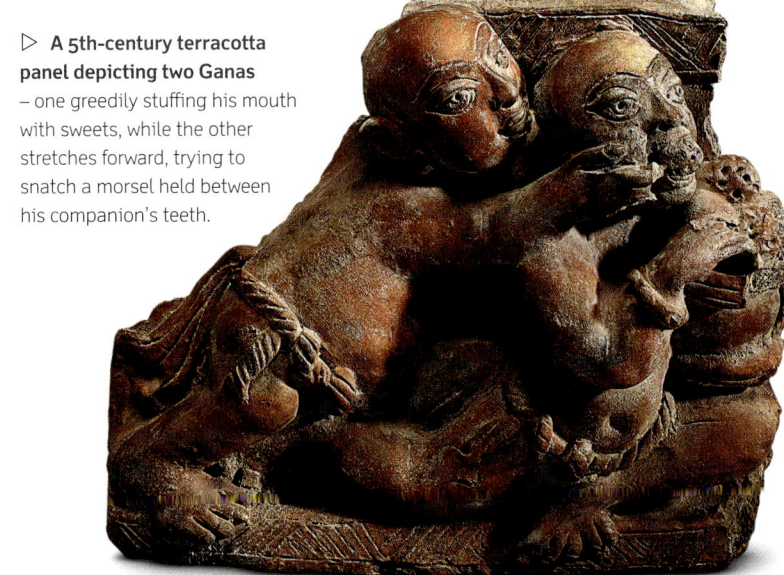

▷ **A 5th-century terracotta panel depicting two Ganas** – one greedily stuffing his mouth with sweets, while the other stretches forward, trying to snatch a morsel held between his companion's teeth.

conveyed in their *abhinaya*, or expressive gestures. They appear very colourful in their *aharaya*, or costumes and makeup.

Textual illustrations

It is interesting how their nature seeps into their portrayal in artworks. Shiva's Ganas are often depicted as small, dwarfish, and terrifying in appearance. Indian Historian Roshen Dalal has highlighted their depictions. There are descriptions in the *Vishnudharmottara Purana* where they are depicted as fat, short, and sometimes shown resting on the left knee. The right leg is bent in a posture later associated with deities like Hanuman, the Vanara god. Sometimes, the right arm is raised in a supporting stance, while the left hand is placed on the girdle at the waist. If they have long hair, it is arranged in curls and spread around the head. They have protruding teeth and bulging eyes, which add to their fierce demeanour. They are often seen wearing two different types of earrings or sometimes just one. Their thighs and bellies are rounded, and they wear frightful ornaments, carry skulls in their hands, and are smeared with fresh blood. Their faces resemble those of dogs, donkeys, swine, and jackals.

In stone

Smith says that these dancing, frolicking, and fighting prodigies of Shiva – ranging from odd and puckish to inexplicable and fiendish, or passive, tranquil, and awe-inspiring – are among the quaintest creations in minor figural art from the 5th–10th centuries. Sometimes, their posture lends a certain rhythm even to stone sculptures. C Sivaramamurti has delineated their appearance in sculptures. He notes

▷ **A wooden sculpture from Tamil Nadu, dating between 1700 and 1900,** depicts a four-armed Gana performing a war dance. His martial nature is evident from the weapons he wields – a club, sword, and shield.

that the Ganas are shown either at the feet or on either side of Shiva as Nataraja, playing four varieties of musical instruments. Sometimes there are even two Ganas flanking Shiva, playing the drum or clapping their hands to keep time, as seen in early Chola sculptures. Among the earliest sculptures of Shiva, from a temple in Bhumara, Madhya Pradesh, there are many dance poses similar to those described in Bharata's *Natya Shastra*, an ancient treatise on drama.

The Ganas inevitably provoke a smile with their shenanigans and their amusing attitude while dancing. They arrange themselves to perform the *karanas* and *angaharas*, or dance sequences, and Shiva, in his bonhomie with them, sometimes presents himself as a dwarf, one amongst them. The sculpture from Nachna, Madhya Pradesh, shows Shiva as Vamadeva, in which he chooses to be a dwarf. The only difference is that he has four hands while they have two. Shiva is depicted as one of his five principal forms: Aghora, Vamadeva, Sadyojata, Tatpurusha, and Ishana. As Vamadeva, with his right leg raised, left hand in *abhaya*, and right hand in *karihasta*, his *jata* or hair is arranged in a cluster of small ringlets, all turned to the right. There is an expression of mirth on his face.

Shiva's inclusive world

From their iconography and mannerisms, it is clear that Shiva seems to be giving importance to those ridiculed or marginalized – the dwarfed, the hunchbacked, or those who behave and look strange. It is not surprising then that brigands, robbers, drunkards, all find that there is something relatable within Shiva. It is important to note too that people from lower castes, no matter how

society considers them impure, are pure for Shiva. All substances find space with him as well. Restrictions do not matter in Shiva's world.

Their chief

The *Skanda Purana* mentions some of the most important Ganas, among them are Ganapati, Nandi, Bhringi, Chandesvara, Chandu, Mundu, Mahaloman, and Mahodara. Shiva appointed Ganesha as their leader. His name reflects this role, as Ganesha – or Ganapati – means "lord or leader of the Ganas".

Sometimes, Nandi, the bull, Shiva's mount, is considered the leader of the Ganas, who ensures order in Kailasha. He is a loyal and most trusted companion, and often looks towards his lord with joy. Even his name is probably derived from the word *ananda*, meaning "joy". The bull symbolizes strength, fertility, and prosperity. Nandi is also a guardian and protector of Shiva's temples and devotees. Usually seated right in front of the lingam, devotees offer prayers with flowers and whisper their wishes in his ear so that he can communicate it to Shiva.

The Ganas denote the tumultuous, undomesticated, and assorted facets of the universe, adding profundity to Shiva's character, and to the universe that Shiva oversees.

> ... the tumultuous, undomesticated, and assorted facets of the universe, adding profundity to Shiva's character ...

▽ Titled *The Wedding Procession of Shri Shankar-ji (Shiva),* this ink drawing was created by Indira Devi, an artist from Madhubani region in Bihar, in 1977. It shows Ganas dancing in their lord's wedding procession.

196 | SHIVA, THE HOUSEHOLDER

A bronze sculpture of Nataraja, from Tiruchchirappalli, Tamil Nadu, captures Shiva in his cosmic dance – one foot lifted in grace. In his hands, the *damaru* beats the rhythm of both creation and destruction. Beside him stands Parvati, serene and poised with a flower in hand – her stillness the perfect counterpoint to his divine motion. On the other side of Shiva is the three legged Bhringi playing the cymbals.

FROM THE TAMIL STHALA PURANAS A lesson in balance

DEVOUT, BUT IMPRUDENT

The Devas and sages venerated the newly married Shiva and Parvati as they sat on Mount Kailasha *(See pp202–03)*. The worshippers sung their praises and paid homage by performing *pradakshina*, or circumambulating them, their heads bowed as the couple smiled and blessed them. All was going well till the arrival of a well-known rishi and truculent bhakta, a devotee of Shiva and Shiva alone – Bhringi.

Bhringi was an ardent devotee. Every morning, after completing his ablutions, he worshipped Shiva as part of his daily rituals. But on this day, he was dismayed. His beloved Shiva no longer sat alone. Bhringi remained undeterred and in conformity with his vow of being an exclusive Shiva worshipper, refused to circumambulate Parvati.

Parvati at this point, still calm, tolerantly informed him, "You are such a wise bhakta, don't you realise we are both the father and mother of the universe and we are two halves of the same truth?" Bhringi ignored her. Miffed, Parvati came up with a plan. She went off to do *tapas*, or penance. As time went by, Shiva was satisfied with her, for she was a great *tapasvini* and was adept at severe penance. Shiva said, "Parvati, you have pleased me with your arduous *tapas*, what do you desire?" She replied in a honeyed tone, "I want to be united with you as half your body, so I can always be near you". The wish was granted and they became Ardhanarishvara, *(See pp166–69)* standing as one body – the right half bearing Shiva and the left half Parvati.

A satisfied and almost smug Parvati waited victoriously for Bhringi. Undaunted, the sage who had done thousands of years of penance of the most austere kind and knew the religious texts like the Vedas and Upanishads, took the form of a beetle, pierced a hole between the two and did a *pradakshina* of only Shiva.

A stunned and angry Parvati announced, "May Bhringi lose all parts of his body that come from the mother. For it is I the mother who has provided all the people of the universe with flesh and blood." Bhringi instantly lost all muscle and was reduced to a heap of bones, thus losing balance and falling humiliatingly on the floor. Unable to get up in this emaciated state, Shiva the compassionate one could not help but feel pity for such an ardent, albeit, imprudent devotee. He gave him a third leg to support his skeletal frame.

Bhringi makes his presence felt in many Shiva–Parvati artworks, skulking around them with his three legs, body bent with protruding ribs. His story emphasizes the crucial congruence between two cosmic forces, the masculine and feminine energies.

In Hampi, Karnataka, the Badavilinga Temple houses a colossal monolithic Shiva lingam, carved from black stone. Legend says a poor peasant woman commissioned it, giving the temple its name – *badava* means "poor" in Kannada. In this image, the temple's priest, KN Krishna Bhat, tends the sacred lingam, a figure of quiet devotion against the monumental stone. Known and respected far beyond the temple walls, he dedicated more than four decades of his life to this service – a living testament to the unwavering devotion Shiva inspires.

△ **Shiva rides the bull Nandi,** wielding a bow in divine grace and power.

THE LOYAL NANDI

Many Hindu deities have faithful helpers, such as the Vanara Hanuman for Rama and the eagle Garuda for Vishnu. Shiva has Nandi, the gentle white bull who, devoted and serene, often sits facing the Shiva lingam, exuding Ananda, a calm delight and embodying loyalty and a readiness to assist.

Some myths say Nandi emerged from the cosmic ocean, but the *Vayu Purana* describes him as the son of Sage Kashyapa and the celestial cow Surabhi. In his anthropomorphic form, he is known as Nandin or Nandikeshvara and was first depicted as a youthful figure with a bull's head. Like Shiva, he has three eyes. Two hands are folded in namaste, while the others hold a deer and a double-bladed battle axe. But, his human body could not withstand the ecstatic energy of his devotion and so Nandi, one of the greatest devotees of Shiva, took the form of a bull.

Gatekeeper of the sacred abode

In temple architecture, Nandi is typically enshrined in a pavilion of his own, facing the sanctum where the Shiva lingam resides. This majestic, milky-white bull represents Shiva's faithful servant, chamberlain, protector, and guardian of the sacred site. Above all, Nandi is Shiva's mount – hence one of Shiva's names, Vrishavahana, "the one who rides the bull".

As leader of Shiva's celestial attendants, the Ganas, Nandi ensures order in Kailasha. During intimate moments between Shiva and Parvati, or while Shiva performed a cosmic dance for her, Nandi often found himself flustered, trying to manage the queue of celestial visitors. As the gatekeeper and crowd controller, Nandi wielded his authority – even over the most exalted beings who were willing to forsake all celestial pleasures just to dwell near Shiva.

Symbol of devotion and strength

Beyond Shiva's mount, Nandi embodies deep meaning. He stands for unwavering devotion, strength, discipline, fertility, and prosperity.

> . . . Nandi was born from the blessing of Shiva himself and was made the head of the Ganas, the celestial attendants . . .

In temples, today, seated right in front of the Shivalinga, Nandi listens patiently as devotees whisper their prayers and deepest desires into his right ear, believing that he will convey them to Shiva himself.

In Hindu iconography, a deity's vahana, or mount, can also represent the lower nature that the god has mastered to maintain cosmic harmony. In one myth, Nandi was once a powerful Asura whom Shiva had to subdue. As a bull, Nandi also symbolizes aggressive male sexuality – yet Shiva, the supreme ascetic and master of yoga, is portrayed as having complete control over such primal forces.

Thus, Nandi is a living symbol of loyalty, restraint, power, and devotion, ever seated before his beloved lord in eternal reverence.

▷ **A colossal Nandi statue** at the top of Chamundi Hills in Mysuru, Karnataka.

MOUNT KAILASHA
AN ICY ABODE

One of the most revered and mysterious mountains in the world rises to 6638 metres (21,778 feet), standing virtually alone on a high plateau in the Ngari prefecture of the Tibet Autonomous Region in China. A part of the Trans-Himalayan range that lies north of the main Himalayan mountains, Mount Kailasha is unmistakeable with its black rock and a distinctive diamond shape overlooking the sparkling waters of the freshwater Mansarovar lake.

This pyramidal black peak bespeaking of sacred geometry and divine architecture with its slopes streaked with glaciers, ice, and snow is one of the most sacred places for Hindus, Buddhists, and Jains.

In mythology
Like many sacred places, Kailasha is imbued with Hindu and Buddhist meanings and is referenced in many religious texts, including the Puranas, with its earliest mention in the Sanskrit epics *Mahabharata* and *Ramayana*. The *Shiva Purana* indicates that Kailasha is the eternal mountain dwelling of Shiva and Parvati. This is where Shiva performs his cosmic dance and engages in deep meditation.

Bearing the epithet Girisha, or lord of the mountains, Shiva sits motionless in deep concentration of the universe, in total absorption, in absolute bliss consciousness and being as Satchidananda. Kailasha is the mountain of pure snow, notes, ethnologist Wolf-Dieter Storl in *Shiva: The Wild God of Power and Ecstasy*, the mountain of white ash, the mountain of salvation.

This is also the site of Shiva and Parvati's divine union, symbolizing cosmic balance and love. Storl writes, it is said that as "Shiva and Parvati approached Mount Kailasha after their wedding ceremony, the wolves began to howl and the ghosts to wail. Forest devils and rock gnomes rolled down the hill slopes laughing insanely and merrily. With wild dancing, drinking, and buffoonery, they celebrated the newlywed couple. Finally, the couple retired to their roofless abode and spent their days in blissful love making."

The centre of the universe
Shiva is said to have chosen Mount Kailasha as his dwelling place, symbolizing ultimate enlightenment and liberation. The mountain is described as a manifestation of divine energy and is believed to be the axis mundi, or the centre of the universe. It is often depicted as a celestial throne and its significance is highlighted through various mythological narratives and scriptures.

Storl writes that it is the "motionless polar star around which the heavens revolve, the resting hub of the cycles of time of the dance of creation and destruction ... the mystical centre where samsara, the wheel of birth and death turns not."

Scholar of religious studies Diana Eck calls Kailasha a "world centring mountain", which is not only the god's abode, but also the "mountain manifestation of Shiva's lingam, the one that pierced the earth in the very beginning of time."

It is not surprising then that Kailasha is considered, in many sects of Hinduism, as heaven, and the ultimate destination of souls. It is why it is often the grand dream and goal of many a Hindu pilgrim to circumambulate the mountain and the lake it faces.

▷ *(clockwise from top left)* **The ancient Tibetan Buddhist monastery Chiu Gompa**, also called Sparrow Monastery, the majestic Mount Kailasha rising in the background; **Pilgrims at Dolma La Pass**, the highest and most challenging point in the Mount Kailasha's pilgrimage circuit; **the coastline of Lake Manasarovar**, nestled at the southern base of Mount Kailasha.

STEEPED IN FAITH

SEEKING RELEASE
It is thought that no one has ever summited Mount Kailasha; climbing is prohibited out of respect for its sanctity. Pilgrims visit here to perform the ritual circumambulation, or *kora*, around the mountain. It is believed to cleanse sins and bring spiritual merit. Meditation at Kailasha is believed to lead to moksha.

IN MYTHOLOGY
Mount Kailasha is often referred to in ancient texts. According to one popular legend, the sacred river Ganga flows from Shiva's matted locks, originating at Kailasha and descending on to the Earth. In the *Skanda Purana*, the mountain was also home to Ganas, sages, and other gods including Indra, the lord of the Devas.

PILGRIM'S WAY
Hindu pilgrims come this way as do the Buddhist, some travelling to Kailasha by way of Lhasa, or through India and the district of Pithoragarh. The *parikrama*, or circumambulation, is a 52-kilometre (32-miles) trek, typically taking three days to complete. The hiking altitudes are more than 4,500 metres (15,000 feet) and the journey is particularly challenging due to the high altitude and rugged terrain.

Rising majestically from the Himalayas, Mount Kailasha in the Ngari prefecture, of the Tibet Autonomous Region in China, is revered by Shaivites as the earthly abode of Shiva. This hallowed peak embodies divine silence and cosmic might. Pilgrims seek emancipation and spiritual awakening by completing the arduous *parikrama*, or circumambulation, around its base. For devotees, Mount Kailasha is more than just a mountain; it is Shiva himself, and a timeless location where heaven meets earth, silence speaks, and the soul surrenders.

I am Pure Consciousness, Bliss, the Self

Nirvana Shatakam, Adi Shankaracharya

4 | SHIVA
THE YOGI

Shiva has been meditating since before time. Through the endurance of self-imposed austerities, he accumulates an immense reservoir of psychic energy – so concentrated it blazes with incandescence.

THE SUPREME ASCETIC

As Yogeshvara, the lord of yoga, Shiva embodies all aspects of yoga – meditation, asceticism, and transcendence. Shiva, as the supreme yogi, does not entirely extinguish the fire of lust, but transmutes it into the fire of asceticism.

Revered as Adiyogi, or the first yogi, Shiva is the origin of yogic wisdom. The term "yoga" first appears in the *Rig Veda*, the earliest known Sanskrit text. However, in the context of harnessing the mind and body, evidence suggests that yogic practices predate the Vedas. Archaeological findings from the Indus Valley Civilization, a prehistoric urban culture of the Indian subcontinent, show seals depicting Shiva-like figures in meditative or yogic postures. These traces of early yogic tradition reinforce the idea of Shiva as the primordial yogi, whose legacy shaped the foundations of yoga.

The knowledge-giver

Later texts, such as the *Shiva Purana*, composed around 10th–11th centuries, portray Shiva not only as the embodiment of yoga, but also as its primordial teacher. In these narratives, he transmits the science of yoga to the Saptarishis, or the seven great sages, who in turn transmit this knowledge to the world.

The *Shiva Samhita*, a classical Sanskrit yoga text attributed to Shiva, presents a comprehensive system of yogic practice. In a dialogue with Parvati, Shiva expounds on millions of asanas along with instructions on breath control, mudras, and spirituality. He also delves into foundational yogic paths such as Hatha Yoga, Raja Yoga, and Laya Yoga.

Over time, many key aspects of yogic thought and practice become associated with Shiva. He is revered as the lord of Pranayama, the art of breath regulation. Meditation mantras such as So'ham ("I am He") mirror the sound of his breath. He is also Omkara, the source of the primordial sound "Aum", which anchors the mind in meditation. As the eternal yogi, Shiva is not only the silent practitioner but also the force behind the transmission and evolution of yoga.

Symbolism of asceticism

A central aspect of yoga is asceticism. It emerged around the 6th–5th centuries BCE as a counterpoint to the ritual actions emphasized in Vedic literature. Various forms of asceticism, such as tapas, meditation, and techniques for altering or withdrawing consciousness, offered a new vision – spiritual knowledge and liberation.

As the divine yogi, Shiva serves as the model and supreme ascetic among the gods. He sits in splendid isolation on a solitary Himalayan peak, absorbed in deep meditation. Detached from worldly concerns, Shiva embodies inner peace, transcendence, and detachment. He represents pure awareness, inner mastery, and perfect stillness – qualities that mirror the yogic state of *samadhi*, in which the mind dissolves into stillness.

Even various Shaiva elements hold yogic significance. Shiva's third eye *(See pp78–79)* symbolizes inner vision and spiritual awakening – core goals of yogic practice. His abode, Mount Kailasha, is the metaphorical "mountain of meditation", representing the ascent of consciousness. Even the Shiva lingam is a symbol of upward-flowing energy and the silent, still mind of *samadhi*, the ultimate yogic state.

The power of asceticism

Shiva has been meditating since before time. Through the endurance of self-imposed austerities, he accumulates an immense reservoir of psychic energy – so concentrated it blazes with incandescence. This energy grows so potent that it periodically threatens the very fabric of existence. One such moment arises after Sati's death *(See pp148–49)* when Shiva retreats into an even deeper state of meditation. His power intensifies to a level that terrifies the gods. To restore balance, they turn to Parvati to draw Shiva back into the world.

It is not through combat or confrontation that Shiva acts, but through sheer meditative force and the blazing current of his inner stillness. When Kama, the god of love, dares to disturb his meditation, Shiva incinerates him with a single glance – a beam of fire from his third eye. Over and over, it is this immense meditative power, neither weapon nor warfare, that becomes the vehicle of Shiva's divine action.

THE SEVEN WISE MEN

The Saptarishis, Brahma's seven mind-born sons, are cosmic custodians who guide humanity through time. Shiva entrusts these semi-immortal beings, living through billions of years, with tasks of spiritual guidance and preserving sacred knowledge.

They may have been born of Brahma, one of the Trinity, a product of his mind, but their connection to Shiva is transcendental. For it is Shiva, according to many traditions, who as Adiyogi or the first yogi, imparts knowledge onto them. The transmission is not just philosophical, but energetic, transformative, and foundational to the spiritual evolution of humanity.

These semi-immortal beings, known as the Saptarishis, or the seven sages, are cosmic custodians entrusted with the task of maintaining balance on Earth, to work in harmony with Shiva and uphold dharma, while guiding humanity through vast cycles of time.

As Mahadev, Shiva allocatess them the tasks of spiritual guidance and preservation of sacred knowledge. It is because of this deep connection to Shiva, and their mastery over time and space, that they are considered higher in rank than many Devas, or gods.

Cosmic guidance

Shiva's cosmic energy guides their spiritual evolution and he bestows upon them knowledge of yoga and the cosmos. Their learning forms the basis of various yogic and Tantric traditions, making Shiva's wisdom the very foundation of Indian spirituality. It is this narrative that highlights Shiva's role in guiding humanity toward self-realization – an instance of cosmic wisdom meeting timeless guardianship.

Beacons of light

The list of Saptarishis varies, depending on the religious text, whether it is *Shatapatha Brahmana*, the *Mahabharata*, *Vayu Purana*, or the *Vishnu Purana*. According to the *Brihadaranyaka Upanishad*, a religious scripture, the Saptarishis are Agastya, Atri, Bharadwaja, Gautama, Jamadagni, Kashyapa, and Vashishtha. In fact, Vedic astronomy identifies the seven stars of Ursa Major, or the Big Dipper, as the Saptarishis.

These sages are archetypes of divine wisdom, each embodying a unique facet of cosmic intelligence. In some accounts, they act as spiritual regulators during times of upheaval. Their yogic power and penance grants them near immortality, allowing them to transcend the cycle of birth and death and serve as beacons of light through the ages.

Each sage channels a ray of Shiva's infinite consciousness through silence, fire, compassion, or cosmic visions and embodies a distinct spiritual archetype, reflecting not only their individual *tapas*, or austerity and wisdom, but also facets of Shiva's own cosmic nature. They carry their own unique aspect of Shiva's teachings to different geographical areas, spreading spiritual wisdom.

Among the Saptarishis, Vashishta is known for his calm wisdom and mastery over the *Brahmavidya*, or knowledge of the absolute. His journey from ego to enlightenment unfolds through his rivalry with Vishwamitra who is incited over the former's divine cow Kamadhenu. The rivalry escalated to a point when they cursed each other and became birds. Eventually they realized the futility of this and reconciled.

Vishwamitra is unique for having earned the title of Brahmarishi, or one who has attained the highest level of spiritual knowledge and awakening. The only one among the Saptarishis

THE SEVEN WISE MEN | 211

◁ **In this vivid miniature painting,** the first avatar of Vishnu, Matsya, the divine golden fish, guides a boat carrying Manu and the Saptarishi through the cosmic deluge. Surrounded by storm clouds and mythical sea creatures, the scene reflects the preservation of life, wisdom, and order amidst chaos.

to rise to the rank through his own merit and intense meditation, Vishwamitra is credited with composing the *Gayatri Mantra*, an empowering hymn of abiding influence.

Atri, the father of Dattatreya, a composite form of Brahma, Vishnu, and Shiva, symbolizing the union of the Trinity, is known for his serene wisdom and deep meditative insight, representing the stillness of consciousness.

Bharadvaja is a sage of immense intellect and scientific temperament. He was a master of Ayurveda, military science, and Vedic hymns. His lineage is associated with the sixth Mandala, or collection of hymns of the *Rig Veda*, and he embodies disciplined inquiry and service.

Gautama is revered for his dharmic clarity and authorship of the Sanskrit text *Gautama Dharmasutra*. He is a symbol of social order and ethical living. Gautama also plays his part in the *Ramayana*. He was married to the beautiful Ahalya. Indra, the lord of the Devas, disguised himself as Gautama and tried to seduce Ahalya. Gautama cursed Ahalya and Indra for their transgressions, turning his wife into stone. It took Rama's touch years later to liberate and absolve her of her sins.

The fiery sage Jamadagni's life is a reflection of the tension between worldly duty and spiritual detachment. The father of Parashurama, an avatara of Vishnu, is often associated with righteous anger and the power of renunciation.

Kashyapa embodies the creative force of the cosmos. His expansive vision and balance between opposing forces mirror Shiva's role as both creator and destroyer. He is considered a progenitor of many beings, including Devas, Asuras, and humans.

THE POWER OF AUSTERITY

Tapas is the inner fire of spiritual transformation and discipline. Shiva, as the ascetic and yogi, is the embodiment and inspirer of this transformative fire that signifies austerity, inner purification and burning away of ego and ignorance.

A path to *gyana kanda*, that is spiritual knowledge or gnosis, could be attained through asceticism, or world renunciation and discipline. This called for *tapas*, a word that comes from the Sanskrit root *tap*, meaning "to heat" or "to burn", symbolizing the inner fire of transformation. In itself, *tapas* refers to intense austerity, inner purification, and the burning away of ignorance. It is not suffering — it is transformation.

Shiva, as the supreme ascetic and yogi, is both the embodiment and the inspirer of this transformative fire. The archetype of *tapas*, he is referred to as Adi Tapasvi, or the first *tapasvi*. Shiva's *tapas* is the fire that purifies, refines, and destroys ignorance. He uses it as a tool to dissolve the ego and karmic residue making way for spiritual rebirth. It's the path from form to formlessness.

Radical dissent

During the Vedic period, rituals held a predominant position within the practice of Hinduism. But, by around the 5th century BCE, it found a rival in asceticism as a form of gaining knowledge. Rituals were no longer the sole path to escape the endless cycle of birth and rebirth, and gain salvation. Instead, asceticism became an alternate source of spiritual knowledge and liberation.

There were a variety of approaches, which included *tapas*, meditation, techniques of altering consciousness or withdrawing it to transcend worldly concerns — all offered a different outlook of the human condition.

However, religious texts held asceticism as antithetical in its radical dissent from Brahmanical orthodoxy. The ashrama system, which divided society into the four stages of life, or ashrams, is believed to have been instituted as a mechanism against the onslaught of renunciation. This division into the student, householder, hermit, and renouncer, or the *sannyasa* was formalized by the time the texts of the Dharmasutras were written. It was made clear that men could take to renunciation after they completed the other stages of life.

Spiritual rebirth

In the ancient texts of the *Rig Veda*, Upanishads and *Atharva Veda*, *tapas* is linked to the spiritual rebirth of sages and gods. The hot climate in India could have been the basis for turning heat into a symbol of struggle.

It is the heat that generates special powers and spiritual development. Hindus believe that the sadhu, or ascetic, is holy because of the accumulated unspent heat generated by his ascetic practices. Hence the sage can burn sins and reduce old karma to ashes, according to German-American cultural anthropologist Wolf-Dieter Storl.

Tapas was not reserved exclusively for the ascetic. Sages, gods, and demons performed *tapas* to gain Shiva's blessings. Asuras like Ravana, Bhasmasura, Tarakasura, Mahishasura, and Andhakasura all gained powers through gruelling *tapas*, but faced calamitous consequences due to its misuse. Philosophically, *tapas* is a process of spiritual incubation, nurturing higher awareness. It is not just physical austerity, but a refinement of consciousness. It's the bridge between *dhyana*, or meditation, and *sakshatkara*, or realization of god. It is a sacrifice, a discipline of consciousness, guiding the practitioner from sensory distraction to lucid awareness. It's not just about renunciation, but refining perception, aligning the mind with *satya*, or truth, and *dharma*, or cosmic order.

Practitioner and inspiration

Shiva is often depicted in deep meditative stillness and intense spiritual austerity on Mount Kailasha, embodying the essence of *nirvikalpa*

THE POWER OF AUSTERITY | 213

samadhi, a state beyond thought and duality. He is both a practitioner and an inspiration for seekers of knowledge. In texts like the *Shiva Purana*, *tapas* is portrayed as a means of burning away karma, attaining spiritual insight, and invoking divine grace. Shiva's own *tapas* is said to be so potent that it sustains cosmic balance and inspires sages across the ages. The *Shiva Purana* emphasizes *tapas* as a path to divine realization. In Shaiva metaphysics, it aligns with *spanda*, or the subtle vibration of consciousness, and leads to *anugraha*, or divine grace.

Parvati, the tapasvin

After Sati's self-immolation, Shiva became averse to marital bonds and so Parvati faced the onerous task of gaining his attention for marriage. She took up the challenge by doing what she knew best and is hence considered a great *tapasvini*.

She meditated with unwavering concentration for 3,000 years, her mind firmly fixed on Shiva. She clothed herself in deer skin, surrounded by fire in the scorching heat of summer, stood on one leg, neck deep in water during the rainy season and the harsh winter and lived on leaves or sometimes air. Detached from nature, Parvati as a *tapasvin* felt no pain, heard no sound, saw no image, tasted no flavour and smelt no odour. She did not eat even a leaf, earning the name Aparna.

Tapas outside of mythology takes on a multitude of forms. In the contemporary world, people choose to experience silence for weeks in retreats or even at home as a form of *tapas*. Women fast for the welfare of their families, sacrificing food, water and performing rituals in the wee hours. Psychologically the individual feels empowered by following Shiva's *tapas* methods even if modified to suit one's individual needs. Shiva is exceptional for he did not follow the path laid out in the texts of the *Brahamanas*, which stipulate the correct time for renunciation. Instead, throughout his life Shiva managed both the life of an ascetic and that of a *grihastha*, the married householder, and therein lies his uniqueness.

◁ **An Indian painting** depicting Shiva in his ascetic form, seated cross-legged in Padmasana on a blooming pink lotus. At his side are his devoted companions – Nandi, the white bull, and Ganesha, his elephant-headed son – symbolizing devotion, strength, and cosmic balance.

In West Bengal and Bangladesh, the spring month of Chaitra comes alive with the pre-harvest Gajan festival, celebrated to invoke fertility in the soil. Devotees, known as sannyasis or bhaktas, use their bodies to invoke the godhead, performing arduous rites that culminate in Charak, the hook-swinging ritual. In this image, devotees are dressed as Shiva, taking part in the festival celebrations. As Shiva is ritually married to Goddess Harakali, the sannyasis form the bridegroom's party, moving through villages with devotion and ceremony. Children add a lighthearted, human pulse, singing:
"We two brothers
Sing songs about Shiva
Grandmother has gone to Gaya and Kashi
So we play the *damaru*."

BHIKSHATANAMURTI

SEEKING ALMS WITH GRACE

He is the radiant, wandering ascetic, who begs for alms. Though naked and austere, he is mesmerizing, embodying the paradox of renunciation and seduction. This rare and powerful form of Shiva, known as Bhikshatanamurti, emerges to atone for *Brahmahatya*, the killing of a Brahmin. This takes place, according to the *Shiva Purana*, when Shiva, in his fierce form as Bhairava, severs Brahma's fifth head to curb his arrogance and commits a grave sin. To atone, he roams the world as Bhikshatana, carrying Brahma's skull as his begging bowl – a divine mendicant seeking purification through humility.

In Hinduism, even the act of begging for *bhiksha* or alms carries profound spiritual meaning. Far from being a social or economic necessity, it is a symbol of renunciation, humility, and detachment. Texts like the *Manusmriti* instruct *brahmacharins* or students to seek food through begging – not just to sustain themselves, but to dissolve ego or *ahankara* and cultivate discipline. It is also an important practice during a young boy's initiation ceremony, that is *upanayan* preparing him with an essential characteristic – humility. For ascetics and monks, begging is not a loss of dignity but a practice of *aparigraha* – non-possession and surrender to divine will. It reflects a life freed from material ties, sustained by faith and interdependence. Once again, Shiva embodies this ideal – as Bhikshatanamurti, the divine beggar who turns renunciation into a cosmic lesson.

The wandering ascetic

In the *Linga Purana*, Shiva assumed this form to challenge false piety. In the Deodar forest, Shiva appeared as Bhikshatana, to confront the arrogance of self-righteous sages. Naked, radiant, and unsettlingly beautiful, he shocked their rigid sensibilities. Though an ascetic, he remained adorned – with serpents coiled at his hips and divine ornaments – exuding a raw, inscrutable seduction. He sought alms from the sages' wives, who responded not with disdain, but overwhelming desire, some even collapsing in longing. Despite his ritual impurity and untouchable status, the women were drawn to him in an instant, revealing the power of divine presence over social boundaries. Just as he appeared as a *Kirata* or outcast hunter in the *Mahabharata*, here too he challenged caste and convention, disrupting orthodoxy with divine spontaneity.

The itinerant god in sacred art

This form appears often in sculpture, with some of the earliest depictions dating to the 7th century, including a terracotta panel from Ahichatra and a carved door jamb in Mathura. He is shown as youthful, four-armed, and bearing a bell, often tied to his foot or hand – a marker once required of outcastes to warn others of their approach.

In narrative art, Shiva is often shown ithyphallic, symbolizing spiritual power and restraint. Sometimes, however, his phallus is depicted small and pendent, suggesting a state beyond both desire and yogic control – a liminal, neutral presence.

He carries the *Khatvanga*, a staff topped with a skull, symbolizing both death and the cosmic axis. In one hand is a skull begging bowl, fused to his palm. At his side walks a dog, symbol of the outcaste – marking him clearly outside orthodox Vedic norms.

In this unsettling form, Shiva unmoved by the emotions he stirs, remains aloof – a god beyond dualities, breaking illusions and exposing the emptiness of pride and dogma.

▷ **An early 13th-century stone sculpture from Tamil Nadu depicts Shiva in ascetic form**, nude except for a yogic sash across his torso and a serpent belt encircling his waist. He has four arms, holding a drum, trident, noose, and a skull begging bowl, said to represent Brahma's severed head. Behind him stands an aggressive dog, the mount of Shiva as Bhairava.

◁ **Indian painter Sundaram Rajam's depiction of the concept of oneness with the divine.** In the foreground, a yogi is shown in deep meditation, seated on a tiger skin. Next to him, the translucent silhouette of Shiva appears, poised to extend his hand to hold the yogi's, symbolizing the yogi's transcendence as he reaches a higher state of consciousness.

NIRVANA SHATAKAM

TO ACHIEVE ONENESS WITH THE DIVINE

Sin or merit can never touch me
Joy and sorrow cannot contaminate me
I know no mantra, I have no sacred pilgrimage to make
I know no scripture nor have I anything to gain through rituals
I am neither the experiencer, nor the experienced, nor the experiencing
I am Shiva, Shiva alone am I.

I have neither likes nor dislikes
Nor have I covetousness nor greed
Nor have I any arrogant vanity nor any competition with anyone
I have not even a need for the four main purposes of life
I am Shiva, Shiva alone am I.

Nirvana Shatakam, from *The Nectar of Chanting* by SYDA Foundation

The 8th-century philosopher Adi Shankaracharya composed the six-verse *Nirvana Shatakam*, also known as the *Atma Shatakam*. It is a profound expression of Advaita Vedanta philosophy, which emphasizes the non-dual nature of reality and the unity of Atman, or the individual self, with Brahman, or the ultimate reality. The hymn asserts that there is no fundamental distinction between the individual soul and the universal self. Serving as a guide to self-realization, the hymn encourages self-reflection and contemplation to transcend the illusory duality of the world and realize one's true, divine nature.

Structure
Each verse begins with the systematic negation of the material and psychological self, such as the body, mind, intellect, senses, and even elements such as earth, fire, and air. In this way, the hymn asserts that the true self transcends all these limitations, revealing that one's essence is beyond the material and psychological realms.

The verses end with the affirmation "*Shivoham, Shivoham*", meaning "I am Shiva, Shiva alone am I". This declaration affirms the individual's identity with the divine consciousness, that is Shiva, representing the ultimate reality. By realizing this unity with the divine, the individual transcends the cycle of birth and death, attaining liberation, a state of eternal bliss and freedom.

The path to oneness
The *Nirvana Shatakam* is often chanted or recited as a form of meditation to aid in the realization of its message. Shiva's inherent power is *chaitanya atma*, or the power of pure consciousness. Therefore, the key to understanding Shiva is through his relationship with consciousness. The quest for the self can only be realized through meditative practices, where one reaches a state of divine oneness and awareness. This is not a worship of Shiva in the traditional sense, but rather a realization that one's true self is not separate from the ultimate reality. By chanting the *Nirvana Shatakam*, the practitioner meditates on the idea that their *aham*, or own essence, is the same as the divine. As a result, the seeker becomes divine in order to worship Shiva, achieving a higher state of awareness and communion with the divine through self-effort.

THE FLOWING LOCKS OF SHIVA

Shiva's *jata* are more than hair – they are symbols of wild ascetic power and cosmic mystery. Twisted into matted coils, this untamed force isn't unleashed, but deliberately bound – reflecting discipline, control, and the mastery of chaos.

Jata, Shiva's matted hair, carries deep metaphysical meaning – serving as a conduit between the earthly and the divine. These tangled braids, wound into rope-like coils or crowned as a *jatamukuta*, reflect Shiva's identity as the supreme yogi – wild, unbound, and untouched by worldly vanity. They represent the fusion of matter and spirit, anchoring Shiva's role as a bridge between creation and dissolution.

Jata as a cosmic symbol

Epithets such as *Jatadhara* – the bearer of matted hair – and *Vyomakesha*, whose hair is like the sky, point to the vastness and elemental force contained within Shiva's hair. In the *Shatarudriya*, a hymn from the *Yajur Veda*, dedicated to Shiva in his form as Rudra, he is called *Kapardin*, likening the spiral of his locks to a cowrie shell, or *kaparda*.

Shiva's unkempt hair resists the order and polish of societal grooming. It is a bold statement of renunciation, a rejection of ego and materialism, and a mark of detachment from worldly constraints.

In yogic symbolism, the *jata* mirrors the *nadis* – subtle channels through which *prana* or life force flows. Just as Kundalini energy rises through the central *Sushumna nadi*, Shiva's locks are said to channel and contain immense spiritual force.

◁ **A *sadhu* or holy man** takes a sacred dip at Gangasagar, where the Ganga meets the sea, during the Makar Sankranti pilgrimage. Thousands of devotees gather for this holy ritual – believed to cleanse sins – at one of Hinduism's most revered confluences.

His *jatas* even catch and hold the powerful river Ganga *(See pp184–85)*, softening her descent to Earth and preventing devastation – an act that symbolizes Shiva as cosmic regulator, balancing destructive power with grace.

Ancient texts such as the *Rig Veda's Keshin Hymn* speak of long-haired sages, the *keshins*, as mystical beings closely associated with Rudra, an early form of Shiva. These ascetic wanderers were said to possess supernatural insight, commune with celestial beings, and exist in altered states of consciousness. Their unshorn hair marked a break from societal norms and a deeper connection to the divine – possibly even fulfilling a shamanic role in early Vedic culture.

In art and culture

In art, Shiva's hair is richly symbolic. In depictions of Nataraja, his locks stream outward like celestial waves, often adorned with the crescent Moon, serpents, ashes, and a tiny figure of Ganga. This wild, yet sacred, image signifies his dominion over time, death, and primal forces.

Hair in many cultures, especially in India, functions as a stand-in for the self, a marker of identity, power, and social status. Its cutting or styling can reflect submission, mourning, rebellion, or spiritual evolution. Among ascetics, uncut hair symbolizes renunciation, while in rituals, shaving one's head – such as after a parent's death – signals transformation.

Shiva's dark, coiled locks are often likened to rain clouds, glowing with the lustre of lightning – a powerful image of both destruction and fertility.

DAKSHINAMURTI

A GURU IS BORN

He is the embodiment of wisdom, yoga, music and spiritual knowledge, and though his name is associated with death – it is not death in the conventional sense, but as a symbol of transformation, the dispelling of ignorance, and the awakening of inner truth.

That is Dakshinamurti, the profound and serene form of Shiva, revered as the ultimate teacher, or Adi Guru. The name translates to mean "the one who faces south", south being *dakshina* in Sanskrit. This is particularly relevant as within Hindu traditions, the southern direction is associated with death and transformation, signifying the dispelling of ignorance and the awakening of inner truth. So, Dakshinamurti faces Yama, or the god of death, and he is called thus because he faced the south when he taught yoga and jnana, or wisdom to rishis, or sages.

Those on the path of learning and self-realization revere the Dakshinamurti form because it is here that Shiva teaches through silence even as the sages sit in rapt attention. He is often depicted seated under a banyan tree, surrounded by sages, with one leg resting on a demon, a symbol of *apasmara*, or ignorance. His mudras, or hand gestures, especially the Chinmudra – also known as Gyan Mudra – have deep historical and spiritual roots in the yogic tradition, symbolizing the union of individual consciousness with universal consciousness.

Blissful dancing

The story goes that once Shiva went into an ecstatic dance in the Himalayas. When his ecstasy became overwhelming and could not match his movement, he would become still. When it allowed him some movement, he danced wildly once again. The gods watching were unable to fathom what was transpiring and left, but Shiva, engrossed in his dance, was oblivious to their presence. But, seven stayed back and when they approached Shiva in Kailasha, they found him seated, leg bent and kept in position by a yogapatta, or strap. One of his hands, which was resting on his right thigh, was holding an *akshamala*. The gods insisted on learning this dance form from him, but Shiva explained that it called for a tremendous amount of preparation. The gods' preparation to master the dance went on for years. One Full Moon day, after 84 years of sadhana, or training, he looked at this group of seven when the sun was moving from the North to the South, during an astronomical period known as Dakshinayana. Shiva watched them for 28 days and by the next Full Moon, decided to become their guru. He turned south to begin the transmission of yogic science and came to be known as Dakshinamurti. In doing so, the first guru was born and that day is celebrated as Guru Purnima, a festival that honours teachers.

Through the ages

Dakshinamurti's depictions in art vary across regions and periods, yet are a consistent reflection of Shiva's role as the divine teacher. Though popular in south India, the beginning was probably in the Gupta period, primarily in Magadh, or modern-day Bihar. This form is typically carved into the southern niche of south Indian Shiva temples. In Kerala's temple murals, Dakshinamurti appears in vibrant colours and intricate detail.

In one of the panels from Ahichatra, a kingdom mentioned in the *Mahabharata*, a four-armed Dakshinamurti is seated with an *akshamala*, or a rosary, in his upper right hand and a vase with vegetation in his upper left hand. The other hands hold nothing. To the left is a female figure, probably Parvati, with folded hands, according to Indian Indologist NP Joshi.

Many statues depicting Shiva's descent into teaching are found in the temples of Tiruvorriyur and Kanchipuram in South India. The one in Kanchipuram has him seated under a banyan tree, on a raised seat, with two deer below and sages gathered around to listen to him preach of dharma or yoga. According to archaeologists TA Gopinatha Rao and RD Banerji, these depictions of Shiva are reminiscent of Buddha's attainment of enlightenment and his first sermon.

Art historians identify several iconographic forms such as the Vyakhyana Dakshinamurti, which is the most common, where Shiva is shown teaching with hand gestures. Then there is the Jnana Dakshinamurti, which emphasizes wisdom, in which he is seen holding a lotus. In the Yoga Dakshinamurti, Shiva is shown in deep meditation, with a yoga *patta*, or strap tied around the knees. In the Vinadhara Dakshinamurti, he is holding a veena, highlighting his mastery of music.

◁ **At the Rathinagiri Hill Temple in Vellore,** Tamil Nadu, seated in serene majesty, Shiva appears as Dakshinamurthi – the supreme guru who dispels ignorance and illuminates the path of wisdom.

A HOME FOR SHIVA

The temples dedicated to Shiva reflect both the austerity of the solitary yogi and the grandeur befitting the cosmic lord and householder.

A HOME FOR SHIVA

Shiva is present across a spectrum of sacred spaces: in ancient caves and mountaintop shrines, in modest rock shelters, in monumental temples, and in the heart of his devotees. This ubiquity reflects the Shaiva understanding that the divine transcends any single form, appearing wherever there is reverence — whether in remote natural settings, humble dwellings, or grand architectural edifices.

Early rock-cut sanctuaries

Caves are natural sanctuaries that, through their very structure, evoke the inner cave of consciousness where Shiva resides as the silent yogi. They mirror the meditative stillness of Shiva as Adiyogi, the primordial yogi. If, fortuitously, a lingam-like stone or rock formation is found within a cave, Shaivites often adopt it as a Shiva domicile, seeing it as a sacred manifestation of

▽ **Majestic and sacred,** the Kailasha Temple at Ellora in Maharashtra, is a monumental tribute and timeless symbol of devotion to Shiva — carved from a single rock to resemble his Himalayan abode, Mount Kailasha.

the divine. One such popular site is the Amarnath Cave Temple *(See pp 296–97)* in Jammu & Kashmir, where the lingam is an ice formation that waxes and wanes with the lunar cycle. Other cave shrines, however, can be far more modest in scale. One of the most well-known is the Tapkeshwar shrine in Dehradun, Uttarakhand, where water naturally drips onto the lingam throughout the year – hence its name, derived from *tap*, meaning "dripping".

Alongside natural rock-cut sanctuaries, many of the earliest temples dedicated to Shiva were caves intricately carved and sculpted into sacred spaces. These spaces were not mere shelters, but sculpted metaphysical realms. The most magnificent is the 6th-century Elephanta Caves in Maharashtra, a vast temple complex with multiple representations of Shiva – Sadashiva, Gangadhara, and Ardhanarishvara *(See pp166–69)*. The entire cave functions as a symbolic mandala of transformation.

Not far away, the Jogeshwari Caves in Maharashtra are among the earliest Hindu cave temples in India. They enshrine a lingam at the far end and feature Shaiva sculptural panels depicting episodes such as Shiva and Parvati's wedding *(See pp164–65)*, them playing the game of dice *(See pp160–63)*, the slaying of Andhakasura, Shiva and Ravana, and forms of Shiva as Nataraja, and Lakulisha. Further south in Karnataka, the Badami Caves, also from the 6th century, are renowned for their striking carving of Shiva as Nataraja. The complex also houses sculptures of Harihara *(See pp46–49)*, Ardhanarishvara, Skanda *(See pp182–83)*, and Ganesha *(See pp176–77)*.

Later than Elephanta, the 8th-century Kailasha Temple at Ellora stands as a monolithic marvel. Carved top-down from a single rock, it represents Mount Kailasha, Shiva's mythic abode, thereby blending architecture with cosmic symbolism.

Sacred geometry

From these early cave sanctuaries, Shaiva architecture developed into structural temples, which became more and more elaborate over time. Sacred geometry guided by principles such as mandala-based designs, the energetic significance of spatial placements, and layouts prescribed by Vastu Shastra, the ancient Indian system of architecture and design, shaped the architecture of Shiva temples. The temple plan reflects cosmic order, with energy centres aligned to the cardinal directions.

Like other Hindu temples, a Shiva temple has a *garbhagriha*, or sanctum sanctorum, representing the womb of the universe. This is where the Shiva lingam resides. The sanctum is usually small, dark, and enclosed, evoking a sense of introspection and awe. Leading up to it is the *mandapa*, a pillared assembly hall where devotees gather to meditate and perform rituals. The journey from the outer *mandapa* to the inner sanctum mirrors the path from external distraction to inner truth.

The exterior of Shiva temples is often richly carved with scenes from Shiva's life and crowned with a soaring tower, the *shikhara* (in North India) or *vimana* (in South India), built directly above the *garbhagriha*. In the Nagara style of North India, the *shikhara* is curvilinear, while in the Dravidian style of South India, the *vimana* is pyramidal. It symbolizes Mount Meru, the cosmic mountain linking Earth and the celestial realm. Many South Indian temples, especially those in the Dravidian tradition, also feature monumental

▽ **Nestled on the banks of the Tons River in Dehradun,** the Tapkeshwar Mahadev Temple is a sacred sanctuary dedicated to Shiva, where a natural cave enshrines an ancient Shiva lingam, echoing centuries of devotion.

△ **Rising gracefully beside the Agastya Lake,** the Bhoothnath Temple in Badami, Karnataka stands as a timeless tribute to Lord Shiva, its stone-carved sanctum echoing with the spiritual legacy of the Chalukya dynasty.

gateway towers known as *gopurams*. These serve as grand thresholds, marking the transition from the mundane to the sacred.

Prominent temples

One of the most outstanding Shiva temples is the Kashi Vishwanath Temple in Varanasi, Uttar Pradesh, a celebrated Jyotirlinga. Here, Shiva is worshipped as Vishwanath and Vishweshwara, the lord of the universe, the most powerful manifestations of the deity.

In southern India's Tamil Nadu, the Brihadeeswara Temple stands as a masterpiece of Chola architecture, one of South India's greatest dynasties. More than just a temple, it is a statement of grandeur, precision, and spiritual depth, housing one of the largest Shiva lingams in India. What makes it intriguing is that it is built entirely of granite, despite the absence of any such stone near the temple site.

Also in Tamil Nadu is the Chidambaram Temple, remarkable for enshrining Shiva not as a lingam but as Nataraja, the cosmic dancer. It was conceived not merely as a shrine but as a cosmic stage where Shiva performs the Ananda Tandava, the dance of bliss. Built by the Cholas, the temple features exquisite carvings of the 108 dance poses from the *Natya Shastra*, the ancient Sanskrit treatise on the arts, making it a sacred site for Bharatanatyam dancers.

Further north, in Madhya Pradesh, the Kandariya Mahadeva Temple at Khajuraho is considered the crown jewel of the region's celebrated temple group – the largest cluster of medieval Hindu and Jain temples in the country. Rising to 31 metres (102 feet), with a soaring *shikhara* surrounded by 84 miniature spires, it dazzles with more than 900 exquisitely carved figures of celestial beings, dancers, musicians, and mythological scenes. Its architectural plan includes a series of pillared halls – *ardhamandapa*, or entrance porch; *mandapa*, or assembly hall; and *mahamandapa*, or main hall – leading to the sanctum. Symbolically, the temple's layout mirrors the human body: the sanctum as the head, the *mandapa* as the chest, and the entrance as the feet.

From humble patrons to powerful royalty, Shaiva temples embody the devotion of a wide spectrum of worshippers, all contributing to the creation of Shiva's sacred abodes.

PANCHA BHUTA TEMPLES

FIVE TEMPLES, ONE DIVINE ESSENCE

They are a sacred constellation of five ancient Shiva temples, each an embodiment of one of nature's five elemental forces – Earth, Water, Fire, Air, and Ether or Space – and centred around a Shiva lingam believed to be infused with the living essence of that element. These Panchabhuta Temples, or the Pancha Bhuta Sthalams, based in southern India, are not just architectural marvels, but profound expressions of Shaivite philosophy, where Shiva is seen as both the source and the harmonizer of nature's primal energies. Together, they reflect a deep philosophical vision – the unity and balance of the natural world with the divine.

For spiritual seekers, visiting all five temples is more than a pilgrimage – it's a journey through the very building blocks of existence, a meditative circuit that connects the soul to the cosmos through the presence of Shiva in each elemental form.

Grounds of devotion

Located in Tamil Nadu's temple town, Kanchipuram, the Ekambareswarar Temple represents Prithvi or Earth and is home to the sacred Prithvi Lingam. In the elemental tradition of the Panchabhuta temples, Earth symbolizes stability, grounding, and the enduring strength of the physical world.

The Jambukeshwarar Temple in Thiruvanaikaval, Tamil Nadu, near the sacred river Kaveri, represents the element of Water in the sacred Panchabhuta tradition. Water symbolizes purity, flow, and the ever-changing, yet life-giving essence of existence. To this day, the sanctum of the temple houses the Appu Lingam, which remains perpetually surrounded by water, even during the driest season. This ever-present spring is a powerful symbol of the eternal stream of consciousness, reminding devotees of the soul's journey toward clarity and truth.

The sacred seat of the Agni Lingam is at the Arunachaleswarar Temple in Thiruvannamalai, Tamil Nadu, and represents the element of Fire, signifying transformation, illumination, and the inner light of consciousness. Fire has been revered since the dawn of civilization. In the *Rig Veda*, Agni is personified as a sacred force – protector, messenger, and purifier. Even today, fire remains central to daily rituals and life transitions in millions of many homes that practice the Hindu faith. It is considered a silent witness or *sakshi*, to truth, whether in sacred ceremonies or the lighting of a simple household lamp.

The Srikalahasteeswara Temple in Andhra Pradesh's Srikalahasti, is home to the Vayu Lingam and represents Vayu or Air – the subtle force of movement, breath, and life itself. Revered as Dakshina Kailasam or the southern counterpart to Mount Kailasha, this temple stands as a masterpiece of Dravidian design, steeped in myth and spiritual symbolism. No one can touch the Vayu Lingam – not even the temple priests – emphasizing the sacredness of what cannot be seen but is always felt – the breath of life, the spirit that moves all things.

The element of space, consciousness, and vastness, Akasha or Ether, finds representation at the Thillai Nataraja Temple in Chidambaram, Tamil Nadu, which is home to the Akasha Lingam. Unlike the other elements, Ether is intangible, formless, and all-encompassing – just like pure awareness. The Akasha Lingam invites the seeker to look inward – to realize that the divine is not only outside, but also within, in the boundless expanse of consciousness itself.

▷ *(clockwise from top)* **The Sri Ekambaranathar Temple,** Kanchipuram, Tamil Nadu. An interior view of the temple's hallway leading to a shrine, showcases the grandeur of Dravidian architecture; **A sacred Shiva temple in Tiruchirapalli,** Tamil Nadu, Jambukeshwara is known for its association with the element of water and rich Dravidian architecture; **A majestic Dravidian-style temple** dedicated to Shiva as Nataraja, reflected in the sacred water tank, the Nataraja Temple in Chidambaram, Tamil Nadu, is a renowned pilgrimage site in South India; **The Srikalahasteeswara Temple in** Andhra Pradesh is a revered Shiva temple in the Chittoor district, known for its spiritual significance and intricate Dravidian architecture; **Devotees gather as the grand chariot procession** honours Shiva during the sacred Karthigai Deepam festival at the historic Chola-era Arunachaleshwara Temple in Thiruvannamalai, Tamil Nadu.

STEEPED IN MYTH

EKAMBARESWARAR TEMPLE
Beneath a sacred mango tree, Parvati shaped a lingam from sand in loving devotion. Touched by her penance, Shiva appeared as Ekambareswarar, the "Lord of the Mango Tree". That very tree still stands, over 3,000 years old, bearing four types of mangoes from one root. A living miracle, it embodies Earth's unity, fertility, and power to sustain life.

JAMBUKESWARAR TEMPLE
As Akilandeshwari, Parvati once teased Shiva during his deep meditation. Sent to Earth to atone, she performed penance beneath a sacred Jambu or Java plum tree, crafting a lingam from the flowing waters of the Kaveri River. Touched by her devotion, Shiva appeared, not in anger, but as a teacher – offering her spiritual wisdom and reaffirming that humility opens the path to grace.

ARUNACHALESHWARA TEMPLE
In a cosmic dispute over supremacy, Vishnu and Brahma sought the beginning and end of a blazing pillar of fire – Shiva's manifestation in the Lingodbhava form. Neither succeeded. The fire stretched beyond comprehension, revealing Shiva as infinite, formless, and beyond ego. In this blaze, truth burned bright – the divine cannot be measured, only surrendered to.

In Hinduism, divinity is not confined to temples or sculpted idols – it can appear anywhere, even in the simplest forms. In this image, a humble Shiva lingam, little more than a stone, has been consecrated amidst the branches of a tree. Devotion is evident in the markings on its surface, the temple bell hung nearby, and the offerings of flowers laid with care, reminding believers that sacredness is more about reverence than form.

◁ **A mural from the Lakshmi Narayana Temple in Orchha,** Madhya Pradesh, depicting Panchamukha Shiva, the five-faced form of the deity. Each face symbolizes a cosmic force, representing his cosmic dimensions and all-encompassing nature.

PANCHAMUKHA

A COMPLETE VISION OF SHIVA

Wrathful, face bulging with the curves of palpable frenzy, the long, thick and untamed moustache – Aghora is the most feared face of Shiva. It is also the most misunderstood. And it's just one of his five faces.

The five faces of Shiva, also known as Panchamukha Shiva or Panchanana, represent his cosmic functions, which correspond to the five elements: earth, water, fire, air and space. This representation of Shiva as the universe signifies his completeness. These faces are Sadyojata, Vamadeva, Aghora, Tatpurusha, and Ishana, each associated with specific elements, directions, functions, shakti, or a specific power and a spiritual meaning.

Together, they form a complete vision of Shiva as the eternal source, sustainer, transformer, concealer, and revealer of all existence. It's a beautiful metaphor for the cycles of life and consciousness. The *Vishnudharmottara Purana*, an encyclopedic Hindu text, speaks of the five faces of Shiva.

The pure Shiva
Ishana is the face of Shiva that faces *akasha*, or the sky. Ishana embodies the power and *tattva*, or essence of Srishti Shakti, or creation. He transcends direction, form, and function. Ishana is the pure Shiva who is untouched and represents liberation, *moksha*, or salvation, and the bliss of cosmic union. When Ishana flows through a person, one no longer identifies with the body or the mind and instead feels an overwhelming love for all beings. At that moment, life and death are seen as passing clouds.

Lifting the veil
Tatpurusha faces east, where the sun rises and awareness awakens. He symbolizes the power of concealment or tirodhana shakti. Tatpurusha is the veil, but serves as a reminder that the veil can be lifted. He is linked to air and reminds us that our true nature is hidden beneath layers of identity and illusion. This face encourages introspection, self-awareness, and an inward journey. Tatpurusha is the inner self and the witness to consciousness who sees all but says little. Tatpurusha governs breath and represents the secret watcher inside all beings. Concealment is one of Shiva's acts that he hides so that we can endeavour to seek it. This face is associated with the *ajna chakra*, or the Third Eye – the portal to intuition, wisdom, and detachment.

Of destruction and regeneration
Aghora faces south – the direction of the ancestral realm and death. It is the face of the sacred fire and is fierce. He is the face of destruction and regeneration that is associated with the dissolution of ignorance, ego, and attachment. He teaches us that destruction is not an end, but a necessary step for rebirth and spiritual evolution. The Aghoris *(See pp284–285)*, who worship this form, believe that there is nothing inauspicious in this world because all that exists is in Shiva himself.

Beauty of existence
Vama means the "left side". If one stands facing east, the north is to our left. Hence, the north-facing Shiva is worshipped as Vamadeva. The left of a person is representative of Shakti, of feminine strength and beauty. In Ardhanarisvara, the goddess is on the left side. Vamadeva, the preserver of harmony, stands for *sthiti shakti*, or the power of preservation. It is associated with healing, grace, and is the sustaining force of the universe. Vamadeva is connected to water and the power of sustenance, for just as water nourishes a seed, this form of Shiva preserves the beauty of existence. This face governs compassion, forgiveness, balance and continuity. The emotional intelligence that lets life blossom represents the heart chakra or *anahata*.

The creator within
Sadyah means "just now" and *jatah* means "just born". Shiva makes his presence felt through the countless souls being born. Sadyojata is the face of birth. The existence of a being starts from birth, hence the Sadyojata face of Shiva is offered prayers first. This face signifies *anugraha shakti*, or the power of manifestation and blessings. Sadyojata symbolises new beginnings, potential and the birth of ideas and forms. He invites us to embrace our creative energy.

HE WHO HAS NO FORM

Beyond all form and name, Shiva exists as silent vastness – unseen, untouched, and utterly free. As *Nirguna*, he is the stillness before sound, the endless space beyond the stars – pure being beyond time, thought, and self.

In the vast tapestry of Hindu philosophy, Nirguna, meaning "beyond attributes", points to a reality that transcends all form, name, time, space, and description. Nirguna Shiva is not a deity confined by attributes, but the boundless essence, the ultimate truth in its purest, formless state. *Nirguna* refers to Brahman in its purest essence – the unmanifest, formless absolute that lies beyond the grasp of thought, language, and even the three *gunas* – *sattva*, *rajas*, and *tamas*. As revealed in the Upanishads, this Nirguna Brahman is not a deity with qualities, but the impersonal, infinite ground of all existence – pure being, consciousness, and bliss – *sat-chit-ananda*, untouched by the limitations of the

Beyond name and form

Shiva emerges from Brahman, the indivisible "One without a second". As *Nirguna*, without form or qualities, Shiva embodies the infinite, formless consciousness that transcends all duality. This vision resonates deeply with Advaita Vedanta, a prominent school of Hindu philosophy, where the ultimate reality is not a god with attributes, but pure, boundless awareness.

Phyllis Granoff, a specialist in Indic religions, highlights how medieval Sanskrit texts, especially Shaivite Puranas and Agamas, portray Shiva through a lens of narrative distancing, presenting him as *nirguna* or formless and *nishkala*, without attributes. These depictions place Shiva at the ineffable reality. His dynamic play between form and formlessness becomes a kind of divine pedagogy – guiding devotees beyond identification with the material body toward a deeper awareness of the self. Francis Xavier Clooney, renowned scholar of comparative theology, in his book *Hindu God, Christian God: How Reason Helps Break Down the Boundaries Between Religions* explores how in turning to the supremely free Shiva, one begins to glimpse their own inner freedom. Through his embodied presence, the body itself is reimagined as a vessel for spiritual awakening.

The formless "absolute"

Shiva is the unnameable – the one who transcends all opposites and eludes the grasp of language and thought. As *Nirguna*, he is beyond all names, forms, and dualities; beyond being and non-being, truth and falsehood, the one and the many. In Hindu thought, the divine is often spoken of as "God", yet Shiva points to something far more elusive: not the known, but the unknowable; not an object of worship alone, but the ultimate mystery of existence itself. In this vision, all human categories dissolve and what remains is a silence in which Shiva – the timeless, formless essence – is both nothing and everything.

Symbolism of the lingam

A deeper understanding of Shiva emerges through the worship of the lingam – a symbol rich with layered meaning. More than a mere object of devotion, the lingam embodies the profound interplay between transcendence and materiality, between form and formlessness. It represents a threshold state: the partial realization of *Sabija Samadhi* – a moment of oneness on the path toward complete transcendence, where all fixed forms begin to dissolve into the mystery of being.

The formless Shiva is *nirguna*, *nishkala*, *arupa*, *alinga* – without qualities, parts, or shape. Yet in the Shiva lingam, especially in its formless aspect, this abstract reality is evoked in a subtle manner. It is *nishkala-sakala*, both without form and with it – a liminal symbol that bridges the infinite Brahman and the tangible, anthropomorphic divine. It is form, and yet beyond form.

In the mystery of Shiva, we are invited to step beyond the boundaries of thought, name, and form into a silence where the eternal dwells. Whether glimpsed through the stillness of the lingam, the vastness of *nirguna* Brahman, or the cosmic dance between presence and absence, Shiva is not merely a god to be worshipped, but a truth to be realized.

MAHA MRITYUNJAYA MANTRA

THE ELIXIR OF IMMORTALITY

Tryambaka we worship, sweet augmenter
of prosperity.
As from its stem the cucumber, so may I be
released from death, not reft of immortality.

Maha Mrityunjaya mantra, from *The Hymns of the Rig Veda* by Ralph TH Griffith

Short and pithy, made up of just these lines, the Maha Mrityunjaya mantra or the Death-Defying mantra is one of the most powerful and revered Vedic chants dedicated to Shiva in his form as Tryambaka, the three-eyed, and an epithet of Rudra. It has many names — the Tryambakam mantra, the Rudra mantra, or the Mrit-Sanjeevani, and has appeared in the ancient Sanskrit texts of the *Rig Veda*, the *Yajur Veda*, and the *Atharva Veda*.

Spiritual essence and purity forms the ethos of the Maha Mrityunjaya mantra; the cucumber metaphor probably suggests effortless detachment from mortal bonds. Ancient texts associate many benefits when chanting this mantra, among them healing, protection from untimely death, and overall well-being, mental peace, and spiritual development.

Ward off evil

The mantra is not just about warding off death, but also overcoming the fear of death and accepting life's transitions. Besides spiritual benefits, chanting the Maha Mrityunjaya mantra regularly relaxes the mind, body, and soul. It also wards off evils like greed and jealousy, while promoting longevity of life. However, the immortality referred to is not physical, but lies in spiritual liberation and eternal consciousness.

The mantra's benefits are maximized when recited 108 times and is said to offer protection from negative planetary influences, and enhance mental clarity, especially recommended during illness or times of crisis. There are many myths associated with this mantra. Among them, the story of Sage Markandeya (See pp112–13) who, destined to die at 16, meditated on this mantra, until Shiva appeared to defeat Yama, the god of death, and protect his devotee. Shukracharya, the guru of the Asuras, used it to revive the dead, giving it the name Mrit-Sanjeevani, the life-restoring herb. It is chanted while smearing *vibhuti*, or holy ash, over the body and while performing a *homa*, a religious offering ceremony.

Potent verses

Mantras are powerful and potent verses or combinations of words or syllables from scriptures that are believed to transform a person's life due to the vibrations emitted when the mantra is repeated. Its recitation creates a subtle atmosphere that induces a sense of enlightenment, peace and fulfilment. The Sanskrit word *japa* is derived from the root *jap*, meaning "to utter in a low voice and repeat internally". It is the meditative repetition of a mantra or a divine name and has many parallels in other religions such as Jainism, Sikhism, and Buddhism.

Japa may be performed while sitting in a meditative posture or while performing other activities, or as part of formal worship in a group. The mantra or name may be spoken softly, loud enough for the practitioner to hear it, or may be recited silently in the practitioner's mind. It is performed almost always with the objective of realizing the truth embodied in the mantra.

▷ **The Maha Mrityunjaya mantra,** arranged here in concentric circles in Hindi, is known as the "Great death-conquering mantra," and symbolizes healing, protection, and liberation from fear and mortality.

ॐ त्र्यम्बकं यजामहे सुगन्धिं पुष्टिवर्धनम् उर्वारुकमिव बन्धनान्मृत्योर्मुक्षीय मामृतात्

South of the Kedarnath Temple in Uttarakhand, perched on a hillock, stands the Bhairavnath Temple, also known as Bhairon Baba Mandir. Here, Bhairava, a fierce manifestation of Shiva, is worshipped as Bhukund Bhairava, the guardian of the snowbound valley. Through the long winter months, when Kedarnath lies closed beneath snow, he watches over the temple and its pilgrims. The Bhairava shrine is a cluster of stone-carved images of the deity, with defined features. Tridents and fluttering flags of orange, red, and white mark the place.

MANY BHAIRAVAS

No image of Shiva embodies as many contrasting iconographic forms as Bhairava. The diverse manifestations are not just symbolic, but deeply woven into ritual, astrology, and spiritual practice.

The diversity in Bhairava arises from his worship across India, Nepal, Tibet, and Southeast Asia, where local traditions have shaped distinct representations – Mahakaal in Tibetan Buddhism, Muthappan in Kerala's Theyyam tradition, and Svacchanda Bhairava in Kashmir. Collectively, the various forms of Bhairava reflect a rich tapestry of spiritual symbolism, cosmic functions, and psychological transformation within Shaivism and Tantric practices.

The eight forms

The eight primary forms of Bhairava, known as the Ashta Bhairava, are described in the Puranas as guardians of the eight cardinal directions. Devotees worship them on Bhairava Ashtami or during specific planetary transits for protection, prosperity, and spiritual growth.

Each form embodies unique powers and attributes. Asitanga Bhairava, the black-limbed guardian of the east, enhances creativity, artistic skills, and prosperity, riding a swan. Ruru Bhairava of the southeast, the protector of animals, fosters compassion, healing, wisdom, and spiritual insight, with the ox as his mount. In the north, Bhishana Bhairava shields devotees from fear and malevolent forces, mounted on a lion, while Samhara Bhairava in the northeast destroys negativity and grants liberation, his faithful companion being the dog. To the south, Chanda Bhairava bestows victory over enemies and success in endeavours, riding a peacock, whereas Krodha Bhairava of the southeast removes obstacles and strengthens courage, mounted on an eagle. In the west, Unmatta Bhairava dispels confusion and mental unrest, with the horse as his mount, while Kapala Bhairava in the northwest frees devotees from legal troubles, riding an elephant.

Diverse forms

Other forms of Bhairava include Kala Bhairava, or the black one; Tamrachuda or the red-crested form; Chandrachuda or the Moon-crested form; and Kapali, the one who holds a skull. Batuk Bhairava is another distinctive form, depicted as a child symbolizing innocence and purity. His actions are free of guile. Popular in household worship, he blesses devotees with wisdom and removes obstacles.

*(1) **A basalt sculpture from 12th-century Karnataka.** Close-up of Kshetrapala, the guardian deity of sacred land in Hindu tradition.*

*(2) **Kali and Bhairava in union, in a watercolour painting from Nepal.** A powerful depiction of Kali and Bhairava in divine union, displaying the fierce aspects of Shiva and Shakti.*

*(3) **The revered shrine of Bhairavnath atop Pearl Hill in Udaipur, Rajasthan.** Honouring a fierce guardian form of Shiva, this sacred site draws devotees seeking protection, strength, and spiritual guidance.*

The most well-known form, however, is Kaal Bhairava *(See pp108–09)*, representing time and cosmic justice. Associated with destruction and transformation, he removes the *bhaya of kaal*, or the fear of time, and stands as the eternal protector of dharma. Kaal Bhairava guards sacred spaces, punishes the wicked, and vanquishes ego, fear, and illusion.

Yoginis and Matrikas

Most Bhairava images are found around Yogini shrines from the 9th century onwards, particularly in Madhya Pradesh and Orissa. The Chaunsatha Yoginis, numbering 64, are female divinities associated with Kali. Agamic texts – Sanskrit scriptures detailing ritual, temple construction, and worship practices – speak of 64 Bhairavas divided into groups of eight, each said to be a consort of a Yogini. Together, they represent the union of Shiva as consciousness and Shakti as energy. The Bhairava images in Yogini shrines typically have a flabby stomach and bear resemblance to the Bhikshatanamurti *(See pp216–17)*.

In some traditions, Bhairava is also considered the leader of the Yoginis. In the temples of Chaunsatha Yogini at Bheraghat in Madhya Pradesh, he stands at the centre, surrounded by the Yoginis arranged in a circular formation. This spatial arrangement symbolizes the cosmic dance of creation and dissolution, with Bhairava as the axis of time and transformation. The relationship between Bhairava and the Yoginis combines cosmic symbolism, spiritual empowerment, and esoteric ritual.

Bhairava is also referred to as the "lord of the circle of mothers", a title reflecting his association with the Matrikas, the divine mothers. As art historian Vidya Dehejia notes in her book *Yogini Cult and Temples*, if there were eight Matrikas, then there were eight corresponding Bhairavas, emphasizing the paired cosmic principle of male consciousness and female energy.

Worship

Bhairava serves as the chief guardian deity in many Shiva temples. In this role, he is known as Kshetrapala, the guardian of sacred spaces – typically depicted naked and awe-inspiring. He is worshipped before the day's regular temple rituals, and temple keys are ceremonially placed before him at the closing time of the temple.

Dehejia highlights the guardian tradition at Kedarnath, where, perched on a vast promontory high above the valley, a cluster of Bhairavas – carved with fearsome and prominent faces – keep watch. Here, he is called Bhairavnatha. Valiant ascetics firmly plant their tridents in the ground here, and from this vantage, the Bhairavas command a view of the glassy glacial cirque below, where Shiva's temple stands.

Bhairava is also central to Tantric practice, particularly in forms such as Kshetrapala, Kaal Bhairava, and Batuk Bhairava. In esoteric traditions, he is worshipped in cremation grounds and embodies the transcendence of fear and the breaking of taboos. He symbolizes mastery over death, impermanence, and the limitations of worldly existence.

▽ **(4) A masked performer as Bhairava, in the Kathmandu Valley.** Through powerful dance and ritual, he channels divine energy, reminding onlookers of Bhairava's role as protector, destroyer of evil, and keeper of sacred order in Nepalese tradition.

(5) An intricate stone carving of Bhairava-Shiva at Rani ki Vav, the UNESCO World Heritage stepwell in Patan, Gujarat. Bhairava is shown here with multiple arms holding various weapons and symbols: a noose, dagger, damaru or small drum, vajra, among others.

(6) A rock-cut sculpture of Bhairava at the Kamakhya Temple in the Nilachal Hills, Guwahati, Assam. He is honoured here as a fierce guardian of this powerful Shakti Peetha, where divine energy and Tantra converge.

SECRETS FROM THE GURU

The Tantras are more than spiritual guides or intricate manuals for ritual, philosophy, and mystical practice. They are intimate conversations between Shiva and Shakti.

Within the Tantric realm, Shiva plays a profound and multifaceted role – not merely as a deity who is to be worshipped, but as the very embodiment of pure consciousness, the masculine principle that complements and completes the feminine energy, that is Shakti.

Within this realm lie the Tantras – sometimes also referred to as Agamas – a class of esoteric scriptures central to several traditions within Hinduism, especially Shaivism, Shaktism, and Vaishnavism. Most were probably composed from the 8th century onwards and developed by the 10th century. They are unique in that there is an almost complete lack of doctrine in them.

In Shaivism, these texts take the form of profound conversations between Shiva and Shakti. The Goddess, as the disciple, asks questions and Shiva, as the master, answers them. For example, in the *Vijnana Bhairava Tantra*, Shakti asks questions about liberation, and Shiva responds with experiential wisdom – not as a superior, but as a loving consort.

Guru is central

The meanings of the Tantras are often elusive. This is because they were compiled within the context of a living, oral tradition and teachings of a guru. They are often considered secrets revealed by the guru, but only after the appropriate initiation of the seeker, one that would have wiped away the power of past actions.

The one who asks the questions and the one who responds with sagacity often shift within Tantra. In the Tantras focused on the Goddess or those of the Shakta tradition, Shiva becomes the seeker, asking the questions, while it is the Goddess who replies and reveals the truth. This narrative structure reflects the importance and centrality of the guru in Tantrism. Just as the Goddess receives wisdom from Shiva, or vice versa, so does the disciple receive wisdom from his or her master, writes British scholar of comparative religion Gavin Flood.

Role of Shiva and Shakti

An important part of Tantrism is where Shiva is seen seated on the Sahasrara Chakra, the highest of the seven focal points of energy in the body. Shakti, on the other hand, is visualized, conceptualized, and experienced as Kundalini, or divine feminine power in the Muladhara Chakra, at the base of the spine.

Tantra is rooted in the sacred union of Shiva as consciousness and Shakti as energy. Their cosmic connection and closeness denote the interchange of tranquillity and energy, and form and formlessness. In advanced Shaiva Tantras, Shiva is not looked upon or treated as a distant god. Instead, the seeker is invited to become Shiva and embody awareness, detachment, and blissful presence. Shiva is not separate from the practitioner. Worship becomes self-realization, recognizing that the divine is within.

Magical powers

While the Tantras often fall into disrepute for their erotic and antinomian elements – ritual sex and the consumption of alcohol and meat by ferocious

▽ **A painting depicting the Sahasrara Chakra**, or crown chakra, positioned at the forehead of a Tantric practitioner. The Sahasrara is symbolized by a thousand-petalled lotus, signifying the pinnacle of spiritual enlightenment. Immediately below it is a peacock with its long, eye-patterned tail, a symbol of illumination and the awakening, associated with the Ajna Chakra, or the third eye.

▷ **A Tantric painting depicts the Ajna Chakra, or third eye**, on the forehead of a Tantric practitioner. From this point, the Kundalini is shown rising towards the crown. The painting's red and grey tones suggest the passionate vitality and life force of Shakti, alongside Shiva's purification and spiritual transformation, respectively.

▷ **The Deity and The Devotee**, an early 20th-century watercolour painting from Pune or Aurangabad, depicts the ascent of the Kundalini through symbolic, esoteric forms. Rising from the base of the body, the energy passes through the throat and the Ajna chakra – marked by a yellow crescent – before reaching the Sahasrara, represented as a red lotus at the crown. From this lotus emerges the face of Mahakaal, mirrored in the figure's lower body. The energy of this ascent appears so intense that the devotees seem to steady the figure, fanning him and holding him in place with firm grips and tridents.

SECRETS FROM THE GURU | 245

The experience of bliss, moksha, and freedom is not just for the higher worlds, but in this world as part of the practitioner's spiritual journey where he is the enjoyer, or the *bhogi*.

deities – most of their contents are of a more sober nature and contain material on a wide range of topics. Primarily ritual texts, Tantras explain the formation of mantras, hierarchical cosmologies, initiations, the evolution of sound, yoga, doctrine, appropriate behaviour, and temple architecture, writes Flood.

It would be apposite to say that the Tantras are concerned with the attaining of magical powers called *siddhis*. The experience of bliss, moksha, and freedom is not just for the higher worlds, but in this world as part of the practitioner's spiritual journey where he is the enjoyer, or the *bhogi*.

Tantric asceticism

The Tantric sects within Shaivism are the Pashupatas, the Shaiva Siddhantas, the Kaulas, and the Kapalikas, to name a few. The ideologies of these groups influenced not only popular religion, but also Brahmanical circles, as seen in 11th-century Kashmir.

The popular cult of the deity Svacchanda Bhairava is influenced by Tantric asceticism, as are the higher social levels of the Brahmans. Indeed, the learned brahman elite, of whom the Shaiva theologian Abhinavagupta was a part, began to transform extreme Tantric ideology into a more respectable religion of the higher castes.

The Tantras present elaborate hierarchical cosmologies that absorb the cosmic hierarchies of earlier traditions. For example, the highest world of the Shaiva Siddhanta, or religious traditions of Karnataka, is transcended by further worlds within Kashmir Shaiva traditions.

▽ **A c.1850 painting from the Punjab Hills** depicts the seven chakras along the body. Rather than the usual abstract or geometric symbols, each chakra contains a divinity, including Ganesha and Brahma. At the base sits a Shiva lingam, while the throat features what appears to be a peacock, the mount of Karttikeya. At the crown, Shiva and Parvati are shown together, symbolizing the union of pure consciousness and dynamic energy.

STIRRING THE SERPENT

The connection between Shiva and Kundalini is a cornerstone of Tantric philosophy. It is astounding to realize that a hidden source of spiritual energy lies within the body – one that, when awakened, is believed to unlock extraordinary potential.

In the Hindu Tantric tradition, Shiva represents pure consciousness – the unchanging, formless awareness that underlies all existence. It resides in Sahasrara, or the crown chakra, the highest energy centre in the human chakra system, located at the top of the head. In contrast, Shakti, the divine feminine, embodies the dynamic, creative energy of the universe, called Kundalini. It is symbolized as a coiled, slumbering serpent resting in the Muladhara Chakra, located at the base of the spine.

According to Tantric philosophy, Shiva without Shakti is inert. He is the potential that requires the spark and the energy to manifest. It is only through the union of Shiva and Shakti that consciousness can express itself in form.

The union

Shiva and Kundalini can be likened to a mystical dance of stillness and energy, and consciousness and creation. Shakti, the dormant Kundalini energy, lies in quiet repose, brimming with raw potential, waiting to be awakened. When awakened, she rises and ascends through the chakras along the Sushumna Nadi – the central subtle energy channel that runs from the Muladhara to the Sahasrara – to seek union with Shiva at the crown.

Kundalini's journey

Kundalini's ascent is not merely energetic, but it is symbolic of the soul's evolution from fragmentation to wholeness and enlightenment. As Kundalini pierces each chakra, she dissolves layers of illusion, ego, and duality. Upon reaching the Sahasrara and merging with Shiva, the practitioner enters Samadhi – a state of blissful unity, where the individual self dissolves into the infinite. The union of Shiva and Shakti signifies the dissolution of duality and the realization of non-dual consciousness.

Techniques for activation

Facilitating Kundalini awakening is a sacred and transformative process that requires patience, discipline, and deep inner alignment. Across yogic and Tantric traditions, several practices are revered for their ability to gently stir this dormant energy and guide it upwards through the chakras. These include specific asanas, or yogic postures, especially those that activate the spine and pelvic region to help prepare the body for energy flow. Poses such as Bhujangasana, or cobra pose; Sarvangasana, or shoulder stand; and Padmasana, or lotus pose are commonly used to stabilize and energize the subtle body.

Pranayama, or breath control, is also central, as breath is seen as the bridge between body and spirit. Techniques such as Nadi Shodhana, or alternate nostril breathing; Kapalbhati, or skull-shining breath; and Bhastrika, or bellows breath are used to purify the *nadis*, or energy channels, and awaken *pranic* force – the vital life energy that sustains all living things and permeates the universe.

Sound is regarded as a direct expression of Shakti and can align the mind with higher consciousness. *Japa*, or mantra repetition, and Nada Yoga, the chanting of sacred sounds such as Om, So-Ham, or Sat Nam, help activate vibrational frequencies that resonate with Kundalini.

Meditation on the chakras, particularly the Muladhara and Sahasrara, can gently coax the Kundalini upwards. *Bandhas*, or energy locks, such as Mula Bandha, or root lock, and Uddiyana Bandha, or abdominal lock, combined with mudras such as Gyan Mudra, or gesture of wisdom, and Khechari Mudra, help direct, stabilize, and contain the rising energy.

Ethical living and self-inquiry are equally important. Practices such as *svadhyaya*, or self-study; *ahimsa*, or non-violence; and *satya*, or truthfulness cultivate the inner purity and steadiness required to handle the intensity of awakening.

▷ **This watercolor painting by the Indian contemporary artist Abhijit Sardar** depicts Shiva applying *alta*, a bright red dye, to Shakti's feet. Here, the *alta* is blood from a human head, placed in a bowl that rests on a coiled serpent. Shiva uses his matted hair for its application. The artwork shows the love between Shiva and Shakti, representing the spiritual journey from primal energy to transcendence.

SHIVA AND SHAKTI

Hindu philosophy emphasizes the relationship between humans and the active energies of the cosmos. In this framework, the balance of Shiva and Shakti represents the divine role in human life. This balance reflects the interconnectedness of all existence, where spiritual growth arises from the harmony of opposing forces.

Theologians often bifurcate the divine into male and female aspects. Shiva is the transcendental, inactive male, who carries out all worldly activities through his immanent, energetic counterpart, Shakti, the divine feminine. However, with the development of Tantrism in the 1st millennium CE, a shift occurred. Tantric philosophy took a logical step based on this cosmic division of labour: If Shakti is the one carrying out all the actions, why not focus on Her as the true force of the universe? As a result, Tantrism subverted Shiva's superior role, elevating Shakti – embodied as goddesses such as Parvati, Durga, and Kali – to the top of the divine hierarchy, acknowledging Her as the animating energy of all creation.

An eternal interconnection

Despite this, the two are inextricably linked. Shiva cannot move without Shakti, and Shakti has no purpose without Shiva. Shiva is the limitless sky – formless and transcendent – while Shakti is the manifest Earth, shaping and sustaining existence. Neither sky nor Earth can exist without the other.

Shiva's epithets, when conjoined with the Goddess, further emphasize their inseparability. Titles such as Umapati, Shivashakti, Girijapati, Umamaheshvara, Gaurishankar, Haragauri, Bhava–Bhavavani, and Rudra–Kali highlight this dynamic union.

Many texts also stress the interdependence of Shiva and Shakti. The *Saundaryalahari*, a hymn composed by Adi Shankaracharya, states "Shiva is only capacitated to act when he is joined with Shakti; otherwise, the god is incapable of even a twitch". This idea is also reflected in sculptures, icons, and paintings. The Ardhanarishvara *(See pp166–69)* form, the lingam and yoni, and the bindu and triangle are all visual representations of their union.

Two forces, one essence

In Tantric cosmology, the entire universe is perceived as being created, penetrated, and sustained by two fundamental forces that eternally exist in a perfect, indestructible union. These principle forces are Shiva and Shakti, the metaphysical divine couple, representing the masculine and feminine principles of cosmic energy, respectively. All life is understood to hold these opposite energies.

Shiva is the silent witness, the unmanifest consciousness energy, symbolizing pure transcendence, while Shakti represents power, active force, and functionality. Together, as cosmic partners, the two generate, maintain, and regulate the universe in coordination. Although Shiva and Shakti are opposites, they also transcend the male–female dichotomy,

> . . . The universe is born from the union of Shiva and Shakti; without their coming together, nothing can exist or persist . . .

forming a psychic totality. This unity is represented in the iconography of Ardhanarishvara, a deity that embodies both male and female attributes in one body. In Shaktism, a Hindu tradition that reveres the Goddess as the supreme being, there is no conflict between men and women. Instead, both realize the Earth through their collective fullness, embodying the equilibrium of the feminine and masculine aspects within a single being. This symbolizes Shiva and Shakti's unity, which brings about harmony, and such balance of energies leads to contentment.

From grief to union

The relationship between Shiva and Shakti is marked by a tension, or rather, a reconciliation, of asceticism and love. This dynamic is most evident in the story of the Shakti Peethas, sacred sites of Shakti worship. After Sati's death, Shiva, overcome with grief, danced uncontrollably while carrying her lifeless body on his shoulders causing havoc in the world. To halt the world's destruction, Vishnu dismembered her body, and the Shakti Peethas emerged wherever parts of her body fell. Sorrowed by this separation, Shiva retreated to the mountains. Eventually, he discovered her in the form of the yoni. Shiva, in turn, took the form of the lingam, entering into her, and thus the two remained united forever. Through the yoni, Sati drew the ascetic Shiva out of his seclusion, making him accessible to the world in the form of the lingam.

◁ **In this watercolour painting by Abhijit Sardar,** Sati reveals her divine powers by manifesting ten fierce forms to guard every direction as Lord Shiva tries to evade Daksha's insult. These 10 goddesses, known as the Dasa Mahavidyas, embody Shakti's boundless strength and cosmic protection, representing the fierce and infinite energy of the divine feminine.

KASHI

WHERE LIFE AND DEATH MEET

Nestled on the banks of the sacred river Ganga in Uttar Pradesh, Kashi is a cosmic sanctuary where time, death, and ego dissolve in the presence of the divine. It's a mood, a mystical rhythm, a kind of pious nonchalance, a *masti*, that flows through the lives of its residents. Here, time softens, ego dissolves, and even death is sacred, as if touched by eternity. To live in Kashi is to feel intimately connected to something vast, ancient, and ineffable.

Now known as Varanasi or Benaras, it is one of the oldest continuously inhabited cities in the world with its earliest history stretching back to the early Vedic period, and its spiritual presence as timeless as the river that flows beside it. The name Kashi comes from the Sanskrit root *kash*, meaning "to shine". More than a name, it is a metaphor — an invocation of illumination and liberation. It suggests not just physical brilliance, but the inner radiance of enlightenment.

Sacred landscape

Kashi is one of the seven holiest cities, Sapta Puri, in Hinduism, a sacred destination for pilgrims seeking *moksha* — the liberation from the cycle of birth and death. At its heart stands Shiva, worshipped here as Vishwanath, the "Lord of the Universe". Every street, shrine, and riverbank echoes with his presence, making Kashi not merely a city but a living embodiment of divine energy.

In the *Jabala Upanishad*, Kashi is described as the abode of Brahman, the supreme reality, where those who die attain liberation without fail. The *Mahabharata* refers to it as the dwelling place of Avimukta, another name for Shiva, the one who never forsakes his devotees. In the *Skanda Purana*, Kashi is extolled as the holiest of cities, centred around the majestic temple of Vishwanath, Shiva as the Lord of the Universe. Surrounding this temple is a sacred constellation of shrines and lingams, believed to have come from all corners of India. Each one is an echo of the divine, creating a spiritual geography where every step is a pilgrimage. Kashi is often called the "City of Light" or the "City of Shiva", believed in legend to have been founded by Shiva himself. Its very stones are said to carry his essence, as reflected in the famous saying: "*Kashi ke kankar Shiva Shankar*" — even the pebbles of Kashi are Shiva incarnate.

City of liberation

For many Hindus, to die in Kashi is to be freed from the cycle of rebirth. Myth says that in one's final moments here, Shiva himself appears, whispering: "What you see is my form ... but now, behold — I enter the unseen, the Sat-Chit-Ananda." With this vision, the soul glimpses Brahman, and liberation, *moksha*, is granted.

Saints and poets have called it the Golden City, where Shiva moves among the dying, whispering salvation into their ears. According to legend, Brahma once weighed Kashi against the heavens — and Kashi was heavier, for it contains the entire cosmos within it. Philosophers like Adi Shankara, Patanjali, and Ramanuja have walked its streets. Buddha gave his first sermon nearby. And still today, Kashi remains a spiritual heartland, a place where death is not an end, but a return to the eternal.

This sacred city, with its burning ghats and timeless rituals, carries an aura of spiritual gravity unmatched anywhere else. It is a living, breathing embodiment of Hindu tradition, an eternal space where the spiritual and material merge.

In Kashi, death is not feared — it is part of life's rhythm. As the saying goes: "*Kashyam maranam mukti*". To die in Kashi is to be liberated.

▷ *(clockwise from top)* **Sacred and eternal,** Varanasi is believed to have been founded by Shiva — a place where life, death, and liberation converge on the banks of the Ganga; **Priests perform the fire ritual or aarti** at Dashashwamedh Ghat, honouring Ganga; **Dedicated to Shiva, Shri Kashi Vishwanath** is believed to be a place where Shiva grants *moksha* or liberation to the soul; **During Chita Bhasma Holi at Manikarnika Ghat, Varanasi,** devotees gather at the cremation grounds to celebrate Masan Holi with ash from funeral pyres.

SACRED MYTHS

RETURN TO KASHI
Banished from Kashi, Shiva waited as King Divodasa ruled under a divine boon. Guided by Vishnu's plan, Ganesha revealed the king's unrest. Enlightened, Divodasa installed a Shiva Lingam and attained *moksha* or the freedom from the eternal cycle of life, death, and rebirth. Shiva returned, reclaiming Kashi as Avimukta – eternal and free. With harmony restored, the Gods rejoiced. The city once again pulsed with cosmic rhythm, a beacon of spiritual liberation.

GUARDIAN OF TIME
In Kashi, Shiva walks as Kaal Bhairava – the fierce lord of time and death. He's no serene sage but a vigilant guardian, flanked by Bhairavas, the loyal guards and protectors. Travellers pray at his shrine, for without his nod, none may enter. Protector, punisher, liberator – he watches all, ensuring only the worthy pass through the gates of the sacred city.

THE LINGAM OF LIGHT
In Kashi, the Ganga flows with Shiva's essence, purifying all it touches. From its depths, a blazing lingam of light pierced sky and earth – Shiva's divine form made manifest. Shrines and lingams mark every corner, echoing his presence. The city itself became sacred, not just a home for Shiva, but Shiva incarnate – a luminous site where heaven, earth, and soul converge.

In Kashi, the holiest city for devotees of Shiva in India, funeral pyres burn along Manikarnika Ghat under the dark cover of night. Death is a sacred journey rather than an end in this context. Under Shiva's watchful eye, devotees believe that death in this ancient city results in *moksha*, or freedom from rebirth. On the banks of the holy Ganga River, the perpetual fire, nourished by centuries of devotion, connects the divine and the earthly.

I am Shiva, Shiva alone am I

Nirvana Shatakam, Adi Shankaracharya

5 | SHIVA
THE DEITY

To worship and believe in Shiva is not to seek him through wealth, but through loftiness of thought, clarity of mind, and the confidence that guidance will come. It is to cultivate autonomy in one's path and the detachment needed at life's most crucial moments.

GOD OF THOSE WHO SEEK

There is a reason why Shiva is so beloved: we are drawn to wonder, to transcend the dullness of everyday life. In worshipping him, the mundane merges with the spectacular, creating a convergence that spawns a spectrum of emotions and heightens experience. Devotion becomes a pathway to amazement, and in revering Shiva, this awe is experienced again and again.

Shiva's stories help us come to terms with the many dimensions of our own lives. As God, he is mighty enough to sustain the cosmos, yet he also shows us how to navigate our smaller, individual worlds. His battles with Asuras reveal strength; his boons and promises remind us of the consequences of compassion; his role as a family man reflects reconciliation; his loyalty to the Ganas affirms acceptance of the strange and marginal; his mastery of dance and rhythm celebrates art; and his deep meditation embodies the inward journey. Through these Shiva teaches us to accept, balance, and harmonize our lives with reality.

Comfort amidst loss

Shaivism acknowledges that paradoxes and contradictions are part of the cosmic fabric. To accept and propitiate Shiva is to recognize the power of the uncontrolled and the fear of the unknown. Therefore, his image brings comfort even in the grief of the cremation ground. There he stands, assuring that life is not over but only making way for a new beginning. Psychologically, his mantra "Aum Namah Shivaya" is the most effective in moments of great loss. To utter it is to experience the peace that comes with knowing everything is ephemeral, that this too shall pass. For had Shiva himself not endured this with Sati? Had he not been reviled by society, punished, and humiliated? Yet he did not let suffering consume him; he moved forward. His coping mechanisms were not always perfect, but even their failings carried lessons for devotees.

The realization of oneness

Through Shaiva myths and artistic expressions, one enters a realm of spiritual values rooted in truth and beauty. Each episode and icon points to Shiva's core qualities – fullness of being and pure consciousness, a state of perfect bliss. This state arises from the realization that one's true self is identical with ultimate reality, an ecstatic experience of divine oneness.

In this realization, a seeker enters into communion with Shiva. From this communion emerges a transformed outlook, marked by conviction, a spirit of sharing, and a nobility that renders the personality radiant and compelling. It nurtures deeper autonomy and a higher awareness.

The path to Shiva

Even though rituals abound in Shiva's worship, it is the idea of becoming one with him that surpasses all other forms of devotion. Unlike many temples in India where deities are covered with heaps of jewellery, Shiva as the lingam remains unadorned and even when represented anthropomorphically. To worship and believe in Shiva is not to seek him through wealth, but through loftiness of thought, clarity of mind, and the confidence that guidance will come. It is to cultivate autonomy in one's path and the detachment needed at life's most crucial moments.

Perhaps the purest way to connect with Shiva is to close the eyes, take a deep breath, and gently emanate the sound "Aum". As the sound-symbol of the absolute, "Aum" is called *anahata*, the uncreated vibration, not produced by any physical function. It connects the individual with universal consciousness, resonating as the cosmic echo of ultimate reality, yet one that can also be experienced within personal reality. It is not to be uttered blindly or mechanically, but with as much depth and inner engagement as one can summon.

TAMIL SHAIVISM

Championed by kings and embraced by the masses alike, Tamil Shaivism rose to become the very heart of Tamil religious life. South India's colossal temples and sacred verses stand as testaments to a devotion that transformed stone into spirit and music into divine presence.

The flavour of Shaivism encountered in South India is somewhat different from the one followed in other peripheries of the country. There is a frenzy, a fervour, and an ardour that can stir even a sceptic. The byproducts of these emotions are the enchanting and heartwrenching poems and art seen on facades and interiors of magnificent temples across South India.

Bhakti movement

Of particular influence in this region was the Bhakti movement, a significant religious and social movement in medieval India, emphasizing devotion to a particular deity. It means having a direct connection to God, bypassing priestly intermediaries and excessive rituals. In South India, it originated around the 6th century CE with the Alvars, the Vaishnavite saints, or followers of Vishnu, and the Nayanars, the Shaivite saints who composed hymns in their vernacular languages, making it accessible. This was a movement that challenged the caste system and promoted social equality by allowing people from all backgrounds to participate in their love for Shiva.

The Nayanars, who belonged to the lower castes, as did the Otuvars, sang hymns to Nataraja icons, which symbolized Brahmanical royalty during festive processions.

This aspect of Tamil Shaivism constitutes the Shaiva Bhakti movement, which refutes caste distinction, asceticism, and formal and ritualistic temple worship, instead adopting a personal and immediate connection with Shiva. The Bhakti movement developed in opposition to lower-caste oppression and was influential, perhaps due to the personal freedom to connect with the lord beyond the control of Brahmin authority.

The Nayanars

Between the 6th and the 9th century, a group of 63 holy men and women from Tamil Nadu devoted their lives to Shiva. The Nayanars – or lord in Tamil – were the canonized saints of the Tamil Shaivas. The saints, some ascetic, some married, were from different backgrounds and all segments of society from the upper castes and classes such as kings, brahmans, and cultivators to the hunters, low-caste musicians, and even outcastes. In contrast to the traditional Hindu caste hierarchy, the saints formed an ideal society, almost like a spiritually egalitarian community of Shiva devotees. United, they were equal in their extreme love and devotion, often travelling together to the numerous temples, and singing in praise of Shiva. Cults developed around these saints, whose devotion to the gods was particularly admired.

Prominent among the Nayanars were Champantar, Apar, and Arurar, the authors of the hymns in the Tevaram, who are celebrated as the principal saint leaders of the Tamil Shaiva sect. The Tevaram, the first vernacular texts in Hinduism, is a heretic and sophisticated tradition of classical Tamil poetry, writes scholar of Sanskrit and Tamil literature Indira Peterson. The saint hymnists include women such as Karaikkal Ammaiyar and Kannapar. Tamil Shaivas consider their works equal to the Vedas as the saints eloquently expressed their love for Shiva, a form of religiosity new in Hinduism.

Although the later Bhakti movements arose primarily as a reaction against Hindu orthodoxy, the early Tamil Bhakti cults saw themselves as the champions of the Tamil Hindu religion. The enemy was not brahmanical Hinduism or Sanskritic religious modes, but Buddhism and Jainism, which were alien to Tamil culture.

A sense of oneness

The Tevaram helped drive out Buddhism and Jainism from the Tamil region, thereby establishing Tamil Shaivism as the main religion, patronized by the kings and practised by the masses. The hymns, which promoted a sense of oneness, were set to Dravidian music and incorporated into temple rituals. The images of the Nayanars are found in many Shiva temples in Tamil Nadu, and they are worshipped as saints even today. The belief is that none of these saints died a natural death – each vanished into the radiance of Shiva when his or her time came.

Kannappar

The paragon of Bhakta devotees, Kannappar holds a special place in the hearts of Shiva devotees. One of the best known stories about Kannappar is the one in the Tamil epic *Periya Puranam* by poet-saint Chekkilar. The story tells of a 16-year-old Kannappar, then a tribal hunter chieftain who had been brought up in the forest and was adept at fishing, hunting, and stealing cattle, all necessary for survival in the wild. Once, while out hunting, he found an abandoned statue of Shiva. Filled with love for the god, Kannappar fed him pieces of meat of a boar that he had killed. He had roasted each piece to make sure it was tender for Shiva. He kicked aside the flowers that a brahman priest had left on Shiva's head. Instead, he gave him the flowers that he had worn and spat out the water from his mouth on the statue. He stayed with the lingam all night and left at dawn to hunt again. The brahman priest returned and immediately removed Kannappar's offerings. To open the brahman's eyes to the love of Kannappar, one of Shiva's eyes began to bleed. To stop the flow of blood, Kannappar gouged out his own eye with an arrow and replaced the god's eye with his. When Shiva made his other eye bleed, Kannappar moved to do the same with his other eye, but Shiva stopped him. Overwhelmed by his devotion, Shiva appeared and placed him on his right, restored his vision, and granted him salvation.

He later became the central figure of a Telugu epic poem Haravilasamu by the well-known 15th-century Telugu poet Srinatha, writes Indian art historian Vidya Dehejia, which depicts his complete absorption in Shiva and the paramount importance of a love that is able to withstand trials.

△ *(left)* **A 14th-century bronze sculpture** of Appar holding a spade, from Thanjavur, Tamil Nadu.

(centre) **An 11th-century bronze sculpture** of Kannappar, from Tiruverkadu, Tamil Nadu.

(right) **A late 14th-century copper alloy sculpture** of Champantar, also known as Sambandar, from Tamil Nadu.

▷ This late 13th-century copper alloy sculpture from Tamil Nadu depicts Karaikkal Ammaiyar in her ascetic form. Emaciated, with a bald head and sagging breasts, she bears a serene expression as she sings Shiva's praises, beating the cymbals in devotion.

KARAIKKAL AMMAIYAR

THE REVERED MOTHER OF KARAIKKAL

He is the One who possesses me.
He stands as the One.
He does not need to know Himself.
His pure matted hair looks like coils made of gold.
He is the place where the gods get their grace.

Karaikkal Ammaiyar in *Arputat Tiruvantati* or Sacred Linked Verses of Wonder, from *Siva's Demon Devotee* by Elaine Craddock

One of the three revered women Nayanar saints and one of the greatest figures in early Tamil literature, Karaikkal Ammaiyar, or Revered Mother of Karaikkal, was known for her severe austerities and her habit of singing to conjure up visions of Shiva dancing. Though she lived in the 6th century, historian Upinder Singh notes that her images started appearing in temples only after the 12th century. In them, she has sagging breasts and swollen veins, protruding eyes, bare white teeth, skeletal legs, and knobbly knees. In some, she holds a pair of small cymbals with a fang-toothed smile and a rapturous gaze, presumably in accompaniment to Shiva's dance.

The hagiography of Karaikkal tells the story of Punitavati, one of the earliest Hindu woman saints who lived in the town of Karaikkal in Tamil Nadu during the 6th century, and left a corpus of her works. She and her husband were devout Shiva worshippers and served him and his devotees until events proved that Punitavati had divine powers. Her husband, shocked and terrified, abandoned her and married another woman. Punitavati prayed to Shiva begging him to turn her into an ugly demon, or *pey*, and to divest her of the burden of her flesh. A miracle occurred and she turned into an emaciated skeletal figure who became known as the mother of Karaikkal. She then embarked on a pilgrimage to Mount Kailasha (See pp202–03), but did not want to defile the path with her feet, and is said to have walked there on her hands. She only begged Shiva to allow her to watch him dance into eternity.

In his praise

Karaikkal left an extensive body of work of 143 poems across three texts, most of which are set in the cremation ground, the only place where she said she could watch Shiva dance. In her poetry, she refers to herself as Karaikkal *pey* or the ghoul of Karaikkal.

In some of her verses, she writes about the cremation grounds in a wild forest of banyan trees, even as she describes the macabre ghoulish denizens of the forest. She talks about the ground being damp with liquid marrow and skeletal ghouls with sunken eyes, who eat half-burnt corpses. In them, she chooses to join the ghoulish creatures of the banyan forest to rejoice in the beauty and radiance of dancing Shiva, having realized the irrelevance of bodily beauty and external surroundings. She writes:

The troupe of ghouls comes together,
extinguishes the funeral fires everywhere, and
joyously feasts on the corpses.
In the terrifying cemetary, the Beautiful Lord
dances holding fire in His hand.

Karaikkal Ammaiyar in Patikam 2 of *Tiruvanlankattu Mutta Tiruppatikam* or *First Sacred Verses on Tiruvalankatu*, from *Siva's Demon Devotee* by Elaine Craddock

THE HEROIC WORSHIPPERS

They derive their name from the stone lingam that they wear around their neck in a silver casket, symbolizing Shiva's presence. The Lingayats do not recognize the Vedas and the priestly caste, instead worshipping Shiva who is considered the supreme self. Their emphasis is on honest work and generosity.

A vibrant and reformist Shaiva movement emerged in 12th century in the southern region of Karnataka as a response to rigid caste hierarchies and Brahmanical orthodoxy. It was not just a spiritual movement, but a bold, social revolution – a social upheaval by and for the poor, the low caste, and the outcaste against the rich and the privileged. It was almost like a rising of the unlettered against the literate pundit. Founded by philosopher, social reformer, statesman and poet, Basavanna, the movement became known as the Lingayat tradition. The focus lay on deep, personalized, direct worship of Shiva and a rejection of temple worship with rituals.

Origins

In South India, the Shaiva Shiddhanta system had eliminated the eccentricities practised by early Shiva followers, and embraced a less ambiguous form of worship, one where the methods of achieving salvation lay in practices such as meditation, penance, and the worship of the lingam.

This changed with the emergence of the Lingayat tradition. Its origins lay in the Virashaiva sect, which had come earlier and was itself a reformed version of Kalamukha, a medieval Shaivite sect. The term *virashaiva* translates to mean "militant" or "heroic Shaivism". Basavanna later developed and inspired the Virashaiva movement, bringing the Lingayat school of thought to life. It shared its roots with the ongoing Bhakti movement, particularly the Shaiva Nayanar traditions. Within the Lingayats, the practice of Shiva worship is distinct. The sect is unorthodox; they do not recognize the authority of the Vedas and the priestly caste. They reject caste discrimination and gender inequality and lay emphasis on *kayaka*, or honest labour, and *dasoha*, or generous sharing, as spiritual practices and encouragement for education, equality, and moral living.

His presence on the person

For the Lingayats, Shiva is identical to the Paramatma, or the supreme self, and they view the lingam as the sole, sacred symbol, thereby opposing pilgrimages, sacrificial rites, and image worship. The lingams embody the essence of Shiva; it is the manifest omnipotence of the divine. The Lingayats carry a stone lingam of Shiva in a silver or gold pendant around their necks, symbolizing his ever-present divinity and enabling a deeply personal form of devotion.

Noted poet AK Ramanujan wrote how Basavanna's attempt at building an egalitarian society clearly indicated that "the love of Shiva cannot live with ritual".

Speaking of and to Shiva

A significant aspect of the Lingayats were the *vachanas* that their saints, such as Basavanna and Akka Mahadevi, composed. They wrote some of the most passionate *vachana* poetry between the 10th and the 12th century, with the local idiom taking the paramount position as Sanskrit, the preferred language at the time, gave way to the more colloquial Kannada. A religious lyric in Kannada free verse, the *vachana* literally translates to mean "saying things said". These poets were not bards or pundits in a court addressing the elite, but men and women speaking to ordinary people of every class, caste, and trade. Much like the Bhakti movements across India, Shiva was

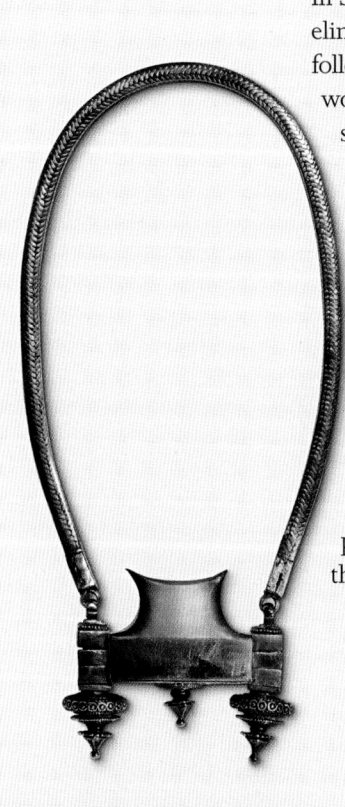

◁ **A 19th-century silver case**, to house a Shiva lingam, belonging to the Lingayat community.

THE HEROIC WORSHIPPERS | 263

> It was not just a spiritual movement, but a bold, social revolution – a social upheaval by and for the poor, the low caste, and the outcaste against the rich and the privileged. The focus lay on deep, personalized, direct worship of Shiva and a rejection of temple worship with rituals.

central to the compositions amongst the Lingayats as well. Their devotional hymns glorified Shiva, emphasizing personal devotion over rituals, making him accessible to all.

Many poets, much like Basavanna and Shiva Ramanatha, brought in their own personal tone and even gave Shiva their own personal name or nickname, indicating the complete intimacy and closeness to their chosen one. Such as in this excerpt by Basavanna, where he wrote:

Keep me at your men's feet
looking for nothing else,
O lord of the meeting rivers.

Basavanna, from *Speaking of Siva* by AK Ramanujan

▷ **A Lingayat from Mysore,** Karnataka, wearing a pendant around his neck that likely holds a lingam, signifying his devotion and connection to the tradition.

LINGAYET.

HINDOO.

MYSORE.

422.

VERSES OF MYSTIQUE

Between the 10th and 12th centuries, some poet saints composed some of the most passionate devotional poetry in Kannada. Akka Mahadevi and Basavanna were among the most celebrated of these mystic poets. Their compositions on Shiva express an intense, personal devotion that transcends ritual and orthodoxy.

Some of the most intense, mystical poetry emerged between the 10th and 12th centuries, many in the praise of Shiva – some deeply sensual, some raw with emotion, others ecstatic in his praise, and yet others brimming with spiritual longing and divine love. Among the authors were four well-known saints, Akka Mahadevi, Basavanna, Dasimayya, and Allama, who were a part of the Lingayat and Veerashaiva traditions. Between them, they wrote *vachana* poetry – short, free-verse devotional verses – dedicated to Shiva, which rejected societal norms and celebrated the divine.

One of the most radical voices among them was Akka Mahadevi, a 12th-century poet and mystic from southern India who composed more than 430 *vachanas* in Kannada. Rarely would one come across a figure so unique. Her life and poetry are a luminous testament to spiritual defiance, feminine autonomy, and ecstatic devotion to Shiva, whom she addressed as Chenna Mallikarjuna, or the beautiful lord, white as jasmine:

O lord white as jasmine
when do I join you
stripped of body's shame
and heart's modesty?

Akka Mahadevi, from *Speaking of Siva* by
AK Ramanujan

Her lover and her husband

Akka Mahadevi's detachment for everything worldly made her scorn clothing, but her love for her chosen god Shiva was rooted in societal norms as she saw him as her husband. She wrote:

People,
male and female,
blush when a cloth covering their shame
comes loose.
    When the lord of lives
lives drowned without a face
in the world, how can you be modest?

Akka Mahadevi, from *Speaking of Siva* by
AK Ramanujan

Her ardour, her loyalty and her boldness were truly remarkable. Besides rejection of societal norms, caste, and ritualism, her devotion to Shiva was that of a lover and husband and often used sensual metaphors to express mystical union.

She became an ardent devotee of Shiva at a young age and considered him her eternal consort. A local Jain king, Kaushika, sought to marry her, and some accounts say she agreed under strict spiritual conditions while others state she refused outright. When he violated her conditions, Mahadevi is said to have walked away from royal life.

> Her life and poetry are a luminous testament to spiritual defiance, feminine autonomy, and ecstatic devotion to Shiva, whom she addressed as Chenna Mallikarjuna, or the beautiful lord, white as jasmine.

◁ **A painting of Akka Mahadevi from the Sangameshwar Temple** in Bagalkot, Karnataka. Her body is modestly veiled by the flow of her long hair and a tripundra adorns her forehead, symbolizing her steadfast devotion to Shiva.

▷ **The Sharana Basaveshwara Temple,** a shrine dedicated to Basavanna, in Kalaburgi district of Karnataka. It features a tiered bell-shaped dome, adorned with intricate carvings, rising from a square base.

Her commitment to Shiva was marked by total renunciation – she shed not only societal roles but even clothing, symbolizing complete surrender to Shiva. She wandered as a naked ascetic, singing praises to Shiva, though legend has it that due to her true love and devotion to Shiva, her body was protected and veiled by long hair.

She went in search of fellow seekers, but her non-conformist ways caused consternation in the conservative society of the time. Even her guru, Allama Prabhu, faced difficulties in including her in the gatherings at Anubhavamantapa in Kalyana, a spiritual parliament where she debated with saints such as Basavanna and Siddharama. She was revolutionary. A woman mystic holding her own among the greatest minds of her time. The saints addressed her as *akka*, or elder sister, a mark of reverence and an indication of her high place in the spiritual discussions. Eventually, Mahadevi retreated to the forests of Srisailam in Andhra Pradesh, where she is believed to have attained union with Shiva.

Defying norms

Akka Mahadevi's 430 *vachanas* and other writings are considered searing and lyrical expressions of spiritual longing, renunciation, and divine love. What sets her apart is not just her poetry, but her life as a living embodiment of *madhurya bhava*, or sweet devotion, where the divine is seen as the beloved form of devotion. She was a towering figure of the Lingayat Bhakti movement, known for her radical devotion to Shiva, her poetic voice, and her fearless rejection of societal norms.

Mahadevi's *vachanas* are raw, ecstatic, and often confrontational, challenging both patriarchy and spiritual complacency. She saw the body as a temporary garment and the soul's union with Shiva as the only truth. Her pursuit of enlightenment is recorded in poems of simple language but intellectual rigour. Her *vachanas* also talk about the methods that the path of enlightenment demands of the seeker, such as killing the "I", conquering desires and the senses. Her nudity was not just symbolic – it was a bold statement of a stripping away of ego, identity, and societal constraint, asserting that modesty is meaningless before the all-seeing divine.

As she wrote:

I love the Handsome One:
  he has no death
  decay nor form
  no place or side
  no end nor birthmarks.
  I love him O mother. Listen.

Akka Mahadevi, from *Speaking of Siva* by AK Ramanujan

Akka Mahadevi is often seen as a proto-feminist figure, challenging patriarchal norms, critiquing the limitations placed on women, and celebrating spiritual freedom. Mahadevi's devotion stands out for its radical intensity, and she shares a deep spiritual kinship with other female mystics who expressed divine love through their own cultural and poetic idioms, such as like Andal, Mirabai, and Lalleshwari or Lal Ded.

A household name in the southern state of Karnataka and celebrated in literature, folklore, and festivals, she is regarded a major female figure in Kannada literature. She remains a symbol of spiritual rebellion and inner liberation.

Breaking barriers

Born into a traditional brahman family steeped in Shaivism, Basavanna rejected rituals and temple worship when he was quite young. As much a spiritual leader as he was a reformer, he championed devotional worship, emphasizing personalized direct worship of Shiva. Much like the strikingly original and impassioned *vachanas* of the time, his work too spoke of Shiva and to Shiva, writes noted Indian poet AK Ramanujan in his seminal translation *Speaking of Siva*.

"The lord of the meeting rivers where three rivers meet that is Kudalasangamadeva" became Basavaanna's chosen god and his own personal name given to Shiva. It appears prominently at the closing of every *vachana* as his signature phrase.

He used his poetry or *vachanas* to promote this social awareness, championing gender equality, widow remarriage, inter-caste relationships, and offering spiritual paths to householders and artisans alike. He introduced new public institutions such as the Anubhava Mantapa, or the hall of spiritual experience, which welcomed men and women from all socio-economic backgrounds to discuss spiritual and mundane questions of life.

In one of his famous vachanas, Basavanna questioned traditionalism while writing:

The tongs join hands.
So what?
Can thy be humble in service
to the Lord?

Parrots recite.
So what?
Can they read the Lord?

Basavanna, from *Speaking of Siva* by AK Ramanujan

△ **An Indian coin featuring Basavanna,** honouring him as a mahatma, or great soul.

△ **A painting depicting Adi Shankaracharya (centre)** surrounded by four disciples, seated by a river. He appears in his typical form – as a monk holding a scripture. His four disciples represent the establishment of the four monastic centres attributed to him. The composition appears inspired by Indian painter Raja Ravi Varma's portrayal of a similar scene.

THE GURU AND THE SANYASI

If there is one figure in Shaivism who most profoundly shaped its philosophy, it is Adi Shankaracharya, the 8th-century reformer and philosopher who redefined how Shiva was understood. He moved beyond rituals, emphasizing oneness with Shiva as the true path to realization.

Shiva and Adi Shankaracharya, one divine, the other human, one the Adiguru and the other the eternal student. While Shiva is the eternal consciousness from which all arises and into which all dissolves, Shankaracharya put forward the Advaita Vedanta, which teaches that the individual soul and the universal reality are one and the same. Together, the guru and his student show the believer the true spiritual path.

Adi Shankaracharya was born in 788 CE in Kerala as a divine boon granted to his parents after their penance to Shiva. He went on to become a prodigious scholar, philosopher, theologian, and the foremost exponent of Advaita Vedanta, a Hindu school of philosophy. Even as a young boy in Kalady, Adi Shankaracharya was spiritual and yearned to become a sanyasi, or monk. But his mother, Aryamba, was reluctant as she feared being alone in her old age.

Divine intervention

Legend has it that one day, while bathing in the river, a crocodile caught Shankaracharya's leg. As he struggled, he cried to his mother, "If you grant me

THE GURU AND THE SANYASI

> The revelation of truth is twofold: one, by appearing in the form society most reviles, Shiva instructs that the divine exists in all, and two, wisdom is not the privilege of the elite.

permission to renounce the world and become a monk, I shall be freed." Terrified and desperate, his mother agreed. Miraculously, the crocodile let go. This moment is seen as the divine intervention of Shiva, who had promised to incarnate himself as Shankaracharya to revive spiritual wisdom.

The crocodile was not just a beast, it was fate, fulfilling a cosmic promise. From that day, Shankaracharya began his spiritual journey, eventually becoming one of India's greatest philosophers.

Another legend has it that the gods pleaded with Shiva to restore dharma, or moral duty, during a time of spiritual decline. Shankaracharya's birth was a divine response to restore spiritual clarity in a time of ritualism and fragmentation, revive the path of Vedic dharma, unify diverse sects, and reassert the primacy of spiritual knowledge over ritualism. The name "Shankaracharya" itself is associated with Shiva, and the concept of the guru–disciple relationship, particularly in the context of Advaita Vedanta, deeply rooted in Shiva worship.

When arrogance turned to reverence

It is said that once, while walking in Kashi, Adi Shankaracharya came face to face with a Chandala, a member of the outcaste community, with four dogs. Shankaracharya ordered him to "move aside" to avoid ritual impurity. But the Chandala responded with a sharp query, "Whom are you asking to move – my body or the Atman, the self? If the self is one and indivisible, how can there be difference?"

The answer crushed Shankaracharya's assumptions and a moment of recognition and reverence followed. The Chandala was Shiva, testing his disciple's understanding of non-duality, or Advaita. It was a spiritual turning point and a lesson in humility. The revelation of truth is twofold: one, by appearing in the form society most reviles, Shiva instructs that the divine exists in all, and two, wisdom is not the privilege of the elite.

The cosmic principle

Shankaracharya revered Shiva as the ultimate reality, or Brahman, and often used Shiva symbolism to explain non-dualism. He achieved self-realization and knowledge, but not through rituals or external worship. One of his main precepts is that reality is singular; all perceived dualities are illusions. He is said to have founded Advaita Vedanta, which teaches that the individual soul, or Atman and the universal reality, or Brahman, are one and the same. Shiva is not merely a deity but is nirguna, or without attributes, the eternal consciousness from which all arises and into which all dissolves. His meditative stillness and cosmic dance symbolize the paradox of motion within stillness – just as Brahman is both immanent and transcendent.

Metaphysical insight

Shankaracharya authored many texts and had several well-known disciples. His devotional hymns to Shiva, such as *Shivanandalahari* (See pp270–71) and *Nirvana Shatakam* (See pp218–19) blend bhakti, or devotion, with knowledge.

Shankaracharya often invoked Dakshinamurti, the form of Shiva as the supreme teacher, who imparts wisdom through silence. In his *Dakshinamurti Stotram*, Shankaracharya praises Shiva as the embodiment of self-knowledge and the destroyer of ignorance. His famous declaration:

"*Aham Brahmasmi*", or I am Brahman, echoes the Shiva principle that all distinctions are illusory.

▷ **The Dakshinamnaya Sri Sharada Peetham in Sringeri, Karnataka**, is one of the four cardinal *pithams*, or monastic centres, established by Adi Shankaracharya to propagate the doctrine of non-dualism. The other three are located in Puri in the east, Dwarka in the west, and Joshimath in the north.

SHIVANANDALAHARI

WAVES OF BLISS

O Lord, Thou Supreme doer of good to all the worlds! May my mind be occupied with Thy lotus-feet, my speech with Thy praise, my hands with Thy worship, my ears with sacred accounts about Thee, my intellect with Thy meditation, and my eyes with the glory of Thy form. Then by which organ would I study books unconnected with Thee!

Verse 7, *Shivanandalahari*, from *Sivanandalahari of Sri Sankaracarya* by Swami Tapasyananda

It is said that the composition known as the *Shivanandalahari* came to the writer from utmost devotional fervour, as a river in flood, wave after wave, billowing a flow that comes in breaking over embankments, the outcome of deliberation, the spontaneous outpouring by poet's experience that is like water welling up and flowing. The idea being that the waves of bliss inundate those who contemplate Shiva, the source of all that is auspicious. "*Lahari*" in the title also suggests that one's endeavour is to not to reach the shore, but to keep floating in the hymns. The metaphor of gushing water suggests the flowing of feelings and the urge to reach god by means of an inspired song:

O Lord, Thou bestower of happiness on thewhole world! All glory unto that current of divine bliss, which, brimming from the river of Thy holy stories, flows into the lake of my mind through the canals of the intellect, subduing the dust of sins and cooling the heat of misery born of wanderings in transmigratory cycles.

Verse 2, *Shivanandalahari*, from *Sivanandalahari of Sri Sankaracarya* by Swami Tapasyananda

The *Shivanandalahari*, a hymn of 100 verses, is attributed by tradition, as are also many others in the same genre, to Adi Shankaracharya. Complete in itself, the text enchants with the simplicity of tone and fervour, fulfilling most needs of bhakti, a prerequisite for all texts coming within this rubric. Amid its repertoire, via the myths it refers to and the epithets that are utilized, one gets an insight into the particular nature of Shiva, popular at a point of time, with a certain section of society.

While the reader does not get a detailed account of Shiva's physical beauty, the joy and bliss to the devotees comes to those who read it, it is said, by listening to the stories of Shiva. In terms of his description, the hymn does not hold back, describing him as majestic, three-eyed and luminous with matted crests and adorned with the crescent Moon. Quivering serpents around his neck and blue-throated, he sits on a humped bull, sporting a doe in one hand, a battleaxe in the second and, with the third, he embraces the Goddess Uma, another name of Parvati.

The devotee's beloved

The important factor of bhakti is its power to bind the human and the divine, not in bonds of duty or domination, but in a relationship of love and protection. The devotee goes into the sacred world of Shiva's daily travails and hopes to alleviate some by suggesting alternatives. The anxious devotee desires to look out for the wellbeing of Shiva's tender feet, soothe him, and perhaps even provide a better vehicle.

The form of bhakti illustrated in this poem is unique and rich in figures of speech, metaphors, and vivid imagery. It demonstrates that bhakti is not opposed to Advaita, but can be its most intimate expression. Shiva is both the object of love and the self to be realized.

THE NATHAS

The Nathas are an important strand of Indian mysticism, known for synthesizing Shaivism, Tantra, Yoga, and Advaita Vedanta. Rooted in the worship of Shiva, the Natha path emphasizes inner transformation as the means to ultimate liberation.

In northern India, during the 2nd millennium CE, an esoteric movement emerged as part of Hindu revivalism – the Natha Sampradaya. Its followers, who call themselves Shiva *gotra*, or originating from Shiva, revere Shiva as Adi Natha, the first teacher and supreme master.

The sect drew a wide range of sub-sects. Scholar of religion DA Pai, in *Religious Sects in Ancient India (Ancient & Medieval)*, mentions various kind of Nathas who take on severe austerities: the Akasmukhis, who keep their faces turned skywards; the Urdhvabahoos, who hold one or both arms aloft for years; the Nakhis, who allow their nails to grow until they pierce the skin; and the Brahmacharis, who renounce the world to live as celibates. Yet, the most well-known are the Natha Yogis, specialists in yogic disciplines which they believe grant them superhuman powers.

Prominent figures

Legends of these powers abound in textual sources such as *Hatha Yoga Pradipika*, with Matsyendranatha, the founder of the Natha tradition, and his foremost disciple, Gorakhnath, at the centre of many accounts. Matsyendranatha was born in Bengal, and some scholars suggest that Gorakhnath too hailed from eastern Bengal. Together, their teachings and miracles spread the fame of the Natha path across India.

◁ **A 19th-century painting** of a yogi practising Hatha Yoga by a lotus pond.

Gorakhnath, who likely lived in Uttar Pradesh's Gorakhpur sometime between the 11th and 14th centuries, became one of the most influential Natha masters. He is credited with founding the Shaiva sect of Kanphata Yogis, or "split-eared yogis", who wear large earrings inserted into slits cut in the hollows of their ears. Gorakhnath's teachings emphasized yoga, ethical living, and inner transformation. He is associated with important yogic texts, such as the *Siddha Siddhanta Paddhati*, which explores consciousness and liberation, and the *Goraksha Shataka*, which records Natha rituals and practices – yogic postures, breathing techniques, and methods to awaken the chakras, or mystical energy centres, and raise the Kundalini, or the latent energy at the base of the spine. The Nathas believe these practices bestow not only spiritual realization but also mystical powers. Because of his detailed teachings on asanas, Gorakhnath is often regarded as the founder of a distinct branch of yoga, the Hatha Yoga, which emphasizes physical postures and breath control as the foundation for higher spiritual practice.

Far and wide

Since both Matsyendranatha and Gorakhnath were associated with Bengal, the Natha gurus greatly influenced the religious life of medieval Bengal, and their cult naturally found expression in Bengali literature, as noted by scholar of religion Kalyani Mallik in *Siddha-Siddhanta-Paddhati and Other Works of Natha Yogis*. By the 15th century, the tradition had spread far beyond Bengal and northern India. In the Telugu-speaking region of Srisailam in South India, the Nathas emerged as influential teachers and wonder-working yogis. Both textual and archaeological evidence indicate that Nath gurus gained popularity among royal families as well as the common people. Regional Nath *parampara*, or traditions, took root here, blending Shaiva, Tantric, and Hatha Yoga practices with the Advaita Vedanta of the early Shaiva schools.

The Natha philosophy

Philosophically, the Natha tradition rests on Advaita Vedanta, the non-dualistic doctrine that holds the individual soul as one with ultimate reality. Yet the Nathas take this further: their goal is not merely enlightenment but complete dissolution — merging into Shiva, the source itself. They aspire to the state of the Avadhuta, where pleasure and pain, virtue and vice, friend and foe no longer hold sway, and fragrant sandal paste and ordinary mud hold the same value. In this way, the tradition offers a spiritual refuge — a royal road to liberation.

Body as a vehicle

The Nathas pursue liberation through inner transformation. Central to this pursuit is the human body. The Nathas see it as a sacred microcosm of the universe. Rather than rejecting it, they use the body as a vehicle for liberation through yogic and alchemical transformation. For this, the guidance of a realized guru is essential. The guru is revered as Shiva incarnate, leading the disciple beyond ego and illusion. The teachings blend yogic discipline, Tantric insight, and Shaiva philosophy, all directed towards total liberation. They are passed on through direct transmission, often in secret or symbolic form. Under the guru's guidance, disciples undertake heterodox and mystical rituals that challenge social conventions in order to transcend duality. These practices involve mantra, yantra, and ritual alchemy, intended to dissolve mental conditioning and awaken deeper truths.

Over time, however, the Natha cult declined in prominence, surviving largely as a small, esoteric community of practitioners.

▷ **This 19th-century watercolour from Mandi, Himachal Pradesh**, depicts a Natha Yogi seated in Padma Asana, or lotus posture, upon a lotus pedestal. His large circular earrings identify him as a Kanphata Yogi of the Natha order. Along the central axis of his body are shown the seven chakras of the body.

TRANSCENDING THE MIND

An important non-dualistic tradition within Shaivism is Kashmir Shaivism, which emphasizes realizing the unity of the self with Shiva through meditation, contemplation, and mindful awareness in daily life. One of its most celebrated proponents was the 10th-century philosopher Abhinavagupta.

From the second half of the 9th century CE, Tantric Shaivism in Kashmir, the northernmost mountain state of India, advanced in various forms to the frontline of Brahmanical thinking. It was a profound, philosophically rich school, a non-dualistic, or Advaita, the tradition within Shaivism that taught the oneness of the Atman, or the individual self, and the universal consciousness, or Shiva. It was mystical, deep, introspective, and radically inclusive of all divine experience. There was no separation between the individual and the divine.

While all Shaiva traditions revere Shiva as the supreme being, Kashmir Shaivism brought a uniqueness to the narrative. Unlike some other paths that emphasize renunciation, Kashmir Shaivism embraced the world as a manifestation of divine consciousness, seeing everyday life as a valid arena for spiritual awakening.

Within the self

The intellectual side of Shaivism, as represented in Kashmir Shaivism, is also known as the Trika system, notes scholar JL Brockington. It does not stress on the need for devotional worship of Shiva, but sees the relationship of Shiva and *jeeva*, or soul, as one. The word *trika* means "triad", referring to Shiva, the absolute; Shakti the divine energy; and the individual soul. While Shakti is important across Shaivism, She is inseparable from Shiva – consciousness and energy are one in Kashmir Shaivism.

In fact, the interplay of the soul and the world is defined as Shiva's dynamic first impulse, arousing himself from his static samadhi in which there is no outer world to manifest. Through this *leela*, or divine play, of Shiva and Shakti – the cosmic dance of creation – he is able to recognize his own universal consciousness. Even though every being has this intrinsic knowledge of Shiva within themselves, it is overshadowed by the mind and its act of incessant thinking. So, to transcend the mind is to find Shiva within oneself.

The Trika tradition's philosophical branch is called Pratyabhijnashastra, or recognition school. The aim of life is to recognize one's identity with the absolute consciousness of Shiva. Liberation, or moksha, then comes through recognizing this truth. At its heart, this recognition is called *pratyabhijna*, the realization that the divine already exists within us.

The transcendence of mind in the Trika tradition can be achieved through *anavopaya*, or disciplining the ego, or through meditative practices and *saktopaya*, or the Kundalini path. In this yogic method, the body's energy centres are activated.

◁ **A carving from the 8th-century** Naranag Temple Complex in Ganderbal district of Jammu & Kashmir. The site, dedicated to Shiva and the Nagas, comprises a cluster of ancient temples.

TRANSCENDING THE MIND | 275

◁ **A mid-19th-century watercolour painting of a Shiva temple in Srinagar, Kashmir.** It features a lingam in the sanctum sanctorum, a statue of Nandi at the entrance, and a flag with Shiva's crescent Moon.

> Unlike some other paths that emphasize renunciation, Kashmir Shaivism embraced the world as a manifestation of divine consciousness, seeing everyday life as a valid arena for spiritual awakening.

Elevation of Shaivism

One of the major figures of Indian philosophy and religion, Abhinavagupta, was deeply rooted in the tradition of Kashmir Shaivism. Born around 950 CE, he did much to elevate Shaivism to a level of sophistication and comprehensive coherence, helping ensure its continued patronage by royal courts and exegesis by learned scholars.

One of his most outstanding works is the *Tantraloka*, a magnum opus and an encyclopaedic treatise on the practice of Trika. It synthesizes ritual, metaphysics, and yogic practice, including Tantra and Vedanta.

He taught that the universe is a manifestation of one supreme consciousness, Shiva. There is no separation between the individual self and the divine. Reality is dynamic, pulsating with divine energy called *spanda*. This vibration is the creative movement of consciousness itself.

In another of his treatises, *Paramarthasara*, he wrote: "Whoever walks the path of Bhairava with pure desire – be they Brahmin or sweeper – becomes one with the Divine." His name, Abhinavagupta, was a title given by his guru, meaning "one who is ever-vigilant and authoritative". Considered by many an incarnation of Bhairava, the fierce form of Shiva, Abhinavagupta emphasized that spiritual realization is not limited by caste, gender, or lifestyle – a radical idea for his time.

Nestled among the snow-capped peaks of Gulmarg, Jammu and Kashmir, the tranquil Mohineshwar Shivalaya temple serves as a sacred guardian of the Himalayas. For Shaivites, it is a potent emblem of heavenly presence and inner quiet, where earth and sky intersect in spiritual harmony. Surrounded by nature's splendour, devotees worship Shiva here uniting with his essence as the cosmic yogi and immortal custodian of the Himalayan world.

▷ **A popular representation** of the mystic poet Lal Ded as seen in what seems to be a hand-written booklet from Kashmir, publisher and artist unknown.

LAL DED

MYSTIC OF KASHMIR

I hacked my way through six forests
until the moon woke up inside me.
The sky's breath sang through me,
dried up my body's substance.
I roasted my heart in passions's fire
and found Shankara!

Shiva lives in many places.
He doesn't know Hindu from Muslim.
The Self that lives in you and others:
that's Shiva. Get the measure of Shiva.

I, Lalla: The Poems of Lal Ded by Ranjit Hoskote

She is Ma Lalla, sometimes, Lalleshwari, Lalla, Lal Arifa, Lalla Yogeshwari, the 14th-century Shaiva mystic and poetess whose legacy burns bright in the spiritual heritage of Kashmir. A devoted follower of Shiva, her deeply personal, soul-stirring verses transcended religious boundaries. Her poetry, rich with insight and raw spiritual intensity, echoed themes of bhakti or devotion, and mystical union, resonating not only with Hindu thought but also deeply aligned with Sufi ideals.

Spiritual journey

Born in the 14th century, the family priest had a big influence on young Lal Ded. Her family had her married by the age of 12, as was the tradition then, into a home that mistreated and neglected her. But, amid hardship, she nurtured an inner detachment and quiet strength. At 26, she left behind domestic life to pursue a spiritual path under her guru, Siddha Srikanth.

In doing so, she defied social norms, renounced material life, and became a mystic, wandering the forests and mountains of the region, often naked, sometimes in rags, chanting the verses that would become her Vakhs. These short, piercing poems, composed in the Kashmiri vernacular, laid the foundation of Kashmiri spiritual literature. They explored self-realization, impermanence, divine unity, and the futility of empty ritual. Lal Ded's poetry challenged caste, gender roles, and religious orthodoxy, and she became a radical voice of spiritual rebellion.

The voice of the people

Lal Ded's verses, known as the Lala Vakhs, were first passed down orally before being written down – short, piercing poems in everyday Kashmiri that distilled profound spiritual truths. Among the earliest works in the Kashmiri language, they are still sung and revered today. Her genius lay in translating the esoteric teachings of Shaiva philosophy, once limited to Sanskrit scholars, into a language the common people could understand and feel.

Though a devotee of Shiva, her vision was expansive. Her verses reveal a reverence for the divine in all forms and a belief that inner awakening, not ritual, is the true path to God. She famously declared: "Temple and image, the two that you have fashioned, are no better than stone."

For nearly 700 years, her legacy has crossed religious boundaries. Revered by both Hindus and Muslims, including the Sufi saint Nuruddin Rishi, Lal Ded is seen as a bridge between Shaivism and Sufism. Her poetry, both fierce and tender, continues to inspire seekers across generations. Affectionately called "Mother Lalla", she remains a symbol of spiritual courage, universal truth, and timeless wisdom.

Her work has inspired poets across cultures and centuries, including figures like Rumi and Jane Hirshfield, and continues to resonate in contemporary spiritual literature. Scholars and translators such as Ranjit Hoskote, Coleman Barks, and Richard Temple have brought her verses to the wider world, revealing the timeless beauty and philosophical depth of her Vakhs.

In Lal Ded's poetry, we find a living wisdom – earthy and ecstatic, stripped of dogma, and illuminated by the fire of inner truth.

THE ESOTERIC SECTS

Shaivism has evolved through diverse esoteric sects, each pursuing unique paths to spiritual insight and liberation. From the ascetic rigour of the Pashupatas to the radical Tantra of the Kapalikas and the scholarly discipline of the Kalamukhas, these sects reflect the rich complexity of Shaivism.

Shiva is often worshipped through esoteric rituals and practices known only to initiated devotees. The Pashupatas, who emerged in Gujarat, Rajasthan, and Madhya Pradesh in the c. 2nd century, were possibly the earliest and one of the most influential of the esoteric sects dedicated to Shiva. Pashupata Shaivism in its early and ascetic forms is not Tantric in the same way as later Shaiva traditions, yet it is considered esoteric as it has symbolic practices such as hidden teachings and secret rituals. They remained popular until the 14th century, by which time the sect had spread even to South India.

The etymology and theology of the Pashupatas reflect the perennial conundrum of existence. In Hindu philosophy, the soul is characterized as a *pashu*, or creature, and life is considered a form of bondage, likened to a *maya jaal*, or veil of illusions, which gives rise to *avidya*, or nescience. This veil obscures the numinous absolute from the individual, whose soul, the *pashu*, is tied by *pasha* – the noose or fetter used to capture an animal – and ensnared in the phenomenal world. The ultimate aim, at life's end, is moksha, or liberation – the loosening and release of the knots, webs, and snares that fetter all of creation. According to Pashupata doctrine, this is possible only through Shiva as Pashupati, the destroyer of *avidya*.

The Pashupata path

To attain moksha, the Pashupatas seek to reduce sins by following certain *vidhis*, or rules of conduct, which often involve inviting public censure. According to the sect's literature, a Pashupata novice progresses through several stages of salvation. In the first stage, he bathes and applies the ashes of funeral pyres three times daily, and performs acts of worship in the temple: laughing, dancing, and singing the praises of Shiva; uttering the sound "*huduk*" while curling the tongue; lowing like oxen and roaring like bulls; making prostrations and circumambulations; and repeating Shiva's names as if in a continuous incantation.

At a higher stage of spiritual proficiency, he abandons the sectarian marks and wanders alone, deliberately provoking the censure of ordinary people. He snorts, trembles as if afflicted by disease, makes amorous gestures towards women, displays moronic behaviour, and speaks nonsensically. In the subsequent stages, meditation gradually comes to the fore, and such eccentricities are abandoned.

The Pashupatas deliberately court dishonour to shock the public and draw attention. They simulate anti social actions so that people slander or mistreat them. By doing this, the Pashupata takes on others' bad karma while passing his good karma to them. This is a highly original and active reinterpretation of the usual concept of karma transfer, which typically involves the inadvertent accumulation of bad karma or the unintentional sharing of good karma. Here, instead, the Pashupata deliberately takes upon himself the burden of bad karma. In reality, the Pashupatas are perfectly sober and chaste, merely miming drunkenness. Today, they survive in limited and localized forms.

Kapalikas

In the 6th century, out of the Pashupata fold evolved the Kapalikas, a Tantric extremist sect that had spread across the Deccan by the 8th century. Their name derives from the Sanskrit word *kapala*, meaning "skull", and they are known as "skull-bearers". As TA Gopinatha Rao notes in his second volume of *Elements of Hindu Iconography*, the form of Shiva the Kapalikas venerate as his

△ **A 17th-century watercolour by the Mughal artist Payag** depicts the Tantric forms of Shiva and Shakti as Bhairava and Bhairavi within a cremation ground – a common motif in Tantric imagery. Bhairavi, crimson in hue, wears a skirt of skulls and bears spearheads as horns as she sits upon a decomposing corpse. Bhairava, his body smeared with ash, appears beside her in the guise of a devotee. The abundance of skull imagery reflects their association with the Kapalikas.

purnarupa, or complete form, is Bhairava, the lord of destruction and fear. They also worship him as Kapalin, the bearer of skulls.

Radical practices

The Kapalikas do not differ greatly from their parent sect in doctrine, for, like the Pashupatas, they practice ritualistic imitation of Shiva's mythical exploits and seek mystical identification with the great god as a path to attaining superhuman powers, or *siddhis*. Where they diverge is in their religious practices, which closely resembles those of Shaktism, particularly in their association with human sacrifice and ritual sexual intercourse, the latter performed in imitation of the eternal union of Shiva and Shakti.

Their practices are intended to transcend social norms and challenge the boundaries between life and death, purity and impurity. The Kapalikas extend the outlandish and antisocial tendencies of the Pashupatas to further extremes. The use of inebriating substances and sexual intercourse as means

282 | SHIVA, THE DEITY

to spiritual realization is part of Kapalika ritual. If the reports of their opponents are to be believed – since no Kapalika texts survive – they engage in transgressive rituals that include eating repulsive foods, consuming meat and alcohol, engaging in sexual rites, frequenting cremation grounds, smearing themselves with the ashes of corpses, adorning themselves with ornaments of human bone, wandering naked, and drinking from *kapalas* used as begging bowls. Their ceremonies are often described as macabre and orgiastic, and may even have involved symbolic human sacrifice, though historical evidence for the latter remains debated.

According to the Dutch Indologist J Gonda, the Kapalikas believe that such practices could yield almost limitless yogic powers, granting the *sadhaka*, or spiritual practitioner, a "yogic glance" – the ability to perceive in Shiva the essential principle of unity and purity underlying all creatures and their actions, even the most gruesome and repugnant.

Sanskritization of Tantric traditions

It seems likely that the Kapalikas systematized ancient fertility rites, linked to spirit and ancestor worship and prevalent among some of the primitive Indian tribes, into an early Tantric pattern of worship. Through their practices, many non-Aryan elements, particularly those rooted in female-oriented cults among the hill tribes of the Vindhyas and Himalayas, may have been absorbed and Sanskritized, even while condemned by Brahmanical orthodoxy. In fact, inscriptions found across the Indian subcontinent suggest that the Kapalikas were held in high esteem by several monarchs and sections of the high-caste elite in

◁ **A Tantric practitioner in Varanasi, Uttar Pradesh**, performs rituals using skulls. This practice was originally associated only with the Kapalikas, but became more common as boundaries between esoteric sects became blurred over time.

the early medieval period, who probably regarded them as authoritative Tantric initiates worthy of respect.

Kalamukhas

Between the 9th and 13th centuries, another Shaiva sect – an offshoot of the Pashupata sect that also shared reverence for Lakulisha (*See pp290–93*) – flourished in the Deccan Plateau, particularly in Karnataka and Andhra Pradesh. These were the Kalamukhas, literally "black-faced" or "death-faced", who, like their predecessors, were associated with cremation grounds and esoteric rituals. Most of what is known about them comes from inscriptions and temple records, often authored by their opponents. Their devotion centered on Bhairava and his consort Chandika.

Though frequently mentioned alongside the Kapalikas, the Kalamukhas have distinct practices and philosophies. Their rites are influenced by Agamic texts – theological treatises and practice manuals of divine worship – yet they also respect the Vedas and are well-versed in Nyaya and Vaisheshika philosophies, which are schools of thought focusing on logic and metaphysics. Unlike the more extreme Kapalikas, the Kalamukhas emphasize asceticism, ritual purity, and social reform. The Kalamukhas believe that both worldly happiness and spiritual liberation could be attained through intense and unconventional rituals, such as eating from a human skull or smearing themselves with the ashes of the dead. They carry a club as a ritual object and also worship Shiva in unusual forms, including one where he is seated in a pot of wine. These practices are likely symbolic, representing detachment from worldly norms and a confrontation with morality and impurity.

The Kalamukhas were among the first professional monks in India, establishing monasteries and temple colleges. Their centres included Balligavi, Chitradurga, Nanjangud, and Vijayawada. According to Sanskritist JL Brockington in *The Sacred Thread*, their sudden decline in the 13th century was likely connected to the rise of the Lingayat movement (*See pp262–63*), which emphasized more egalitarian and socially integrated forms of Shaivism.

THE AGHORIS

ASCETICS OF THE DEAD

They are the holy men of the dead, living on the edge of life and death. They command attention in their presence – unabashedly nude, ash-besmeared, and confident in their spiritual powers. Once in a while, on occasions such as the Kumbh Mela, they emerge in large numbers, though they are rarely seen otherwise, retreating soon after into years of hibernation. They embody the impermanence of life, the illusion of duality, and the power of spiritual detachment. Above all, they aspire to become one with Shiva.

The Aghoris belong to a monastic order of ascetic Shaivite sadhus. They are among the most enigmatic and radical Shaiva sects, known for their extreme practices. Traditionally, the Aghoris were followers of Dattatreya, an incarnation of the trinity of Brahma, Vishnu, and Shiva. Today, it appears that over the years, all the extreme Shaiva sects gradually merged and evolved into what is now known as the Aghori tradition.

Origins
The origins and history of the Aghoris are shrouded in mystery. Even so, their beginnings can be traced. Baba Keenaram, a Shaivite ascetic, founded the sect in Uttar Pradesh. Miraculous signs marked his birth and he lived for 150 years, passing away in the second half of the 18th century. He authored key texts such as *Viveksara* and *Ramgeeta*, and devotees consider him an incarnation of Shiva.

The Aghoris trace their roots to the ancient non-Puranic Kapalikas and Kalamukha, which emerged between the 7th and 8th centuries. These sects are known for radical Tantric practices, including the worship of fierce deities, use of intoxicants, and performance of sacrificial rites. In a way, the Aghoris are the sole surviving sect of the Kapalika tradition.

Their beliefs
The Aghoris follow a monistic philosophy, believing that everything in the universe is one and emanates from Brahman, the ultimate reality. They hold that every person's soul is Shiva – the supreme manifestation of Brahman – but is veiled by eight major bonds that cause ignorance and suffering. These bonds are sensual pleasure, anger, greed, obsession, fear, hatred, pride, and discrimination. Aghoris seek to break free from these bonds and attain liberation, by realizing their identity with Shiva.

Their practices
Rooted in Tantric traditions, Aghoris, similar to their Shaivite predecessors, engage in rituals considered contradictory to orthodox Hinduism. They pursue spiritual liberation by embracing what society typically rejects – death, impurity, and taboo. They believe liberation comes from transcending dualities such as purity versus impurity. By deliberately engaging with the impure, the polluted, and the abhorrent, they affirm that all is a manifestation of Shiva and that nothing is inherently evil or sinful. Through these practices, they aim to attain altered states of consciousness and perceive the illusory nature of conventional categories.

Aghoris also seek to transcend the duality of life and death by associating with the dead and the dying. They often live near cremation grounds, meditate on corpses, smear their bodies with ashes from funeral pyres, and use *kapalas*, or human skulls, as bowls and ritual objects, symbolizing detachment from the physical world. Some consume alcohol or meat, not out of depravity, but to break societal conditioning and confront mortality. Their practices are secret, passed down from guru to disciple, and can be mentally and spiritually dangerous without proper guidance.

▷ **Cultural markers are key to identifying** those who follow the Aghori belief system, such as human skulls and ash-smeared bodies.

Naga Sadhus are ascetics devoted primarily to the worship of Shiva. At the Kumbh Mela, they become the focal point of attention, captivating onlookers with their distinctive appearance – ash-smeared bodies, matted hair, and minimal clothing – evoking Shiva as the ultimate yogi.

FROM ASHES TO ASHES

Shiva is often depicted smeared with ash, symbolizing his dominion over death and the fleeting nature of the material world. In this ash-covered form, he embodies both renunciation and the power of transformation, reminding devotees that all physical forms ultimately return to dust.

A multilayered symbol, ash can be beyond human experience. It is the substance of things that are completely burnt, when matter has ceased to exist, and a symbol of the impermanence of life. It is the final state from which the spirit attains freedom. In a metaphorical and spiritual sense, it indicates the transience of beings and the permanence of the supreme – Shiva – who is always smeared with ash.

Ashes are the shining remains of what has been consumed. They are the solid essence of the combustion of fluid oblation of purificatory fire, and the supreme manifestation of primal matter, writes American Indologist David Gordon White. To wear Shiva's ashes is to clothe oneself with his all-encompassing mystery.

The myth behind the fire

It is believed that Shiva first took to wearing ash following his incineration of Kama, who Shiva reduced to ashes by a mere glance from his third eye (See pp80–81). Kama was punished because he was trying to enflame Shiva with passion for Parvati while the god was in severe penance. This proves that the fires of yoga, or *yoga agni*, are greater than those of burning erotic passion, or *kama agni*. Another theory is that Shiva smeared his body with Sati's ashes after she immolated herself at her father, Daksha's yagna (See pp148–49).

Shiva destroys the universe with fire with a glance from his third eye at the end of each era and then purifies it by sprinkling it with ashes. Ashes are in step with his function of universal destroyer. He is fabled to have burnt the universe, Brahma, and Vishnu, and then rubbed the ashes over his body.

Ritual offerings

Bhasma literally means "that which has been reduced to ash" and is used to describe the ash after it has been offered to a deity. In India, some ascetics, such as the Aghoris (See pp284–85), use *khak*, or cremation ash, as *bhasma*, a post-ritual purification that symbolizes transcendence of fear and ego. *Bhasma* can be used internally or externally.

Khak or *vibhuti* also refers to the ashes from the sacred fires that the sadhus bathe with everyday. This is symbolic of ascetic liminality. A householder applies *vibhuti* on his forehead during worship. *Vibhuti* is made from burning dried wood, cow dung, and other sacred materials in a consecrated fire, or *homa*. The ash that is collected after the Ayush Homan, a ritual to invoke the god of life, contains 54 herbal ingredients.

Applying ash signifies the annihilation of desire, and the overcoming of opposition. It reunites fire and *soma*, or a sacred drink, thus symbolizing the union of male and female, too.

Its application is also said to regulate the seven chakras in the body, which is the basis for good health. The religious text, *Padma Purana*, glorifies *bhasma* as the essence of three *gunas*, or attributes: *sattva*, or purity; *rajas*, or passion; and *tamas*, or inertia. These are personified by Brahma, Vishu, and Shiva. It is stated in the *Padma*

> To wear Shiva's ashes is to clothe oneself with his all-encompassing mystery.

Purana that *bhasma* purifies the incantations and, when applied to different parts of the body, is capable of destroying sins committed by the different organs.

The final wisdom
Ash also conveys a sense of death and dissolution of the material world. Shiva wears ash to remind us of the impermanence of life. We are all here in this world for a short span of time; this realization will help decrease worldly desires and increase compassion.

Shiva is also the lord of the cremation ground and he undertakes the task of imparting wisdom to the dying and dead. At the cremation ground, he bends over the dead whispering the Taraka Mantra, where *taraka* means "boat", as this mantra is believed to ferry one across the river of birth and death to the far shore.

Once the body is cremated, ashes become indistinguishable and identical. With caste, colour, name, and form unknown, there is unity among differences and so, Shiva is the destroyer, as he dissolves diversities in the quest for absolute unity. Everything can fuse and then blend. Shiva neither loves nor hates any part of his creation. This is the essence of all life.

△ **This early 19th-century painting from Gujarat** depicts Indrani, Indra's wife, carrying the infant Rishabhanatha on Indra's elephant mount in a grand procession to Mount Meru for his lustration rites, while Apsaras dance and blow horns. According to mythology, after Marudevi gave birth to Rishabhanatha, Indra and Indrani temporarily took the baby to perform the ceremonial rites, returning him afterwards to his mother.

PARALLEL TRADITIONS

It is not uncommon to find different religions and traditions existing side by side, shaping and influencing one another. In this exchange, the Shaiva expression shares intriguing parallels with both Buddhism and Jainism. Some of these connections are subtle, while others are strikingly overt.

Across the interactions of Shaivism with Buddhism and Jainism, two figures stand out: Rishabha, the first Jain Tirthankara and founder of Jainism, and Lakulisha, the Shaivite revivalist of the Pashupata sect. Rishabha reflects ascetic ideals closely aligned with Shiva, while Lakulisha's image and teachings often invite comparison with Buddha.

> Rishabha is frequently depicted with a bull as his emblem, a natural parallel to Shiva, whose mount is Nandi, the bull.

Rishabha

The *Shiva Purana* mentions Rishabha as an incarnation of Mount Kailasha, while the *Linga Purana* esteems him as one of Shiva's 28 avatars. In Vedic literature, the term "*rishabha*" signifies the bull and is an epithet for Rudra, a fierce form of Shiva. Rishabha is frequently depicted with a bull as his emblem, a natural parallel to Shiva, whose mount is Nandi, the bull. Religious studies experts suggest that early Rishabha traditions may have influenced Shiva worship. The similarities are evident: both are ascetic figures immersed in meditation and detachment from worldly affairs. It is not only Hindu texts but also Jain scriptures that invoke Rishabha as Rudra or Shiva, suggesting a shared spiritual lineage that bridges sectarian boundaries.

Lakulisha

If there is any entity within the Shaiva order who bears clear historicity, it is Lakulisha. He lived around the 1st–2nd century CE and his followers consider him the 28th and last incarnation of Shiva. A saint and teacher, Lakulisha revived and systematized the ancient Pashupata sect. By the early medieval period, he was deified and worshipped as a cultic form of Shiva, with sculptural evidence from the 6th century CE attesting to his prominence.

Early images of Lakulisha, particularly from Madhya Pradesh and Gujarat, often portray him as ithyphallic – an iconographic choice not of eroticism, but of ascetic power. The erect phallus symbolized brahmacharya and seminal retention, representing control over the senses and complete carnal renunciation.

Later depictions emphasize Lakulisha's connection with Shiva more explicitly. Two additional arms were added, enabling him to hold Shiva's attributes such as a rosary and a trident, along with mudras signifying his role as a teacher. In one image, he is shown seated on an inverted lotus framed by two pilasters. His right hand holds a *bija puraka*, or citron fruit, and a *chatradanda*, a staff associated with Shaivism, while his left hand carries a club and a bound Vedic manuscript. His hair is carefully locked, and his simple ornaments underline his ascetic character.

Association with Buddha and Mahavira

The early images of Lakulisha are mostly two-armed, unlike other divinities in the same temples who typically bear at least four arms. Indian archaeologist and epigraphist DR Bhandarkar, the first to draw attention to the Puranic data on Lakulisha, in his article "An Eklingji Stone Inscription and the Origin and History of the Lakulisa Sect", interpreted this as evidence of Lakulisha's historical reality. Before being elevated into a divine figure, he was remembered as a historical personality, much like Buddha or Mahavira.

An early image from Bilaspur in Chhattisgarh depicts Lakulisha not with a prominent phallic symbol, but as a serene ascetic, his hairstyle reminiscent of both the Buddha and Mahavira. Jain and Buddhist iconography echoes through Lakulisha's forms, emphasizing shared ideals of renunciation. Puranic literature describes Lakulisha as a lifelong brahmacharin, while sculptors often placed him in the Dharmachakra Mudra, a timeless symbol of Buddha's teachings, evoking his role as a preacher of dharma, in this case, Shiva-dharma. As Indian historian JN Banerjea observed in *The Development of Hindu Iconography*, one such Lakulisha image even mirrors depictions of Buddha performing the Great Miracle at Shravasti, a sacred ancient site where Buddha displayed his spiritual supremacy.

△ **A stone sculpture** depicting an ithyphallic form of Lakulisha

Conflict

Lakulisha's relationship with Jainism and Buddhism also carried an element of competition and opposition. As Indian scholar of philosophy RN Nandi notes in *Social Roots of Religion in Ancient India*, Lakulisha was positioned as a counter to rival Jain and Buddhist preachers, particularly in peninsular India. Conflicts between his sect and these traditions surface repeatedly in sectarian literature, epigraphs, and sculpture of the early medieval period.

The imagery of Lakulisha reflects this dynamic. In Lakulisha's iconography, the club is his most distinctive attribute. His name means "the holder of *laguda*, or club". It is an offensive weapon, and its association with a religious teacher such as Lakulisha seems intended as a symbolic threat to rival sects. In South India, the chief opponents of the Shaiva order was Jainism. Unlike northern depictions, where the club is shown loosely resting on his arm to suggest inaction, South Indian sculptures portray Lakulisha gripping it firmly. This posture conveys militant readiness, reflecting the need to confront the challenges posed by Jain and Buddhist traditions. In regions where Shaivism faced little opposition, Lakulisha is typically represented in a more pacific attitude.

Pashupata–Lakulisha doctrine

Beyond this polemical role, however, Lakulisha's lasting contribution lay in the doctrinal foundations he gave to the Pashupata school of Shaivism. The Lakulisha-Pashupata system was the first Shaiva school to assume a distinct denominational form. Later branches of Shaivism would develop and refine its doctrines, but Lakulisha's sect endured in some form until the 15th century.

Texts such as the *Pashupatasutra* and *Ganakarika* outline its central tenets: three realities – *pashu*, or the individual soul; *pati*, the lord; and *pasha*, the world – as separate and distinct. The path to enlightenment has five stages of practice: the first two outwards, the next three inwards, involving meditative discipline. Yet, despite rigorous effort, salvation rests on the grace of God.

SPIRITUAL POWER, NOT SEXUAL ENERGY

According to the Pashupata–Lakulisha school of thought, the path of asceticism does not deny sexual urges but transforms this energy, redirecting it away from procreation and pleasure toward wisdom, freedom, and bliss. The penile erection symbolizes the principle of *urdhva retas*, the upward ascent of vital energies or fluids. Mastery over seminal fluid is believed to bring mastery over all passions, culminating in desirelessness through ascetic practice and yogic sadhana, and ultimately leading to supreme mystical cognition or samadhi. The upward-pointing phallus, signifies not only the retention of seed once "stirred" but also its upward movement – through the spinal cord to the brain – where it is transformed into creative substance and absorbed as the thought of awakening. As such, the symbol represents the ascent and transmutation of vital sexual energy into mental power, a channeling of the procreative into the creative faculty. Thus, the pictorial rendering of the ascent of vital energy should not be mistaken for fertility or sexuality.

▷ **A 7th-century stone sculpture from Bhubaneshwar,** Odisha, depicts the two-armed Lakulisha seated in a yogic posture on an inverted lotus, holding his characteristic weapon, the laguda. As is typical of Odia depictions, he is flanked by two of his four principal disciples, the earliest propagators of the Pashupata doctrine. Beneath his seat are two ascetics – one holding a skull-topped staff, the other a trident.

PARALLEL TRADITIONS | 293

The Lakulisha–Pashupata system was the first Shaiva school to assume a distinct denominational form. Later branches of Shaivism would develop and refine its doctrines . . .

VANKESHVARA

THE MOST SPECTACULAR IMAGE OF A GOD EVER

Eight feet tall, it stands at the entrance of the 6th-century Devarani Temple in Tala in Chhattisgarh's Bilaspur district, a statue with curious, distinctive features. Made of stone, it has five tiers of large round faces with a range of intricate and detailed animals – from frogs and crocodiles to lizards and crabs – carved across the body. A tortoise head takes the place of an erect penis, and a snake curls around the waist like a belt.

The figure features five distinct tiers of faces: a single head at the top; two bald, moustachioed faces on the chest; a large, round, bald face forming the belly; four bald, grinning faces on the thighs; and two animal heads on the knees.

Historian and Indologist Hans Bakker provides fascinating details about the image. This large male creature wears a turban, made of serpent coils. There are two snake hoods protruding over his shoulders on either side of the head. The ears have peacocks with fanned tails as ornaments. A lizard forms his nose while its hind legs become the brows. The eyes are like eggs or modelled on a frog who can open its eyes wide. The mouth is a crocodile. The moustache is a fish, the chin a crab, and the knees possibly lions. The arms, shaped like elephant trunks, emerge from the mouth of a gaping crocodile. The fingernails are adorned with the mouth of a snake. A tortoise head forms the erect penis and a snake forms a belt over his waist.

A matter of identity

There are many speculations regarding its identity, but the key could lie in the unusual epithet found in the Kalachuri dynasty inscriptions, Vankeshvara. This was probably a name for Shiva in the classical dialect of Prakrit. Vankeshvara means "the lord of vagabonds", derived from the word *vanka*, or wandering. Vankeshvara could imply Shiva who is accompanied by an army of vagabonds. Prior to the advent of the Kalachuri dynasty of the 6th century, mostly aborigines inhabited this area. It is very likely that Vankeshvara was adopted from their pantheon. He was probably an aboriginal, a local deity believed to exercise influence. It seems that the Kalachuris adopted him as their tutelary god to prevent him from doing any harm to them.

This one of a kind statue could look like a Yaksha, or nature spirit, but with the *raudra*, or aggressive, expression on its face. Hence the name, Rudra-Shiva. It may also be inferred that Vankeshvara is Shiva, because, just as Shiva is known as Pashupatinath, or the lord of the animals, Vankeshvara too has animal figures sculpted on his body.

This sculpture is unusual, as such distinctly folk-style depictions are rare in stone. The multiple faces across the broad body are striking. Its form is hard to identify, though it most closely resembles Bhairava (See pp240–41) in a style typical of Dakshina Kosala, or perhaps represents Shiva as envisioned by an unorthodox sect.

Recent evidence proposes that this image could be a Gana or an attendant of Shiva, as described in the *Skanda Purana*. Bakker has tentatively proposed that this could perhaps be a composite Shaiva-Gana figure.

However, it is no coincidence that the statue was discovered in Tala, an epithet of Shiva according to the *Shivasahasranama* (See pp38–39). *Tala* means "the form of *patala*, or the netherworld"; a clear indication of its chthonic connection to this type of Shiva.

AMARNATH

A METAPHOR FOR SPIRITUAL ASCENT

First, he left Nandi, the bull, at Pahalgam. Then, he released the Moon from his hair at Chandanwari. He bid adieu to his snake on the banks of the Sheshnaga lake, and to his son Ganesha at Mahagunas Parvat, or Mahaganesh Mountain. And, at Panjtarni, he left behind the five elements: earth, water, air, fire and sky. Then, as a symbol of sacrificing the Earthly world, he performed the Tandava, his energetic divine dance.

It was only after giving up all his worldly attachments that Shiva entered the Amarnath Cave with only Parvati as his companion. There, he manifested into a lingam of ice and Parvati became the yoni, or the womb of creation.

Shiva chose this remote cave to narrate the *Amar Katha*, the secret of immortality, to Parvati, away from all living beings to preserve the sanctity of this divine disclosure. He left behind his companions and ornaments along the route, and today, each location in Jammu and Kashmir is a stop on the pilgrimage trail.

A shrine of ice

Nestled in the Liddar valley of the Himalayas in Kashmir, the Amarnath Cave Temple is one of the most sacred Hindu pilgrimage sites. The large cave with a natural ice formation in the shape of Shiva's lingam is considered *svayambhu*, or a natural lingam. The ice formation seems to grow and shrink with the lunar cycle, peaking during the Full Moon in the Shravan months of July and August, which is when devotees embark on the pilgrimage.

This phenomenon is seen as a metaphor for the cosmic rhythm reflecting Shiva's eternal presence. The journey itself – through rugged terrain, glaciers, and steep ascents – is considered a test of faith and endurance, symbolising the soul's quest for liberation. The cave is not just a physical destination – it's a symbolic womb of transformation. Shiva's narration of the *Amar Katha* is said to contain the essence of *moksha*, or liberation from the cycle of birth and death and so the pilgrimage itself becomes a metaphor for spiritual ascent, shedding worldly attachments as one climbs toward divine truth. The melting and re-forming of the ice lingam is seen as a cosmic rhythm – birth, dissolution, and renewal.

▷ *(clockwise from top)* **Pilgrims gather outside the sacred Amarnath Cave,** nestled 4419 metres (14,500 feet) high in the Himalayas, to worship the icy lingam symbolizing Shiva; **Pilgrims' camps dot the valley** below the legendary Zoji La Pass, a gateway on the challenging Amarnath Yatra route. This high-altitude road carries thousands of devotees each year through rugged Himalayan terrain toward the sacred Amarnath Cave; **The sacred ice Shiva lingam** stands in the heart of the Amarnath Cave, an awe-inspiring natural formation that draws thousands of pilgrims in a journey of devotion and faith.

MYSTICAL LEGENDS

COAL TO GOLD
According to popular belief, a shepherd named Buta Malik discovered the Amarnath cave in the 15th century. Buta Malik encountered a saint who gave him a bag full of coal. On returning home, he discovered that the coal had miraculously turned into gold. Overwhelmed with gratitude, he went back to thank the saint, but instead stumbled upon the Amarnath cave.

HOLY CAVE
Deep in a secluded cave, the Asura king Banasura attempted to disrupt Shiva's tranquil meditation. But Shiva, calm and powerful, defeated the raging Asura with a single glance. Banasura was impressed by Shiva's might and fled, leaving Shiva to bless the cave itself. Since that day, the cave has become sacred, a timeless haven of divine calm and strength.

CHRONICLES OF KASHMIR
Philosopher Adi Shankara is said to have gone to the site in the 9th century and the site is mentioned in the *Nilamatia Purana* and the *Rajatarangini*, the old chronicles of Kashmir. Sanskrit texts like the *Amarnath Mahatmya* mention the cave, suggesting its significance dates back many centuries.

Amidst snow-laden peaks and biting winds, Hindu devotees embark on the perilous journey to the sacred Amarnath Cave in Baltal, east of Srinagar. Carved by nature and revered as divine, the ice Shiva lingam within the cave symbolizes Shiva's eternal presence. This *yatra* or pilgrimage, fraught with danger and devotion, is more than a test of endurance – it is a deeply spiritual quest to encounter the divine presence in its most pure, untouched form.

LORD OF THE HERBS

Whether it is bel leaves from the most sacred among the pantheon of revered trees in Vedic dharma, or preparations from the hallucinogenic cannabis, or the flowers and fruits from the deadly dhatura plant, the offerings made to Shiva within the Shaiva tradition, are deeply rooted in folklore, ritual practice, and symbolic interpretation.

The offering of leaves and fruit, often during festivals such as Maha Shivaratri, when they are placed gently by the lingam, suggests Shiva's transcendence over worldly attachments and the extremes of existence. In fact, Shiva is also called Aushadhishvara or the lord of herbs and consciousness-changing drugs .

The three-leaf bel

It goes by many names: Bel, bael, bilva or wood apple and its trifoliate form symbolizes the trishula and everything threefold. To some it represents the three syllables of the sacred sound of Aum, or Shiva's three eyes, to others it means the three *gunas*, namely *sattva*, *rajas*, and *tamas*, or the threefold nature of the universe, the trinity of creation, sustenance and dissolution, that is Brahma, Vishnu, and Shiva. But, to offer it to Shiva means devotion, surrender and desire for spiritual growth.

A part of the citrus family, the tree is supposed to be Shiva's favourite and is frequently planted next to Shaivite shrines. In fact, one of Shiva's many names is Bilvadandin, or carrier of the wood apple. Besides using the leaves to worship the god, devotees honour the tree itself by offering it rice and lighting lamps by its trunk.

△ **At a quiet ghat in Varanasi,** a Shiva lingam and the vigilant Nandi receive tender offerings – marigolds, incense, and water – symbols of devotion flowing as endlessly as the Ganga beside them. In this sacred moment, Shiva is honoured not in grandeur, but in the simple, eternal rhythm of daily worship.

Legend has it that Shiva received the bel leaf after he consumed the poison Halahala that emerged during the churning of the cosmic ocean *(See pp 124–25)*. Another story from the *Skanda Purana* tells of how the tree emerged in Bihar's Mandrachal mountain after sweat from Parvati's forehead dropped to the ground. It is believed that Parvati resides in the tree and each part of the tree embodies her divine forms, from the roots to the fruit. Offering one Bilva leaf equals offering a thousand lotus flowers to Shiva.

Altering perceptions

While there is no direct reference in the Puranas to Shiva consuming hallucinogens in the modern pharmacological sense, his association with substances like bhang and dhatura, is deeply rooted in folklore in Shaivite traditions.

In Sanskrit, *dhat*, from dhatura, means "gift". According to the *Vamana Purana*, the dhatura flower emerged from Shiva's chest, symbolizing its divine and transformative nature. Though a highly toxic hallucinogenic plant that can cause delirium, it is also known as Shivashekhara or Shiva's crown because Shiva is the master of poisons, the drinker of Halahala, the conqueror of death, or Mrityunjaya. Similarly, bhang, a preparation made with cannabis seeds, is often offered to the god during festivals. While not explicitly described as hallucinogens in the scriptural texts, these are psychoactive and have been linked to altered states of consciousness. Their use is symbolic of Shiva's transcendence over worldly attachments and his role as the lord of ascetics and yogis.

Rather than promoting substance use, these stories often serve as metaphors. Shiva's acceptance of toxic or intoxicating offerings symbolizes his ability to transform poison into nectar – just as he did when he drank the deadly Halahala to save the universe.

So, the Puranas do portray him as a deity who embraces and transcends the extremes of existence – including substances that alter perception. However, this is more about spiritual symbolism than pharmacological indulgence.

GATEWAYS TO THE GODS

While yatras are arduous journeys to sacred places for spiritual growth, the pilgrimage site is called a *tirtha*, which literally means a "crossing". Metaphorically, a *tirtha* is a divine crossroad, where the divine meets the mortal.

Some journeys are undertaken to pay obeisance, others are for penance, and many are long and difficult, a response to the *bulava*, a divine call. Across India, the devout undertake these yatras, literally meaning journeys or pilgrimages, to sacred places, for many reasons – to purify the self or seek blessings, to honour the departed and the ancestors, or to deepen one's connection with the divine. Sometimes, the arduous journey itself is considered an act of devotion, the physical and emotional challenges becoming a part of the worship and so, spiritually rewarding.

The places the pilgrims seek are *tirthas*, literally fords or crossings, and in the metaphorical sense mean spiritual crossings or a gateway, where the gods are close. These are spiritual gateways – where the divine and the earthly meet.

Tirthayatras, that is embarking on a yatra to visit a *tirtha*, have been a sacred tradition in many devout Hindu households and, as mythologist Devdutt Pattanaik rightly notes, these places can quite easily map the geography of India. Much like the Devi, or the Goddess, and Vishnu and their many avatars, Shiva too has his own set of prescribed *tirthayatras* – some deep in the mountains, others closer to towns and cities, but each bound to the larger Shiva mythology.

A place for worship

Among the most famous of all pilgrimages in India is the Char Dham Yatra, in the mountains of Uttarakhand, covering four places – Badrinath, Kedarnath, Gangotri, and Yamunotri. Of these, Kedarnath is linked to Shiva as one of his most famous temples, involving a high-altitude trek of 16 kilometres (10 miles). There is a similar trek to the Amarnath Cave in Jammu & Kashmir, which has a natural ice formation, believed to be in the shape of a lingam.

There is also a pilgrimage that takes the devotee through the seven holy cities or the Sapta Puri Yatra, a circuit for those seeking liberation from the eternal cycle of life and death. The cities within this are connected to Vishnu, Shiva, and the Devi, and include Varanasi, Haridwar, Dwarka, Ujjain, Kanchipuram, Mathura, and Ayodhya.

The Thiruvathira is a pilgrimage in the southern Indian states of Kerala and Tamil Nadu that takes place in December–January and marks Shiva's birthday and his cosmic dance. It is believed that Parvati performed penance to reunite with Shiva, and their reunion is celebrated as Thiruvathira. Shiva's son, Karttikeya or Murugan has his own yatra in Tamil Nadu, as does Ganesha, whose *tirtha* is known as Ashtavinayaka, or eight Ganeshas, across eight temples in the western state of Maharashtra.

A journey of devotion

One of the most popular yatras that the devotees of Shiva undertake is the Kanwar Yatra, where the bhaktas, known as Kanwariyas, carry water from the Ganga as offerings to their chosen Shiva temple. This typically takes place in the month of Shravan, from around mid to late July, and is dedicated to Shiva. Legend has it that Shiva cooled the burning poison in his throat with water from the Ganga. Devotees emulate this by carrying water from the Ganga to pour over Shiva lingams.

During the Kanwar Yatra, devotees walk barefoot to the Ganga and fetch water in a *ghada*, or pot, carrying it back to their local Shiva temples to pour over the lingam. The pots are balanced on a *kanwar*, or a beam with a basket hanging from each end, and is held on the shoulder. The *kanwar* can be suspended from poles or trees but it should not be placed on the ground until the temple is

△ **Yatras need not always be about journeying to a sacred site** – they can also honour the deity through a ceremonial procession. Here, devotees carry Lord Kedarnath from Ukhimath, the deity's winter seat, to Kedarnath, pausing at Guptkashi, Phata, and Gaurikund, before culminating in the grand opening of the Kedarnath Temple for pilgrims.

reached. The *kanwar* is elaborately decorated with colourful flags, strings and golden festoons. In Tamil Nadu, the *kanwar* is decorated with peacock feathers.

The Night of Shiva

One of biggest days to celebrate Shiva is Maha Shivaratri or the night of Shiva, which marks the night of the New Moon on the 14th day of Phalguna, which signifies the arrival of spring. Two myths are closely associated with this festival.

The first is connected to the night that Shiva and Parvati were married. The second is that this was the day Shiva manifested himself as a pillar of light. It is believed that Shiva is in a robust mood that night and will fulfil any wish as long as the devotee does not eat or drink anything and stays awake the whole night washing the lingam every three hours with milk, yoghurt, ghee, honey, and water, all the while chanting his mantra. Placing thorn apple, or *bilva*, leaves on the lingam also pleases Shiva. The *Skanda Purana* describes the beginning of the Shivaratri *vrata*, or fast, connecting it to the myth of a vicious man Chandu who often terrorized people.

One day, while hunting, night fell and, afraid that he would be a victim of wild animals, he climbed a *bilva* tree. Distressed by the cold and hunger, he passed the night in strict wakefulness. The night happened to be Maha Shivaratri. At the foot of this tree, the leaves of which are sacred to Shiva, there was a lingam. Chandu was so uncomfortably perched that his constant fidgeting made leaves fall on the lingam. This involuntary worship pleased Shiva and Chandu was cleansed of his sins. Keeping vigil and fasting through the night is believed to grant Shivatattva, the essence of Shiva.

THE MUSE DIVINE

Shiva is not just a deity, but a muse – offering endless inspiration through his many forms: the fierce destroyer, the meditative yogi, the loving consort, and the primal source of rhythm and creation.

Artists, playwrights, and dancers have long engaged with Shiva's mythos and philosophy, making them their fulcrum for creativity. From the entire spectrum of his moods, whether it is fury or detachment, to the extensive lore deeply entwined with the many Hindu divinities, Shiva gives artists a veritable wealth of creative inspiration. It is not surprising then that there is a pan-Indian presence in the art and aesthetics of Shiva – from the refined bronze sculptures from the Chola kingdom in the south to Bengal's Kalighat paintings in the east. He appears in countless artistic traditions, with depictions ranging from fierce and ecstatic to serene and meditative, sometimes tender, sometimes absurdly human. A perfect example is ancient India's poet Kalidasa and his epic poem, the beautiful and sensuous Kumarasambhava, where Shiva and Parvati are involved in the birth of their son Skanda Karttikeya.

Personification of rhythm

Several classical Indian dance forms deeply embody Shiva's mythology, especially his cosmic role as Nataraja, the Lord of Dance. Shiva in Tamil Nadu's classical dance form Bharatanatyam is captivating – he's not just a deity, but the personification of rhythm, cosmic energy, and transcendence. The dance form reveres him as Nataraja whose Ananda Tandava, or dance of bliss, symbolizes the cycle of creation, preservation, and destruction. Bharatanatyam dancers channel Shiva's moods – Raudra, or fury, Shanta, or peace, and Adbhuta, or wonder, to evoke deep emotional resonance and sacred movement.

The Kuchipudi dance form from Andhra Pradesh often includes dramatic enactments of Shiva legends, like his marriage to Parvati or the destruction of Tripura, the three Asura cities created by Tarakasura's sons. The dance also dramatizes Shiva's

battles and cosmic dances. The ritual dance of Theyyam in Kerala also features a manifestation of Shiva, known as Pottan. Although it predates classical Hinduism and retains tribal and animist elements, it has absorbed Shiva's mythology. Episodes where Shiva appears as the low-caste Chandala to Adi Shankaracharya are retold through Theyyam, emphasizing emotions such as humility, transformation, and the constant possibility of divine presence in unexpected forms.

The warrior within

Kerala's Kalarippayattu, often spelled Kalaripattu, is not just a martial art, but also a living embodiment of myth, ritual, and spiritual philosophy deeply entwined with Shiva's cosmic energy. According to legend, Shiva created Kalarippayattu as a sacred art of warfare. He taught it to Nandi, his devoted bull, and later his son Karttikeya, or Murugan, to defeat the Asura Tarakasura. These traditions don't just depict Shiva – they channelize his energy, symbolism and spiritual resonance through movement, rhythm, and storytelling. Legend has it that Shiva passed this knowledge to sages like Agastya and Parashurama, who spread it across South India with the latter credited with founding 108 Kalari schools.

Fierce energy

Bengal's Kalighat paintings reinterpret Shiva in contemporary, socially resonant ways and offer a bold, expressive, and often unconventional lens on Shiva. Emerging in 19th-century Kolkata, patuas or scroll painters, created these works and sold them as devotional souvenirs. But they were also social commentaries, satirical critiques, and emotional portraits of divine and human life.

A striking example from the late 1800s shows Shiva with five heads, each representing a cosmic function – creation, preservation, destruction, concealment, and grace. The paintings play with folk humour, showing Shiva in exaggerated or humanized forms, sometimes even poking fun at religious hypocrisy or societal norms.

▽ **At the Battery Dance Festival in New York City,** the sacred syllables of the Shiva Panchakshara Stotra come alive through the graceful rhythms of Kuchipudi. Each movement echoes Shiva's divine dance as Nataraja blending devotion, storytelling, and cosmic energy in a timeless tribute.

Kalaripayattu, the oldest surviving martial art, originated in Kerala around the 3rd century BCE. According to legend, Shiva and Parvati, witnessing a battle between a lion and an elephant, gleaned the secrets of combat from the animals' movements. Shiva passed this knowledge to Parashurama – the sixth avatara of Vishnu – who created the land of Kerala and taught the art to its early inhabitants. The discipline embodies Shiva's dual aspects: fierceness and stillness, blending combat with consciousness. In this image, two warriors practise Kalaripayattu on the seashore, using it as their open-air *kalari*, or training ground.

THE MODERN ICON

Shiva's popularity has sustained through centuries, cultures, and philosophies. His qualities of self-awareness and transcendence, and his attributes of inclusivity appeal to today's youth who seek clarity in a chaotic world.

▽ **(1) A vivid image of Shiva** graces the back of an autorickshaw in Jaipur, reflecting how deeply the divine weaves into the everyday rhythm of life in Rajasthan.
(2) A captivating mehndi design of Shiva and Parvati adorns a palm, symbolizing divine love and spiritual union.
(3) During the Mahakumbh in Allahabad, a foreign devotee reveals a striking tattoo of Shiva on his back, an enduring mark of devotion that transcends cultures.

Shiva isn't just God – he's a vibe. He is the aura, when you step into a Shiva sanctuary. He's the embodiment of inner power, rebellion, and peace, all rolled into one. The popularity of Shiva never really waned, it just metamorphosed while adjusting to changed circumstances.

His appeal spans centuries, cultures, and philosophies and he remains a beloved deity who continues to inspire fiction, pop culture, and art. Writers have written books to unpack his iconography, his mythology has been fictionalized and serialized in popular paperbacks, religious television shows, and movies. Sitarists who play for Shiva, singers who sing for and of Shiva, and motivational speakers who speak of Shiva all have an eager and attentive audience made up of the devout, casual enthusiasts and the occasional sceptic.

Influencers, musicians, and spiritual teachers often reference Shiva across social media, music videos, and motivational content. Artists move beyond literal depictions to explore Shiva's essence through abstraction. Bold brushstrokes, swirling forms, and vibrant colours evoke his cosmic energy and dual nature of creator and destroyer. In Shiva's iconography every element – trident, serpent, crescent Moon, third eye – is loaded with meaning. Modern artists emphasize these visually-striking symbols to explore themes like awakening, power and transcendence.

The art of Shiva

Shiva's many symbols have become inspirations for jewellery across genders – from the lingam, the trishula, or trident, and Nandi, Shiva's sacred bull, around the neck to bracelets embossed with the *panchakshari*, or the five syllables, Aum Namah Shivaya. The god has also become a popular subject for permanent body art with tattoos that depict Shiva in different poses and forms, sometimes meditating, and sometimes ready to go to war. Each symbol represents strength, transformation, and resilience. Practices like yoga, breathwork, and chanting mantras like the Aum Namah Shivaya have become popular tools for stress relief and emotional grounding.

Shiva has also featured in iconic roles in mainstream Hindi films, where he is portrayed with good-natured irreverence – from the iconic Hindi song "Jai Jai Shiv Shankar" featuring the intoxicated protagonists in the midst of revellers with people who appear to be Shiva's ganas to the famous film *Sholay* featuring a comic sequence between the two main actors and a rather large Shiva statue.

All are welcome

The devotees visiting the Kumbh Mela increase and temples dedicated to the god, located in different parts of India have become popular holiday destinations – from the Mahakaleshvara Temple in Ujjain, to the Kashi Vishwanath in Varanasi, to Kedarnath in the Himalayas.

Mondays being Shiva's precious day, is popular with many believers seeking a handsome partner like Shiva. Festivals like Maha Shivaratri are celebrated with youth participation, blending devotion with dance and music. Besides the temples dedicated to Shiva, large, freestanding statues of Shiva in his various forms, have been built, such as the 369 feet high one in Nathdwara, Rajasthan, called the Statue of Belief, or the Vishwas Swaroopam.

Shiva is the ultimate outsider: wild-haired, ash-smeared, meditating in the Himalayas and indifferent to societal norms. For people navigating conformity and pressure, Shiva's detachment and defiance offer a powerful symbol of freedom and authenticity, making the god more than just a spiritual trend, but a cultural wave that blends ancient mysticism with modern identity.

▽ **(4) Amid the vibrant Mylapore Festival in Chennai,** intricate kolam designs bloom across the streets, ephemeral offerings of devotion to Shiva drawn in rice flour.
(5) On the shores of Puri, a fleeting masterpiece rises from the sand, an intricate artwork paying homage to Shiva. Shaped by the elements, it mirrors Shiva himself: timeless yet ever-changing.
(6) Vibrant murals painted by artists from the "Delhi Art Street" collective, on the walls of a Delhi home reflect nature and daily life. Amid the scenes, echoes of Shiva emerge, the eternal ascetic who dwells both in the wild and among the people.

PANCH KEDAR

WHERE GODS DWELL IN THE HIMALAYAS

Garhwal in the northern state of Uttarakhand and nestled in the Himalayas, is a region of staggering natural beauty and deep spiritual resonance. Towering peaks like Nanda Devi rise above a landscape of snow-capped mountains, lush forests, and deep river valleys, painting a scene both wild and serene. But Garhwal is more than just a feast for the senses, it's Devbhoomi, the "Land of the Gods". It is home to ancient shrines that make up some of Hinduism's most revered pilgrimage sites. Among them are a group of five temples, scattered across the remote folds of the region, accessible mostly by foot, in the midst of forests and surrounded by snow-clad peaks.

These are the Panch Kedar, a group of temples dedicated to Shiva, each linked to myth, legend, and devotion, forming a mystical trail where faith and wilderness converge. They are not a destination, but a pilgrimage into the heart of divinity, a place where Earth and heaven seem to touch.

The sacred five

Kedarnath, Tungnath, Rudranath, Madhyamaheshwar, and Kalpeshwar together make up the five sacred temples of Panch Kedar. They are not just architectural wonders, but living echoes of the *Mahabharata*, shaped by remorse, myth, and divine pursuit.

After the brutal Kurukshetra war, the Pandavas, haunted by the bloodshed of their kin and so many other people, sought forgiveness from Shiva. On Krishna's counsel, they journeyed to the Himalayas, hoping for redemption. But Shiva, disillusioned by the fratricidal violence, refused to forgive so easily. To avoid them, he assumed the form of a bull and tried to disappear into the remote wilderness. When Bhima recognized the divine disguise and tried to catch him, Shiva vanished into the earth. Moments later, his body re-emerged — not whole, but in five separate parts, each surfacing at a different location in the mountains. The Pandavas, accepting even this fragmented blessing, built shrines at each site that are today known as the Panch Kedar, each a symbol of penance, perseverance, and the elusive nature of the divine.

Penance in stone

Kedarnath, Tungnath, and Rudranath are stone marvels built in the Nagara architectural style, a distinct style of North Indian temple architecture characterized by its beehive-shaped tower, *shikhara*, square sanctum, *garbhagriha*, and absence of elaborate boundary walls or gateways.

The most prominent of the Panch Kedar, Kedarnath is located near the source of the Mandakini River at a height of 3,583 m (11,755 ft). The lingam here strikingly resembles a bull's back. As part of the Char Dham Yatra and one of the 12 Jyotirlingas, it holds immense spiritual weight. At Tungnath, perched at a height of 3,680 m (12,073 ft) the arms of Shiva surfaced. It is adorned with beautiful ancient stone carvings and commanding breathtaking mountain views. Set in a natural rock temple amidst dense forest and alpine meadows, Rudranath at 3,600 m (11,811 ft), is deeply revered for its serene and spiritual atmosphere. Surrounded by snow-capped peaks, Madhyamaheshwar lies in a remote valley at a height of 3,497 m (11,473 ft) and is known for its peaceful solitude and natural beauty. Kalpeshwar is nestled in a valley at a height of 2,200 m (7,217 ft) and is reached through a picturesque trek.

Pilgrimage to these shrines is not merely a religious ritual — it is a physical and inner journey through some of the most rugged and remote parts of the Indian Himalayas. The yatra is demanding, yet is considered one of the most rewarding spiritual undertakings in Hinduism.

▷ *(clockwise from top left)* **Draped in sacred cloth and guarded by tridents,** these twin ancient shrines within the Kalpeshwar Temple complex quietly echo the timeless presence of Shiva; **A sacred stillness surrounds** the stone temple of Shiva at Madhyamaheshwar in Rudraprayag; **Tungnath is the third temple** in the Panch Kedar pilgrimage circuit. It is said that the site was discovered by the Pandavas, who built a temple as penance after the Kurukshetra war; **Rudranath Temple,** where the face of Shiva is worshipped, stands draped in marigolds and silence, gazing over snow-laced peaks; **Bathed in moonlight, Kedarnath Temple** stands as a sacred beacon where Lord Shiva is worshipped in timeless stillness at one of India's holiest shrines.

SHRINES BETWEEN SNOW AND SKY

RUDRANATH
Hidden deep within shadowy Himalayan forests, in the Chamoli district of Uttarakhand, Rudranath is where Shiva's face is said to have risen from the earth. Mist curls around ancient rocks believed to bear his features. The air hums with ancestral whispers. More than a temple, Rudranath is a mirror for the soul – a place where seekers confront the divine within and beyond.

MADHYAMAHESHWAR
In a serene Himalayan valley, surrounded by snow-clad peaks in the Rudraprayag district of Uttarakhand, lies Madhyamaheshwar, the sacred place where Shiva's navel and stomach surfaced after he tried to hide from the Pandavas. Born of myth and penance, this quiet shrine humbles the soul. Here, the air is thin, the silence profound, and the divine presence is felt in the very pulse of the earth.

KALPESHWAR
Tucked in a quiet Himalayan nook in the Urgram Valley of the Chamoli district in Uttarakhand, Kalpeshwar marks the spot where Shiva's hair emerged from the earth. The smallest of the Panch Kedar, it welcomes pilgrims year-round – no high peaks to conquer, only the self. Here, seekers find an intimate doorway to the divine, where wild nature and ancient myth whisper softly in the wind.

High in the Garhwal Himalayas, beneath the towering peak of Mount Shivling, lies Tapovan, where a sacred Shiva lingam stands as a timeless symbol of creation and cosmic energy. Here, amidst snow-kissed peaks the celestial river Ganga is believed to have descended, flowing from Shiva's matted locks to purify the earth. The trishula or trident planted in the earth stands as Shiva's symbol of clarity and transcendence, cutting through ego, illusion, and desire. Tapovan, from *tapas*, austerity, and *vana*, forest, is the realm of spiritual practice, reflection, and union with Shiva, the eternal yogi who dwells beyond all distractions.

GLOSSARY

Agamas
A collection of sacred texts in Hinduism, the Agamas outline rituals, temple construction, deity worship, yoga, and spiritual practices. Distinct from the Vedas but equally authoritative within their respective sects, they provide practical guidance for religious life and are central to the development of temple culture and devotional worship in Hinduism.

Asuras
These are supernatural beings with immense powers who were constantly in conflict with the Devas, or the gods. According to one myth, Varuni, the goddess of liquor, emerged during the churning of the ocean, and liquor was claimed by the gods. Thereby, gods came to be called Suras, that is with liquor, and their opponents Asuras, that is those without liquor.

Atman
The soul or the principle of life which is believed to be imperishable and present in all creation. It is different from the physical body, mind, and consciousness. According to Advaita Vedanta, it is the same as the Brahman, the essential energy of the cosmos.

Brahman
The focal metaphysical concept of Hindu philosophical thought, which has been defined in several ways. It is the essence of the universe, the cosmic principle within and behind all existence, the ultimate unchanging reality, and the absolute consciousness.

chakras
In yoga, they are the mystical energy centres in the body, usually believed to be seven in number. It is also used to refer to a discus or a wheel, which is a very powerful and deadly weapon wielded by Vishnu, the preserver, and all his avatars.

Chola bronzes
A renowned collection of bronze sculptures created during the Chola Dynasty, 9th to 13th centuries, in South India, especially Tamil Nadu. Most Chola bronzes depict Hindu deities, particularly Shiva in his cosmic dance form as Nataraja, and were used in temple rituals. They are considered iconic examples of Indian metal art and religious sculpture.

Devas
Heavenly divine beings worshipped by Hindus, Jains, and Buddhists. The male form is known as Deva, while the female is called a Devi. The Devas and the Devis have to be regularly propitiated with prayers and offerings by human beings. The root of the word "*Deva*" comes from the word div, which means to shine.

Dhangars
The Dhangars are a traditional pastoral and herding community found in parts of Karnataka, as well as in Maharashtra and other regions of western and southern India. In Karnataka, Dhangars are primarily known for their occupation as shepherds and cattle herders, and they play a vital role in the region's agrarian and rural economy. They have a rich oral tradition, including folk songs and stories tied to pastoral life, and often worship deities such as Shivaji Maharaj, Birappa, and forms of Shiva.

dharma
Hindu scriptures describe dharma as a way of life that follows the path of righteousness. The objective of dharma is the attainment of moksha or ultimate liberation.

Elamite civilization
The Elamite civilization, c. 2700 BCE–539 BCE was an ancient culture centred in present-day southwestern Iran, with key cities such as Susa. While primarily studied in relation to Mesopotamian civilizations, some speculative theories attempt to link the Elamites to Vedic or Hindu traditions, often through proposed linguistic or cultural connections between Elamite, Dravidian, or Indo-Iranian groups.

gunas
In Indian philosophical systems, the *gunas* are the three fundamental qualities that govern all nature and human experience: sattva, – purity, harmony, knowledge; rajas – activity, passion, restlessness; and tamas – inertia, darkness, ignorance. Spiritual progress involves cultivating sattva while reducing rajas and tamas.

iconography
In Hindu traditions, iconography refers to the symbolic representation of deities, concepts, and stories through visual forms, such as statues, paintings, carvings, and ritual diagrams. Each deity is depicted with specific attributes; gestures, or mudras; vehicles, or vahanas; weapons; and postures, which convey their unique powers, roles, and cosmic functions. For example, Shiva is often shown with a trident, crescent Moon, third eye, and seated in meditation or dancing as Nataraja.

Kalighat paintings
A style of Indian painting that emerged in the 19th century around the Kalighat temple in Kolkata, West Bengal. Originally created as souvenirs for temple visitors, Kalighat paintings are known for their bold brushwork, vibrant colours, and satirical themes. They often depict Hindu deities, mythological stories, and scenes

GLOSSARY | 315

from everyday life, sometimes with social or political commentary. This art form played a key role in the evolution of modern Indian art.

kalpa
In Hindu cosmology, a kalpa is a vast unit of time, representing a single day in the life of Brahma, the god of creation. One kalpa equals 4.32 billion years and includes the full cycle of creation, preservation, and dissolution of the universe. At the end of each kalpa, the cosmos is dissolved, only to be recreated in the next cycle. Each kalpa contains 14 manvantaras, or ages of Manus, and countless yugas, or smaller epochs.

Kundalini
A Sanskrit term meaning "coiled one", referring to a form of primal energy believed to reside at the base of the spine. In yogic and Tantric traditions, Kundalini is envisioned as a dormant spiritual force that can be awakened through practices such as meditation, breath control, and mantra. Its rising through the chakras is said to lead to spiritual awakening, heightened consciousness, and union with the divine.

moksha
Refers to liberation of the Atman from the cycle of birth, death, and rebirth. In most Hindu traditions, moksha is the ultimate goal of life.

mudras
Symbolic hand gestures made by deities. It is derived from the Sanskrit word "*mud*" that means joy and "*ra*" that means produce. As a result, mudras mean gestures that produce joy and happiness. Many of the goddesses in their iconography are seen showing these. The most popular ones are the boongiving and the fear-not mudras.

Nagara style of architecture
The Nagara style is one of the three main schools of Indian temple architecture, primarily found in North India. Characterized by its distinctive curvilinear tower, or *shikhara*, rising directly above the sanctum, or *garbhagriha*, the Nagara style emphasizes verticality and compact form. Key features include: A *mandapa*, or pillared hall, connected to the sanctum and rich stone carvings depicting deities, myths, and motifs. This style flourished from the 5th century onwards and is prominent in iconic temples such as Khajuraho, Konark, and Bhubaneswar.

Pahari style of paintings
A school of Indian miniature painting that developed in the Himalayan hill kingdoms of North India, particularly in present-day Himachal Pradesh and Jammu & Kashmir, between the 17th and 19th centuries. Pahari paintings often depict Shiva in serene and intimate settings, such as with his consort Parvati on Mount Kailash, in family scenes with Ganesha and Kartikkeya, or in meditative or ascetic forms.

Prakriti
In Hindu philosophy, Prakriti refers to primordial nature or matter – the dynamic, creative energy that gives rise to the material universe. It is the unmanifested source of all physical and mental phenomena, including the body, mind, and emotions. Prakriti is often seen in contrast to Purusha, the eternal, unchanging consciousness. While Purusha is the passive observer, Prakriti is the active force that evolves into all aspects of creation.

Purusha
In Hindu philosophy, Purusha refers to the cosmic spirit, universal consciousness, or the eternal Self. It is the unchanging, passive, and pure awareness that exists beyond time, space, and material reality. In the *Rig Veda*, Purusha is described as a cosmic being whose body was sacrificed by the gods to create the universe – this myth explains the origin of the world and the four varnas, or social orders.

Rajput style of paintings
A traditional style of Indian miniature painting that flourished in the royal courts of the Rajput kingdoms of North and Central India from the 16th to 19th centuries. The Rajput style frequently portrays Shiva in various forms, such as Nataraja, Ardhanarishvara, or in family scenes with Parvati and Ganesha.

Sthal Puranas
Sthal Puranas are sacred local texts or oral traditions in Hinduism that recount the mythological, spiritual, and historical significance of a particular temple, shrine, or sacred site; *sthal* means place in Sanskrit. These texts often describe the origin of the temple, miracles of the deity, visits by sages or gods, and the benefits of worshipping at that site. They are typically associated with major pilgrimage centres, especially in South India, and help embed pan-Indian deities such as Shiva or Vishnu into regional cultures.

Trinity
In Hindu philosophy, the Trimurti refers to the cosmic trinity of three principal deities who embody the three fundamental aspects of the universe: Brahma – the creator, responsible for the creation of the cosmos; Vishnu – the preserver, who sustains and protects the universe; and Shiva – the destroyer or transformer, who dissolves and regenerates existence. Though distinct in role, they are ultimately seen as different manifestations of the same supreme reality, that is Brahman.

INDEX

A

Abhayamudra 31
Activity 41, 52, 89, 234, 288, 300, 314 *see* Rajas
Adhyatma Ramayana 28
Adi Natha 272
Adi Shankaracharya 59, 67, 128, 146, 219, 248
Advaita Vedanta 5, 219, 234, 272, 273
Agamas 12, 61, 234, 242, 314
Agastya 305
Aghora 194, 233
Aghoris 233, 284
Agni 24, 37, 83, 119, 136, 137, 179, 228
Ahalya 211
Aham 219
Aham Brahmasmi 269
Ahimsa 246
Ajna Chakra 78, 233, 242
    see also Third Eye Chakra
Akka Mahadevi 263–67
Alinga (without shape) 58, 235
Allahabad 308
Alms *see* Bhiksha
Amarnath 226, 296, 297, 299, 302
Amarnath Cave 226, 296, 297, 299, 302
Amarnath Cave Temple 226, 297
Amarnath Yatra Route 296
Ambernath 55
Amrita (Nectar of Immortality) 125, 128, 129
Ananda (Bliss) 66, 92, 100, 195, 201, 227
Ananda Tandava 92, 100, 227
Andhra Pradesh 41, 60, 64, 69, 89, 133, 228
    Chittoor 61
    Mallara 41
    Srikalahasteeswara Temple 228
Anubhava Mantapa 266
Anugraha (Grace) 88, 90, 213, 233
Anugraha shakti 233
Aparigraha 219
Aparna 213
Apasmara Purusha 95
Appar 92
Apsaras 81, 290
Ardhanarishvara 38, 47, 48, 49, 142, 162, 166, 167, 168, 169, 197, 226, 248, 249
Arjuna 28, 33, 74
Arthavada 84
Arulmigu Mutharamman Temple 190
Arunachaleshwara Temple 228
Arupa 235
Asau devta 24
Ashta Bhairava 240
Assam 241
    Guwahati 241
    Kamakhya Temple 241
Asura
    Apasmara Purusha 95
    Gajasura 9, 14, 22, 23, 119
    Hiranyakashipu 49
    Kamalaksha 119
    Tarakaksha 119
    Tarakasura 119, 180, 212, 304–305
    Tripurasura 14, 92, 119
    Vidyunmali 119
Atharvashikha Upanishad 25
Atharvashiras Upanishad 25
Aum Namah Shivaya 12, 256
Avahana (Invitation) 61
Ayyanar 44
Ayyapan 44

B

Badami Cave 100, 226
Badrinath 302
Badva 199
Bagalamukhi 186
Baidyanath 69
Banasura 297
Bandhas 246
Banyan 170, 223, 260
Basavanna 266
Bateshwar 170
Bel (Bilva) 300–301, 303
Bengaluru 33, 326
    Someshwara Temple 33
Bhadrakali 88
Bhagiratha 185, 169
Bhairava 9, 11–12, 15, 23, 41, 77, 109–111, 116, 164, 216, 239, 240–241, 245, 251, 281, 283, 295
    Ashta Bhairava 240
    Astinga 240
    Batuk 240
    Bhairava Ashtami 240
    Bhishana 240
    Bhukund 239
    Chanda 240
    Kala 240
    Kapala 240
    Krodha 240
    Ruru 240
    Samhara 240
    Svacchanda 240, 245
    Unmatta 240
Bhairava Ashtami 22
Bhairavi 186, 189, 281
Bhairavnath 155, 239, 240
    Mula Bandha 246
    Uddiyana Bandha 246
Bhairavnath Temple 239
Bhairon Baba Mandir 239
Bhaktapur 60
Bhakti 25, 104, 180, 256–258, 262–263, 266, 269, 271, 279
Bhakti movement 258, 262–263, 266
Bhang 20, 164, 301
Bharadvaja 211
Bharata 99
Bhasma 67, 69, 250, 288–289
Bhasma Arti 67, 69, 250
Bhasmasura 14, 135, 212
Bhastrika 248
Bhiksha (Alms) 190, 216
Bhikshatanamurti 216, 241
Bhoothnath Temple 227
Bhringi 162
Bhubaneshwar 292
Bhuvaneshvari 186
Bilaspur 291, 295
Bilva *see* Bel
Bliss *see* Ananda
Brahma 13, 40–45, 47, 55, 58, 59, 66, 72–73, 84, 89–91, 103, 107, 109, 115–116, 119–120, 133, 137, 144, 147, 149, 152, 173, 179, 189, 192, 210–211, 216, 229, 245, 250, 300, 315, 322
Brahman 15, 41, 42, 49, 58, 59, 90, 91, 109, 146, 168, 219, 234, 235, 245, 250, 259, 284
Brahma Vaivarta Purana. 173
Brihadeeswara Temple 112, 227

C

Chaitra 156
Chandanwari 236
Chandika 283
Chandra (Moon God) 69, 130
Chandrabadni Temple 155
Chakra
    Ajna 242
    Muladhara 242

Sahasrara 242
Charak 138
  puja 214
Char Dham 155, 203, 310
  Char Dham Yatra 155, 302, 310
Chaunsatha Yoginis 11, 109, 241
Chenna Mallikarjuna 264
Chhattisgarh 291, 295
Chhinnamasta 186
Chidambaram Temple 100, 227–228
Chittoor 61
Chiu Gompa 138

D

Daksha 5, 14, 58, 72, 73, 84–86, 88–89, 115, 130, 137, 144, 149, 189, 249, 288
Dakshinakali 186
Dakshinamurti 6, 223, 269
  Stotram 269
Dakshinayana 223
Dakshina Kailasam 228
Dakshina Kosala 295
Damaru 8, 99, 103, 167, 169, 192, 197, 214, 241
Daruvana 22, 37, 58, 162
Dasara 190
Dasoha 262
Dattatreya 42–43, 211, 284
Dehradun 10
Deogarh 69
Deva 26, 38, 74, 78, 86, 88, 122–128, 135, 136, 151, 152, 179, 197, 202, 210, 211, 314
Devarani Temple 295
Devbhoomi 310
Dharma 44, 55, 81, 86, 115, 117, 142, 146, 210, 223, 241, 269, 291, 300, 314
Dharmachakra Mudra 291
Dharmashasta 44
Dhatura 300–301
Dhumavati 186

Doleshwar Mahadev Temple 60
Dolma La Pass 202
Dravidian 64, 226, 228, 258, 314
Duladeo Temple 55
Durga 11, 78, 145, 248, 322
Dushtuti 78
Dussehra 190
  Kulasai Dasra 190
Dwarka 269, 302
  Tapkeshwar Mahadev Temple 10, 226

E

Ekambareswarar Temple 228
Elephanta Caves 107, 226
Ellora Caves 31, 69
Epigraphia Indica 47

F

Festivals
  Battery Dance 305
  Champa Shashti 133
  Charak Puja 138
  Chithirai 156
  Gajan 214
  Gudi Padwa 89
  Guru Purnima 223
  Karthigai Deepam 228
  Maha Shivaratri 152, 158, 300, 303, 309
  Tirukalyanam 156

G

Gajan festival 214
Gajasura 9, 14, 22, 23, 119
Ganas 26, 31, 61, 86, 88, 93, 116, 146, 149, 152, 161, 173, 176, 192–195, 201, 203, 256, 309
Ganesha 6, 31, 37, 45, 55, 73, 100,107, 146, 164, 169, 172–173, 175–176, 183, 195, 226, 245, 251, 296, 302
Ganga 6, 8, 12, 15, 37, 48, 51, 62, 109, 115–116, 127–128, 136, 144, 146–147, 168–169, 185, 203, 250, 251, 253, 301–302, 313
Ganga River 15, 62, 185, 203, 253,
Gangasagar 221
Gangotri 60, 127, 185, 302
Goddess Ganga 6, 8, 12, 15, 37, 48, 51, 62, 109, 115–116, 127–128, 136, 144, 146-147, 168–169, 185, 203, 250, 251, 253, 301–302, 313
Gangotri 60, 127, 185, 302
Garbhagriha 226, 310,
Garhwal 66, 69, 155, 310, 313
Gaumukh 127
Gaurikund 302
Girija 142
Girisha 202
God
  Aghora 194
  Agni 24, 37, 83, 119, 136, 137, 179, 228
  Bhadrakali 88
  Brahma 13, 40–45, 47, 55, 58, 59, 66, 72–73, 84, 89–91, 103, 107, 109, 115–116, 119–120, 133, 137, 144, 147, 149, 152, 173, 179, 189, 192, 210–211, 216, 229, 245, 250, 300, 315, 322
  Durga 11, 78, 145, 248, 322
  Ganga 6, 8, 12, 15, 37, 48, 51, 62, 109, 115–116, 127–128, 136, 144, 146–147, 168–169, 185, 203, 250, 251, 253, 301–302, 313
  Ganesha 6, 31, 37, 45, 55, 73, 100,107, 146, 164, 169, 172–173, 175–176, 183, 195, 226, 245, 251, 296, 302
  Girija 142
  Hanuman 27, 93, 201
  Harakali 214
  Indra 24, 57, 74, 88, 56, 179, 203, 211, 290
  Ishana 25, 194, 233
  Kali 11, 12, 78, 92–93, 176, 186-190, 240-241, 248
  Lakshmi 14, 45, 152, 233
  Parvati 9, 11, 14–15, 27–28, 31, 33, 37, 45–49, 59, 69, 73, 78, 81, 88, 92, 95, 116, 120, 136–137, 143–147, 150–176, 179–183, 197, 201–202, 208–209, 223, 226, 245, 248, 271, 288, 296, 301–304, 307–308, 315, 324
  Pashupatinath 280
  Rudra 5, 9–13, 22, 24, 25, 27, 35, 53, 57, 58, 72–77, 86, 90, 92, 136, 142, 157, 183, 189, 221, 236, 248, 291, 295, 320, 322, 323,
  Sadyojata 194
  Shakti 11, 36, 37, 49, 53, 90, 122, 145, 155, 186–187, 233, 240–242, 246, 248–249, 274, 281
  Shiva 8–31, 33–69, 71–128, 130–138, 141–205, 208–291, 295–313, 315, 322–324
  Tatpurusha 194
  Vamadeva 194
  Vishnu 9, 13, 14, 26, 27, 37, 38, 40–51, 55, 58, 59, 66, 73, 84, 86, 88,119, 122, 125, 129, 135, 137, 144, 147–149, 152, 155, 157, 173, 176, 189, 192, 201, 210, 211, 229, 233, 249, 251, 258, 284, 288, 300, 302, 307, 314, 315

INDEX

Goddess
Durga 11, 78, 145, 248, 322, 185, 203, 250, 251, 253, 301–302, 313
Ganga 6, 8, 12, 15, 37, 48, 51, 62, 109, 115–116, 127–128, 136, 144, 146–147, 168–169, 185, 203, 250, 251, 253, 301–302, 313
Girija 142
Kali 11, 12, 78, 92–93, 176, 186–190, 240–241, 248
Lakshmi 14, 45, 152, 233
Parvati 9, 11, 14–15, 27–28, 31, 33, 37, 45–49, 59, 69, 73, 78, 81, 88, 92, 95, 116, 120, 136–137, 143–147, 150–176, 179–183, 197, 201–202, 208–209, 223, 226, 245, 248, 271, 288, 296, 301–304, 307–308, 315, 324
Shakti 11, 36, 37, 49, 53, 90, 122, 145, 155, 186–187, 233, 240–242, 246, 248–249, 274, 281
Uma 11, 37, 86, 142, 160, 164, 183, 271
Gomati 69
Gopuram 226
Gorakhnath 272
Gorakhpur 272
Grace *see* Anugraha
Grishneshwara 66
Grishneshwar Temple 66
Grishneshwar Temple 66
Gudimallam lingam 60, 64
Gujarat 66, 68, 69, 241, 280, 290-291
Dwarka 69, 269, 302
Nageshwara Temple 68, 69
Gunas
Rajas (Activity) 41, 52, 89, 234, 288, 300, 314
Sattva (Purity) 41, 52, 89, 234, 288, 300, 314
Tamas (Inertia) 41, 52, 89, 234, 288, 300, 314
Guru 48, 119, 128, 181, 223, 238, 242, 245, 266, 268–269, 272–273, 275, 279, 284
Allama Prabhu 266
Guru Purnima 223
Guru Purnima 223
Guwahati
Kamakhya Temple 241

H
Halahala (Kalakuta or poison) 35, 115, 122, 125, 164, 301
Hanuman 27, 193, 201
Harakali 214
Haravilasamu 259
Haridwar 127, 128, 302
Hariharapitamahasurya 55
Harivamsha 47
Hatha Yoga 208, 272–273
Heart Chakra (Anahata) 233, 257
Himalayas 28, 47, 66, 68, 69, 78, 90, 95, 112, 128, 143, 152, 155, 180, 205, 223, 277, 283, 296, 309, 310, 313
Hiranyakashipu 49
Homa 236, 288
Huduk 280

I
I, Lalla: The Poems of Lal Ded 279
Iccha Shakti 53
Indra 24, 57, 74, 88, 156, 179, 203, 211, 290
Indrani 290
Inertia *see* Tamas
Initiation Ceremony *see* Upanayana
Ishana 25, 194, 233

J
Jaipur 308
Jamadagni 211
Jambukeshwarar Temple 228
Jammu & Kashmir 259, 277, 296, 302, 315
Japa 236, 246
Jharkhand 69
Deogarh 69
Jnana 53, 223
Jnana Dakshinamurti 223
Jnana shakti 53
Jogeshwari Caves 226
Joshimath 269
Jwala Prabha 99
Jyotir (Light) 66
Jyotirlinga 66–69, 137, 155, 227, 310

K
Kaal Bhairava 109, 251
Kailasha 22, 27, 30–32, 89, 92, 116, 120, 122, 143, 156, 160, 164, 173, 192, 195, 197, 201–205, 209, 212, 223, 225–226, 228, 260, 291
Kaivalya Upanishad 25
Kalachuri dynasty 11, 295
Kalady 268
Kalagnirudra Upanishad 25
Kalakuta *see* Halahala
Kalamukhas 280, 283, 323
Kalaripayattu 33, 44–45, 83, 223, 240, 268, 305
Kali 11, 12, 78, 92-93, 176, 186-190, 240–241, 248
Kalidasa 60, 180, 304
Kalighat 144, 147, 173, 304–305, 315
Kalpeshwar 310–311
Kalyana 266
Kamadeva 73, 78, 81, 117,119, 136, 145, 186, 209,288
Kama 73, 81, 117, 145, 209, 288
Kamala 186
Kamalaksha 119
Kamakhya Temple 241
Kanchipuram 64, 157, 223, 228, 302
Kandariya Mahadeva Temple 227
Kannapar 259
Kanphata Yogis 272
Kanwar Yatra 127, 302
Kanwar 127, 302–303
Kanwariyas 127, 302
Kapala 280, 283–284
Kapala Bhairava 240
Kapalabhati 246
Kapalikas 109, 245, 280–281, 283–284, 323
Kapalin 281
Kapila 185
Karaikkal Ammaiyar 258, 260
Karnataka 27, 38, 89, 92, 100, 133, 199, 201, 226–227, 240, 245, 262–263, 265, 267, 269, 283, 315
Kartikkeya 31, 37, 69, 136, 146, 164, 169, 172–173, 179–180, 245, 302–305
Kashi 69, 127, 162, 214, 227, 250–253, 269, 309 *see* Varanasi
Kashi Vishwanath Temple 69, 127, 227
Kashi Vishwanath Temple 69, 127, 227
Kashmir 274, 296
Shaivism 305, 306
Kashmir Shaivism 305, 306
Kashyapa 201
Kaurava 26, 28
Kayaka (Honest Labor) 262
Kedarnath 28, 60, 66, 68–69, 155, 239, 241, 302, 309–310
Kerala 33,44, 45, 83, 223, 240, 268, 302, 304–307
Shabari Hill 45
Khajuraho 55
Duladeo Temple 55
Kandariya Mahadeva Temple 227
Khandoba 12, 41, 132–133, 183, 323
Khechari Mudra 246
Kiratarjuniya 28, 33
Kora 203
Kriya shakti 53
Ksheersagar (Ocean of Milk) 122
Kudalasangamadeva 267
Kulasai Dasara 190
Kulasekarapattinam 190
Arulmigu Mutharamman Temple 190
Kumarasambhava 180, 304
Kumbha Mela 128–129, 284, 286, 309
Kumbh 128–129
Kundalini 122, 221, 242, 244, 246, 272, 274, 314
Kunjapuri Devi Temple 155

L
Laguda 292
Lake Mansarovar 202
Lake Sheshnaga 296
Lakhey 111
Lakshmi 14, 45, 152, 233
Lakshmi Narayana Temple 233
Lakulisha 19, 226, 283, 291–293, 322
Lasya 92, 93
Shringara Lasya 92
Lingam 8, 11–13, 20, 23, 25, 27–28, 35, 37–38, 56–67, 69, 100, 112, 130, 142–143, 155, 157, 195, 199, 201–202, 209, 225–230, 235, 245, 248–251, 257, 259, 262–263, 275, 296, 299–303, 309-310, 313

INDEX | 319

Gudimallam 60, 64
Manusha 60
Shiva 227
Svayambhu 60
Lingayat 20, 133, 262–264, 266, 283
Lingodbhava 37, 59, 66, 115, 117, 122, 137, 229
Lingodbhavamurtis 64

M
Madhurya Bhava 266
Madhya Pradesh 11, 26, 49, 55, 61, 66, 69, 107, 164, 180, 184, 227, 233, 241, 280, 291
Duladeo 55
Kandariya Mahadeva 227
Khajuraho 55
Lakshmi Narayana 233
Mahakaleshwar 66, 67, 69, 107
Orchha 233
Madhyamaheshwar 310, 311
Mahabharata 9, 26, 28, 38, 58, 60, 66, 69, 74, 129, 136, 202, 210, 216, 223, 250, 310
Mahaganesh Mountain 296
see also Mahagunas Parvat
Mahagunas Parvat 295
See also Mahaganesh Mountain
Mahakaal 69, 106, 107, 122, 161, 186, 240, 244
Mahakaleshwar Temple 66-67, 69, 107
Mahakavya 35
Mahakumbh 129, 308
Mahamrityunjaya Mantra 236
Mahaprasthanika Parva 28
Maharashtra 23, 41, 51, 55, 61, 66, 69, 89, 96, 107, 120, 133, 152, 175, 225–226, 302
Grishneshwar Temple 66

Puratan Shivalaya Temple 55
Mahashasta 44
Maha Shivaratri 35, 152, 303
Mallikarjuna 68, 69, 264
Mandakini River 310
Mandapa 226, 227, 315
Manikantha 44
Manikarnika Ghat 53, 250, 234
Mansarovar 202
Manu 211
Manusha lingam 60
Manusmriti 216
Markandeya 47
Matangi 186
Mathura 48, 64, 167, 216, 302
Matrikas 152, 241
Matsya 211
Matsyendranatha 272
Mithya 44
Mohenjo-daro 18–21, 57
Mohini 27, 44, 49, 135, 173
Moksha 90, 106, 146, 203 293, 233, 245, 250–251, 253, 274, 280, 296, 314
Moon God see Chandra Mountain
Himalayas 28, 47, 66, 68, 69, 78, 90, 95, 112, 128, 143, 152, 155, 180, 205, 223, 277, 283, 296, 309, 310, 313
Kailasha 22, 27, 30–32, 89, 92, 116, 120, 122, 143, 156, 160, 164, 173, 192, 197, 202–205, 209, 212, 225–226, 228, 260, 291
Mahaganesh 296
Meru 69, 119, 125, 290
Vindhya 69
Mount Kailasha 22, 27, 30–32, 89, 92, 116, 120, 122, 143, 156, 160, 164, 173, 192, 197, 202–205,

209, 212, 225–226, 228, 260, 291
Mount Meru 69, 119, 125, 290
Mount Shivling 313
Mudras 12, 99, 183, 208, 223, 246, 291, 314, 315
Gyan 223, 246
Khechari 246
Mula Bandha 246
Mulabandhasana 19
Muladhara Chakra 242, 246
Murugan 12, 173, 183, 302, 305
Mylapore 309
Mysore 23, 92, 263, 327

N
Nabhi 69
Nada yoga 104, 246
Nadatanumanisam Sankaram 104
Nadi Shodhana 248
Naga Sadhus 12, 128, 286
Aghoris 284–285
Nagara 226, 310, 315
Nageshwara Temple 68, 69
Nandi 6, 15, 19, 23, 28, 40, 48, 68, 88, 143, 160–161, 164, 169, 172, 195, 200, 201, 213, 275, 291–292, 296, 301, 305, 309, 323
Nara 69
Narada 69, 149, 161–162, 173
Naranag Temple 274
Narasimha 9, 44, 51
Narayana 69
Nashik 69
Nataraja 66, 92–101, 103, 137, 183, 192, 194, 197, 221, 226–228, 258, 304, 305, 315, 323
Nathas 272–273
Nathdwara 309
Natya Shastra 99, 194, 227
Navel see Nabhi

Nayanars 258
Nectar of Immortality see Amrita
Nepal 60, 109, 145, 240
Bhaktapur 60
Doleshwar Mahadev Temple 60
Netherworld see Patala
Newar 111
Nilamatia Purana 297
Nilarudra Upanishad 25
Nirguna 234–235, 269
Nishkala 58, 234, 235
Nishkala-sakala 58, 235
Nishumbha 167
Ngari prefecture 202, 205

O
Ocean of Milk (Ksheersagar) 122
Omkara 69
Omkareshwar Temple 69

P
Palani Hills 173
Pancha bhuta 228
Panchakshari 309
Panchamukha 20, 233
Panchamukha Shiva 233
Panchamukha Shiva 233
Panch Kedar 28, 310, 311
Pandava 26, 28, 60, 69, 310, 311
Panjtarni 298
Paramatma 62
Parashurama 305
Parikrama 203, 205
Parvati 9, 11, 14–15, 27-28, 31, 33, 37, 45–49, 59, 69, 73, 78, 81, 88, 92, 95, 116, 120, 136–137, 143–147, 150–176, 179–183, 197, 201–202, 208–209, 223, 226, 245, 248, 271, 288, 296, 301–304, 307–308, 315, 324
Uma 37

Pashu 280, 292
Pashupata 245, 280–281, 283, 290–293
Pashupati 9, 20, 19–23, 280
Pashupati seal 20, 21
Pashupatinath 280
Patala (Netherworld) 125, 185, 295
Periya Puranam 259
Pithoragarh 203
Poem
Haravilasamu 259
I, Lalla 279
Kumarasambhava 180, 304
Raghuvamsha 66
Rasamanjari 146
Shivanandalahari 10, 77, 95, 269, 271
Prakriti tattva 233
Pralaya 91
Pramathas 86
Pranayama 209, 246
Pratyabhijnashastra 274
Pratyabhijna 274
Pratyahara 144, 147
Prayagraj 27, 127–128, 179, 284
Puranas
Bhavishya 55
Bhagvata 44, 125
Brahma Vaivarta 173, 322
Ganesha 173
Kurma 44, 322
Linga 36, 37, 38, 47, 291, 322, 208, 322
Mahabhagvata 189
Markandeya 112, 187
Nilamatia 297
Padma 44, 288, 322
Shiva 27, 36–38, 51, 66, 69, 119, 120, 135, 151, 176, 202, 208, 213, 216, 291, 322, 250
Skanda 49, 55, 151, 173, 179, 195, 203, 250, 295, 301, 303, 322

Tamil Sthala 197
Tamil talapuranas 156
Vamana 44, 301, 322
Vayu 44, 185, 201, 210, 322
Vishnu 44
Vishnudharmottara 55, 193, 233, 322
Puratan Shivalaya Temple 55
Puri 309
Purity *see* Sattva
Pushpak Vimana 27

R

Raghuvamsha 66
Rajas (Activity) 41, 52, 89, 234, 288, 300, 314
Rajasthan 19, 53, 60, 169, 179, 240, 280, 308–309
Rajatarangini 297
Rakshasa 26, 28
Raktabija 92, 93, 187
Rama 26, 28, 31–33, 43, 44, 69, 104, 201, 211
Ramacharitamanas 28
Ramanathaswamy Temple 66
Ramayana 26, 28, 66, 202, 211
  Adhyatma Ramayana 28
  Krittibasi Ramayana 28
Rameswaram 66
Rasamanjari 146
Rathinagiri Hill Temple 223
Ravana 5, 26–31, 69, 115–116, 192, 212, 226
Rig Veda 9, 22, 24, 25, 57, 76, 136, 208, 211–212, 221, 228, 236, 315, 323
Rishabhanatha 290
  Rishabha 290–291
Rishikesh 62, 89
River
  Ganga 15, 37, 62, 109, 127, 128, 179, 185, 203, 221, 250–253, 301, 302, 313

Gomati 69
Mandakini 310
Narmada 61, 69
Sarasvati 128
Yamuna 128, 170
Rudra 5, 9–13, 22, 24, 25, 27, 35, 53, 57, 58, 72–77, 86, 90. 92, 136, 142, 157, 183, 189, 221, 236, 248, 291, 295, 320, 322, 323
Rudrabhishekam 35
Rudranath 310–311
Rudraprayag 157, 310–311

S

Sabarimala 45
Sabija Samadhi 235
Sadhana 223, 292
Sadyojata 104, 194, 233
Sage
  Agastya 305
  Bharadvaja 211
  Bharata 99
  Bhrigu 58
  Bhringi 162
  Jamadagni 211
  Kapila 185
  Kashyapa 201
  Markandeya 17
  Narada 69, 17
  Parashurama 305
  Saptarishis 208, 210
  Upamanyu 58
Sahasrara Chakra 242, 244, 246
Sahuti 76
Saint
  Akka Mahadevi 263, 264–267
  Appar 92
  Basavanna 262–263, 264–267
  Lalleshwari 279
  Siddharma 266
Saptarishis 208, 210
Samadhi 81, 175, 209, 213, 235, 246, 274, 292

Sambandar 259
Samhara 41
Sannyasis 214
Sapta Puri Yatra 302
Sati 12, 14, 37, 58, 84, 88, 86, 88, 90, 92, 115, 143–145, 147–152, 155, 189, 197, 209, 213, 242, 249, 257, 288
Sattva 41, 52, 89, 234, 288, 300, 314
Shabari Hills 45
Shaiva 11–15, 19–21, 37, 49, 51, 56-57, 59, 64, 66, 88, 90, 92, 104, 107, 115, 127, 138, 142, 170,173, 183, 190, 192, 209, 213, 225–227, 242, 245, 257–258, 262, 264, 272–274, 279, 280, 283–284, 290–295, 300
Shaivism 10–13, 15, 19, 24, 43, 55, 240, 242, 245, 256, 258-259, 262, 267–268, 272–275, 279-280, 283, 290–293
  Kashmir 305, 306
  Tamil 258–259
Shakti 11, 36, 37, 49, 53, 90, 122, 145, 155, 186–187, 233, 240–242, 246, 248–249, 274, 281
Shakti Peethas 249
Shankaranarayana 49
Sharabha 9, 51
Shasta 44
Shatarudriya 24, 221
Shikhara 66, 226, 227, 310, 315
Shiva, forms of
  Ardhanarishvara 166–167
  Bhairava 240–241
  Bhikshatanamurti 216–217
  Dakshinamurti 222–223
  Harihara 46–47
  Hariharapitamahasurya 54–55

Kaal Bhairava 108–111
Kalyanasundarmurti 152–153
Khandoba 132–133
Kiratarjuniyam 32–33
Nataraja 98–101
Panchamukha 232–233
Pashupati 22–23
Rudra 74–77
Shankara 174–175
Sharaba 50–51
Vankeshvara 294–295
Veerbhadra 86–89
Shiva Purana 5, 27, 36–38, 66, 69, 72, 84, 90, 135, 151, 176, 202, 208, 213, 216, 291, 322
Shiva Ramanatha 263
Shivaratri 35, 284, 303
Shiva Samhita 208
Shivatattva 303
Shivashekhara 301
Shivasahasranama 9, 295
Shivanandalahari 10, 77, 95, 269, 271
Shravan 59, 127, 296, 302
Shravasti 291
Shringara Lasya 92
Shumbha 187
Shvetashvatara Upanishad 25, 322
Siddharma 266
Siddhis 128, 152, 245, 281
Sita 69
Skanda Purana 49, 55, 151, 173, 179, 195, 203, 250, 295, 301, 303, 322
Soma 6, 288
Somaskanda 183
Someshwara Temple 33
Somnath Temple 66, 68–69
Spanda 213, 275
Srikalahasteeswara Temple 228
Srinagar 275, 299
Srinatha 259
Srisailam 266, 272
Srishti 41

Sthala vriksha 61
Sthiti 41
Sushumna Nadi 221, 246
Svacchanda Bhairava 240, 245
Svadhyaya 246
Svayambhu 60–61, 68, 296

T

Tala 295
Tamas 41, 52, 89, 234, 288, 300, 314
Tamil Nadu 30, 61, 66, 69, 89, 95, 98, 100, 112, 135, 156–157, 173, 183, 190, 193, 197, 216, 223, 227, 258–259, 260, 302–304, 315
  Arunachaleshwara Temple 228
  Ekambareswarar Temple 228
  Jambukeshwarar Temple 228
  Kulasekarapattinam 190
    Arulmigu Mutharamman Temple 190
  Ramanathaswamy Temple 66
  Tamil Shaivism 258
  Thillai Nataraja Temple 228
  Vellore 223
    Rathinagiri Hill Temple 223
Tamil Shaivism 258
Tandava 27, 90, 92–95, 100, 103, 187, 227, 296, 304
  Ananda 92, 100, 227, 304
  Rudra 90, 92
  Shiva Tandava Stotram 27, 116
  Urdhva 92, 187
Tantra 12, 189, 241–245, 272, 275, 280

Vamakeshvara Tantra 189
Vijnana Bhairava Tantra 242
Tantraloka 275
Tapas 27, 151-152, 161, 175, 197, 209-210, 212–213
Tapasya 33, 135, 185
Tapkeshwar Mahadev Temple 10, 226
Tapovan 313
Tara 186, 189
Tarakaksha 119
Taraka Mantra 289
Tarakasura 119, 180, 212, 304, 305
Tatpurusha 194, 233
Tattva 233
   Prakriti 233
Temple
   Arulmigu Mutharamman 190
   Arunachaleshwara 228
   Bhairavnath 239
   Chandrabadni 155
   Ekambareswarar 228
   Jambukeshwarar 228
   Kamakhya 241
   Kandariya Mahadeva 227
   Kashi Vishwanath 227
   Kedarnath 239, 302, 310
   Kunjapuri Devi 155
   Lakshmi Narayana 233
   Mahakaleshwar 66, 67, 69, 107
   Nageshwara 68, 69
   Omkareshwar 69
   Puratan Shivalaya 55
   Ramanathaswamy 66
   Rathinagiri Hill 223
   Someshwara 33
   Srikalahasteeswara 228
   Tapkeshwar Mahadev 10, 226
   Thillai Nataraja 228
   Tryambakeshwar 66, 69
Tevaram 92, 258
Thanjavur 44, 112, 259

Thillai Nataraja Temple 228
Third Eye Chakra (Ajna Chakra) 78, 233, 242
Thiruirattai Manimalai 260
Thiruvathira 302
Tirruvorriyur 223
Tirtha 109, 128, 302
Tiruvaalangadu Padigam 260
Tiruverkadu 259
Trans-Himalayan range 202
Triaksha 78
Trident 8, 19–22, 52–55, 60, 87, 89, 103, 122, 128, 133–135, 148, 151, 167, 169, 176, 183, 189, 216, 239, 241, 244, 291, 292, 308–313, 315
Trika system 274
Trimurti 40-43, 55, 315
   Samhara 41
   Srishti 41
   Sthiti 41
Trinetra 78
Tripundra 52, 53, 60, 61, 119, 167, 190, 265
Tripura 52, 119, 122, 304
Tripurasundari 146, 186, 189
Tripurasura 14, 92, 119
Trishula 12, 20, 31, 52–55, 300, 309, 313
Tryambaka 20, 78, 236
Tryambakeshwar Temple 66, 69
Tungnath 310

U
Uddiyana Bandha 246
Ujjain 61, 66, 67, 69, 107, 128, 302, 309
   Mahakaleshwar Temple 66, 67, 69, 107
Ukhimath 302
Uma 37, 86, 142, 160, 164, 183, 259, 271
Umamaheshwara 248
Upamanyu 58

Upanayana (Initiation Ceremony) 216
Upanishad 24
   Atharvashikha 25
   Atharvashiras 25
   Kaivalya 25
   Kalagnirudra 25
   Nilarudra 25
   Shvetashvatara 25
Urdhava 92, 95, 187, 292
Urdhvalinga (Ithyphallic) 19
Urdhva retas 292
Urdhva Tandava 92, 187
Urgram Valley 311
Uttarakhand 10, 89, 164, 170, 250, 272, 283, 284
   Bhairavnath Temple 239
   Dehradun 10
   Tapkeshwar Mahadev Temple 10, 226
   Kedarnath Temple 239, 302, 310
Uttar Pradesh 63, 290

V
Vachanas 263, 264, 266, 267
Vaidya 69
Vaidyanath 69
Vaidyanathan 24, 76
Valmiki 28
Vamadeva 194, 233
Vana (Forest) 133
Vanara 193, 201
Vankeshvara 11, 295
Varanasi 11, 53, 69, 109, 227, 250, 283, 301, 302, 309 *see also* Kashi
Vastu Shastra 226
Vedas 13, 24, 25, 36, 43, 55, 58, 72, 73, 84, 104, 106, 119, 197, 208, 258, 252, 262, 283, 314
Vasuki 120
Veerbhadra 41, 72, 77, 84–89, 115, 137, 149
Vibhuti 53, 236, 288
Vidyunmali 119

Vijnana Bhairava Tantra 242
Vimana 27, 226
Vinadhara Dakshinamurti 223
Vindhya 69
Vishnu 9, 13, 14, 26, 27, 37, 38, 40-51, 55, 58, 59, 66, 73, 84, 86, 88, 119, 122, 125, 129, 135, 137, 144, 147–149, 152, 155, 157, 173, 176, 189, 192, 201, 210, 211, 229, 233, 249, 251, 258, 284, 288, 300, 302, 307, 314, 315
   Mohini 27, 44, 49, 135, 173
Vishnudharmottara Purana 55, 168, 193, 233, 322
Vishwanath 69, 127, 227, 250
Vishweshwara 227
Vrata 303
Vyakhyana Dakshinamurti 223

Y
Yajur Veda 24, 221
   Shatarudriya 24, 221
Yama 112, 223, 236,
Yamunotri 302
Yatras 127, 155, 296, 299, 302, 310
   Amarnath 296
   Kanwar 127, 302
   Raj Jat 155
Yoga 12, 15, 42, 104, 147, 179, 201, 208, 272, 208–210, 223, 245, 246, 272, 273, 288, 309, 314, 323
   Hatha 208, 272–273
   Laya 208
   Nada 104, 246
   Patanjali yoga sutras 147
   Raja 208
   Yoga Patta 223
Yoga Dakshinamurti 223

Yoga Patta 223
Yoni 25, 56, 58–60, 142, 248, 249, 296

Z
Zoji La Pass 296

BIBLIOGRAPHY

Primary sources

Bhatt. G. P. ed. *The Skanda Purana, Part 1. Ancient Indian Tradition and Mythology*. Delhi: Motilal Banarsidass Publishers Private Limited, 2024.

Craddock, Elaine. 2010. *Siva's Demon Devotee*. New York: SUNY Press.

N. A. Deshpande. ed. *The Padma Purana, Part 1. Ancient Indian Tradition and Mythology*. Delhi: Motilal Banarsidass Publishers Private Limited, 1990.

Gambhirananda, Swami, tr. with the Commentary of Sankaracarya. *Svetasvatara Upanisad*. Calcutta: Advaita Ashrama, 1995.

Gambhirananda, Swami, tr. with the Commentary of Sankaracarya. *Vishnudharmottara Purana, Shvetashvatara Upanishad*. Calcutta: Advaita Ashrama, 1986.

A. S. Gupta. ed. *The Vamana Purana. Ancient Indian Tradition and Mythology*. Benaras: 1968.

Shastri, J. L. ed. *The Brahma Purana, Part 1. Ancient Indian Tradition and Mythology*. Delhi: Motilal Banarsidass Publishers Private Limited, 2014.

Shastri, J. L. ed. *The Kurma Purana, Part 1. Ancient Indian Tradition and Mythology*. Delhi: Motilal Banarsidass Publishers Private Limited, 1998.

Shastri, J. L. ed. *The Linga Purana, Part 1. Ancient Indian Tradition and Mythology*. Delhi: Motilal Banarsidass Publishers Private Limited, 1990.

Shastri, J. L. ed. *The Siva Purana, Part 1. Ancient Indian Tradition and Mythology*. Delhi: Motilal Banarsidass Publishers Private Limited, 1986.

Sri Sankaracarya. *Sivanandalahari*. Madras: Sri Ramakrishna Math, 1985.

G. V. Tagare. ed. *The Vayu Purana, Part 1. Ancient Indian Tradition and Mythology*. Delhi: Motilal Banarsidass Publishers Private Limited, 1987.

Secondary sources

Bajpai, K. D. and Rao, M. Birla Museum: *Catalogue of the Shiva Gallery*.

Bakker, Hans T. *The Vakatakas*. Groningen: Egbert Forsten, 1997.

Banerjea, J. N. *Pauranic and Tantric Religion*. Calcutta: University of Calcutta, 1966.

Banerjea, J. N. *The Development of Hindu Iconography*. New Delhi: Munshiram Manoharlal Publishers Pvt Ltd, 1986.

Bhattacharyya, N. N. *History of the Tantric Religion*. New Delhi: Manohar Publishers, 1982.

Bhattacharyya, N. N. *Indian Demonology: The Inverted Pantheon*. Delhi: Manohar Publishers, 2000.

Bhandarkar, D. R. "An Eklingaji Stone Inscription and the Origin and History of the Lakulisha Sect." *Journal of the Bombay Branch of the Royal Asiatic Society*, Bombay, 1905–07.

Brockington, J. L. *The Sacred Thread*. Edinburgh University Press, 1996.

Calasso, Roberto. *Ka: Stories of the Mind and Gods of India*. London: Vintage Books: 1999.

Campbell, Joseph. *The Power of Myth*. New York: Doubleday, 1988.

Cashford, Jules. *The Moon, Myth and Image*. London: Cassell, 2003.

Chaturvedi, B. K. *Shiva*. New Delhi: Books for All, 1996.

Chitgopekar, Nilima. *Encountering Sivaism: The Deity, the Milieu, the Entourage*. Delhi: Munshiram Manoharlal Publishers Pvt Ltd, 1998.

Chitgopekar, Nilima. *Rudra: The Idea of Shiva*. New Delhi: Penguin Books, 2007.

Chitgopekar, Nilima. *The Book of Durga*. Penguin India, 2003.

Chitgopekar, Nilima. *The Reluctant Family Man: Shiva in Everyday Life*. Penguin, 2021.

Clooncy, Francis Xavier. *Hindu God, Christian God: How Reason Helps Break Down the Boundaries between Religions*. OUP USA, 2010.

Craven, Roy C. *Indian Art: A Concise History*. London: Thames and Hudson, 1976 (repr. 1987).

Dalal, Roshen. *The Penguin Dictionary of Religion in India*. New Delhi: Penguin, 2006.

Dandekar, R. N. *Vedic Mythological Tracts*. Delhi: Ajanta Publications, 1987.

Dehejia, V. *Slaves of the Lord: The Path of the Tamil Saints*. New Delhi: Munshiram Manoharlal Publishers Pvt Ltd, 1988.

Dehejia, V. *Yogini Cult and Temples: A Tantric Tradition*. New Delhi: National Museum, 1986.

Dehejia, Vidya; Coburn, Thomas B. *Devi: The Great Goddess: Female Divinity in South Asian Art*. Washington DC: Arthur M. Sackler Gallery, Smithsonian Institution in association with Mapin Publishing, Ahmedabad and Prestel Verlag, Munich, 1999.

Doniger, Wendy. *Siva, the Erotic Ascetic*. New York, 1980.

Doniger, Wendy. *The Hindus: An Alternative History*. New York: Penguin, 2009.

Doniger, Wendy. *Women, Androgynes, and Other Mythical Beasts*. University of Chicago Press, 1980.

Dowson, John. *A Classical Dictionary of Hindu Mythology and Religion*. Delhi: Rupa Publications, 2009.

Easwaran, Eknath. *The Upanishads*. Nilgiri Press, 2007.

Eck, Diana L. *Encountering God: A Spiritual Journey from Bozeman to Banaras*. Beacon Press, 1993.

Eck, Diana L. *India: A Sacred Geography*. New York: Harmony, 2013.
Eliade, Mircea. *Yoga: Immortality and Freedom*. Princeton University Press, 2009.
Flood, Gavin. *An Introduction to Hinduism*. Cambridge University Press, 2004.
Goldberg, Ellen. *The Lord Who is Half Woman: Ardhanarisvara in Indian and Feminist Perspective*. Albany: SUNY Press, 2002.
Griffith, Ralph T. H, tr. *The Hymns of the Rigveda*. Kessinger Publishing, 2006.
Harshananda, Swami. *Hindu Gods and Goddesses*. Madras: Sri Ramakrishna Math, 2002.
Haydon, A. Eustace. *Biography of the Gods*. Macmillan, 1941.
Heehs, Peter, ed. *Indian Religions: The Spiritual Traditions of South Asia*. Delhi: Permanent Black, 2006.
Jayakar, Pupul. *The Earth Mother: Legends, Goddesses, and Ritual Arts of India*. Harper Collins, 1990.
Kaimal, Padma. "Shiva Nataraja: Shifting Meanings of an Icon." *The Art Bulletin*, Vol. 81, No. 3, Sept 1999.
Kinsley, David. *Hinduism: A Cultural Perspective*. Prentice Hall, 1982.
Kinsley, David. *Tantric Visions of the Divine Feminine: Dasa Mahavidyas*. Motilal Banarsidass Publishers, 2022.
Kosambi, D. D. *The Culture and Civilisation of Ancient India in Historical Outline*. Vikas Publishing House Pvt Ltd, 1997.
Johnson, Donald and Jean. *God and Gods in Hinduism*. New Delhi: Arnold-Heinemann, 1972.
Kramrisch, Stella. *Exploring India's Sacred Art*. Motilal Banarsidass Publishers, 1994.
Kramrisch, Stella. *The Presence of Siva*. Princeton: Princeton University Press, 1981.
Lorenzen, David. *The Kapalikas and Kalamukhas: Two Lost Saivite Sects*. Berkeley: University of California, 1972.
Madan, T. N, ed. *India's Religions*. Oxford University Press, 2011.
Maxwell, T. S. *The Gods of Asia: Image, Text, and Meaning*. Oxford University Press, 1997.
Monier-Williams, Monier. *A Sanskrit-English Dictionary*. Canny Press, 2024.
Nandy, Ashis. *Time Warps: The Insistent Politics of Silent and Evasive Pasts*. Permanent Black, 2004.
Nandi, R. N. *Social Roots of Religion in Ancient India*. K. P. Bagchi, 1986.
Pattanaik, Devdutt. *7 Secrets of Shiva*. Westland, 2016.
Pattanaik, Devdutt. *Devlok with Devdutt Pattanaik*.
Pattanaik, Devdutt. *Myth = Mithya: A Handbook of Hindu Mythology*. Penguin India, 2006.
Pattanaik, Devdutt. *Secrets from Hindu Calendar Art*. Westland, 2009.
Ramanujan, A. K., tr. *Speaking of Siva*. Penguin Books, 1973.
Rao, T. A. Gopinatha. *Elements of Hindu Iconography*, vol 1 pt II, Gyan Publishing House, 2021.
Ratnagar, Shereen. *Understanding Harappa—Civilization in the Greater Indus Valley*. Tulika Books, 2017.
Ray, H. C. *Dynastic History of Northern India*. Munshiram Manoharlal Publishers Pvt Ltd, 1973.
Saraswati, Chandrasckharendra. *Saundaryalahari*. Bharatiya Vidya Bhavan, 2001.
Singh, Karan, ed. *Shiva: Lord of the Cosmic Dance*. Speaking Tiger, 2022.
Singh, Upinder. *A History of Ancient and Early Medieval India*. Pearson Education India, 2009.
Sivaramamurti, C. *Nataraja in Art, Thought and Literature*. New Delhi: National Museum, 1976.
Smith, David. *The Dance of Siva*. Cambridge University Press, 1996.
Sontheimer, Gunther-Dietz. *King of Hunters, Warriors, and Shepherds: Essays on Khandoba*. Manohar Publishers and Distributors, 1997.
Srivastava, Smita S. *Cults of the Bull in North India: A Socio-Religious Study up to A.D. 500*. Unpublished Ph.D. thesis.
Storl, Wolf-Dieter. *Shiva: The Wild God of Power and Ecstasy*. Simon & Schuster, 2004.
Swahananda, Swami. *Hindu Symbols*. Sri Ramakrishna Math, Advaita Ashrama, 2003.
Swami, Sivananda. *Lord Shiva and His Worship*. The Divine Life Society, 2008.
SYDA Foundation. *The Nectar of Chanting: Sacred Texts and Mantras Sung in the Ashrams of Swami Muktananda*. New York, SYDA Foundation, 1978.
Tapasyananda, Swami, tr. *Saundarya Lahari: Of Sri Shankaracharya*. Chennai: Sri Ramakrishna Math, 1987.
Viswanathan, Ed. *Am I a Hindu?* New Delhi: Rupa & Co, 1993.
Wilkins, W. J. *Hindu Mythology, Vedic and Puranic*. Fingerprint! Publishing, 2023.
Woerner, Gert, ed., Schuhmacher, Stephan, ed. *The Encyclopedia of Eastern Philosophy and Religion: Buddhism, Hinduism, Taoism, Zen*. Shambhala, 1994
Younger, Paul. *The Home of Dancing Siva: The Traditions of the Hindu Temple in Citamparam*. The University of Chicago Press, 1999.
Zimmer, Heinrich. *Myths and Symbols in Indian Art and Civilization*. Princeton University Press, 1992.

Acknowledgments

About the author
Dr Nilima Chitgopekar is a historian of religion. She has authored seven books, in addition to editing one volume and contributing numerous essays and articles to books and journals. She has been a professor of history at Delhi University for more than four decades and has delivered lectures worldwide, most recently at Harvard University. She has also been the recipient of several prestigious fellowships, including those from the Oxford Centre for Hindu Studies, the Charles Wallace India Trust, and the USIS. Dr Chitgopekar has featured in and collaborated on BBC documentaries and radio programmes. Committed to bringing Hindu mythology to a wider audience, she has also been involved in creating several online films. Through her writings and digital presence, she strives to bring academic discourse into the mainstream, so that anyone could engage with the labyrinthine religions of India.

Author's acknowledgments
Writing this book has been one of the most rewarding, almost magical, experiences of my life. It would not have been possible without the help of many people. I wholesomely thank all the various teams at Dorling Kindersley (DK) who worked with me – **Neha**, **Bhavika**, **Aarushi**, **Sumedha**, and **Geetam** from the art team; **Suhita**, **Rhea**, and **Priyal** from the cover team; **Janashree** from the editorial team; and the sales team.

To **Aparna**, I am grateful for her quiet confidence. To **Chitra**, who made this book happen and has always been so enthusiastic with her unwavering support. I am deeply grateful to my editor, **Vatsal**. His meticulous and painstaking eye for detail is unmatched and his consideration and helpfulness with long discussions and insights, very often, went beyond the role of an editor.

I am grateful to my mother **Mira Gupta**, who, with her joy of folk music, sang and provided me with apt songs on Shiva and Parvati. I am very appreciative of **Dr Amita Paliwal**, who cheerfully helped me with translating the songs. To my son **Dhruv**, who gets involved in myriad ways every time I start writing, who listens carefully, and whose enthusiasm has backed this book continuously. To **Tara**, my daughter-in-law, for her love, joy, and constant excitement around the book.

To my husband **Deepak**. This book could not have been written without him being part of it every single day. His pride in my work and his support are what I treasure more than anything else.

To my readers, who have been waiting eagerly for this book and whose deep connection with my writing has urged me on. I am very thankful.

Publisher's acknowledgments
The publisher would like to thank **Gavin Flood** for writing the foreword; **Chitra Subramanyam** and **Vatsal Verma** for content planning; **Tarun Khanna** for proofreading and indexing; **Devayani Shahane** for editorial support; **Tarinee Awasthi** for translating verses from *Nadatanumisam Sankaram* on *p104* and *Kumarasambhavam* on *p180*; **Nain Rawat** for his assistance in procuring the Garhwali folk song on *p155*; **Samrajkumar S** and **Manpreet Kaur** for picture research administration support; **Rajoshi Chakraborty** and **Devika Pagay** for design support; and **Satish Gaur** and **Umesh Singh Rawat** for pre-production support.

Every effort has been made to acknowledge those individuals, organizations, and corporations that have helped with this book and to trace copyright holders. DK apologizes in advance if any omission has occurred. If an omission does come to light, DK will be pleased to insert the appropriate acknowledgment in the subsequent editions of the book.

ACKNOWLEDGMENTS | 325

The publisher would like to thank the following for their kind permission to reproduce their photographs:

(Key: a-above; b-below/bottom; c-centre; f-far; l-left; r-right; t-top)

1 The Cleveland Museum Of Art: Purchase from the J. H. Wade Fund. **2 Alamy Stock Photo:** Pictures From History / CPA Media Pte Ltd. **4 Los Angeles County Museum of Art:** South and Southeast Asian Art. **8 Alamy Stock Photo:** Dinodia Photos RM. **10-15 Unsplash:** João Vítor Duarte (texture Background). **18 Bridgeman Images:** National Museum of Karachi, Karachi, Pakistan. **20 Getty Images:** Moment / fahadee.com (bl). **The Metropolitan Museum of Art:** Purchase, Nathaniel Spear Jr. and James N. Spear Gifts, 1986 (tl). **21 Dorling Kindersley:** Aditya Patankar / National Museum, New Delhi. **22 Getty Images:** Archive Photos / Pierce Archive LLC / Buyenlarge. **23 Philadelphia Museum of Art:** Gift of Ann and Donald McPhail, 2018. **24-25 Getty Images / iStock:** Nastasic / DigitalVision Vectors (t). **26 The Cleveland Museum Of Art:** Purchase and partial gift from the Catherine and Ralph Benkaim Collection; Severance and Greta Millikin Purchase Fund. **27 Getty Images:** Sanjay Kanojia / NurPhoto. **28-29 Getty Images:** Sepia Times / Universal Images Group. **30 Dreamstime.com:** Alinamd (t/sky), Klodien. **31 Philadelphia Museum of Art:** Purchased with the Stella Kramrisch Fund, 2005 (br). **32 Alamy Stock Photo:** Chronicle. **32-33 Dreamstime.com:** Arthit Marsing (background). **33 The Metropolitan Museum of Art:** Rogers Fund, 1970 (br). **34-35 Alamy Stock Photo:** Sunil Sharma / ZUMA Press Wire. **36-37 Alamy Stock Photo:** The History Collection. **38-39 Unsplash:** Pixelbuddha Studio (background). **39 Unsplash:** Arun Prakash. **40 Wellcome Collection**. **41 Getty Images:** Hulton Fine Art Collection / Culture Club. **43 Wellcome Collection**. **44 Alamy Stock Photo:** Peter Horree. **45 Wellcome Collection**. **46 Getty Images:** Pictures From History / Universal Images Group. **47 Bridgeman Images:** Lowe Art Museum / Gift of Leo S. Figiel, M.D. (br). **48 Alamy Stock Photo:** piemags. **49 The Art Institute of Chicago:** Pritzker Collection. **50 Dreamstime.com:** Evgeniy Fesenko. **50-51 Dreamstime.com:** Tanwa Na Thalang (background). **51 Dreamstime.com:** EPhotocorp (br). **52-53 123RF.com:** kues (background). **Dreamstime.com:** Dmitry Rukhlenko. **54 Getty Images / iStock:** Satish Parashar. **54-55 Unsplash:** Wesley Tingey (background). **56-57 Getty Images / iStock:** Derikjohn. **58 The Cleveland Museum Of Art:** John L. Severance Fund (bl). **59 The Cleveland Museum Of Art:** Purchase and partial gift from the Catherine and Ralph Benkaim Collection; Severance and Greta Millikin Purchase Fund. **60 Alamy Stock Photo:** imageBROKER / dad fotos (tl); Amit Machamasi / ZUMA Press Wire (tr). **Getty Images:** Frank Bienewald / LightRocket (tc). **61 Alamy Stock Photo:** Pep Roig (tl). **Dreamstime.com:** Rupendra Rawat (tr). **Getty Images / iStock:** Mayur Kakade (tc). **62-63 Getty Images:** Frédéric Soltan / Sygma. **65 American Institute of Indian Studies. 66-67 Dreamstime.com:** Anil Dave (bc). **Getty Images:** AFP / Sam Panthaky / Stringer (tc). **67 Dreamstime.com:** Anil Dave (ca, cb); Saiko3p (bc). **Shutterstock.com:** Md Niazuddin Nawaz (tc). **68 Getty Images:** Sunil Magariya / Hindustan Times. **72-73 Unsplash:** João Vítor Duarte. **74-75 Depositphotos Inc:** michelangeloop. **76-77 Unsplash:** Johannes Plenio. **78-79 Dreamstime.com:** Graphics.vp. **80-81 The Metropolitan Museum of Art:** Purchase, Anonymous Gift, 2013. **82-83 Shutterstock.com:** Chitranakshatra. **84-85 Alamy Stock Photo:** Niday Picture Library. **86-87 © The Trustees of the British Museum. All rights reserved**. **88 Alamy Stock Photo:** Edwin Binney 3rd Collection / The San Diego Museum of Art / The Picture Art Collection. **89 Alamy Stock Photo:** Arunabh Bhattacharjee (br). **90-91 Muskan Agrawal:** @madu.draws. **92 Shutterstock.com:** PRIYA DARSHAN (bl). **93 Wellcome Collection**. **94 Dreamstime.com:** Kruglovorda. **95 Alamy Stock Photo:** imageBROKER / Muthuraman V (b). **96-97 Library of Congress, Washington, D.C.:** Underwood & Underwood. **98-99 Los Angeles County Museum of Art:** South and Southeast Asian Art. **100 Depositphotos Inc:** mcmorabad. **101 Getty Images:** Soltan Frédéric / Sygma. **102-103 Shutterstock.com:** Alex Erofeenkov. **105 Getty Images:** R. Satish Babu / AFP. **106-107 Getty Images:** Hulton Archive / Heritage Arts / Heritage Images. **108 Leiden University Library, The Netherlands**. **109 The Metropolitan Museum of Art:** Zimmerman Family Collection, Gift of the Zimmerman Family, 2012 (br). **110-111 Alamy Stock Photo:** Lieze Neven. **112-113 Getty Images / iStock:** Mayur Kakade. **114-115 Dreamstime.com:** Iuliia Selina. **115 Wellcome Collection:** (br). **116 Getty Images:** Heritage Art / Heritage Images. **117 Alamy Stock Photo:** World History Archive (r). **118-119 Rasa United:** Inni Singh. **120-121 Getty Images:** Godong / Universal Images Group. **123 Anag Kumar / Brogen:** www.brogen.in. **124-125 Art by S. Rajam Courtesy Himalayan Academy, Hawaii**. **126-127 Alamy Stock Photo:** Prabhat Kumar Verma / ZUMA Press, Inc.. **128-129 Getty Images:** Niharika Kulkarni / AFP (b). **Shutterstock.com:** Ritu's Angle (tc). **129 Shutterstock.com:** tscreationz (bc). **130-131 Getty**

Images / iStock: wing-wing. **132 Wellcome Collection**. **133 Getty Images:** Universal History Archive / Universal Images Group. **134-135 Getty Images:** Pierce Archive LLC / Buyenlarge. **136-137 Ankita Biswas:** @bhairava_rises. **138-139 Shutterstock.com:** Mushfiqul Alam / NurPhoto. **142-143 Unsplash:** João Vítor Duarte (background). **144 Alamy Stock Photo:** The Picture Art Collection. **145 Dreamstime.com:** Aliaksandr Mazurkevich. **146 The Metropolitan Museum of Art:** Gift of Dr. J. C. Burnett, 1957 (tl). **147 Alamy Stock Photo:** Penta Springs Limited / Artokoloro. **148 The Metropolitan Museum of Art:** Purchase, Friends of Asian Art Gifts, 2021. **149 Dreamstime.com:** David Pillow (br). **150 The Ganesh Shivaswamy Foundation:** From the Collection of Hemamalini & Ganesh Shiaswamy, Bengaluru. **151 Getty Images:** Sepia Times / Universal Images Group. **152-153 Getty Images / iStock:** Satish Parashar. **154-155 The Ganesh Shivaswamy Foundation:** From the collection of Hemamalini and Ganesh Shivaswamy, Bengaluru. **156-157 Alamy Stock Photo:** NV Studios (tc). Getty Images: Mel Longhurst / VW Pics / Universal Images Group (b). **157 Alamy Stock Photo:** BOISVIEUX Christophe / hemis.fr / Hemis (tc). **158-159 Getty Images:** SAJJAD HUSSAIN / AFP. **160-161 Unsplash:** Pixelbuddha Studio (background). **160 Government Museum and Art Gallery, Chandigarh**. **161 Wellcome Collection**. **162-163 The Metropolitan Museum of Art:** Purchase, Nancy Fessenden Gift, 2019. Unsplash: Pixelbuddha Studio (background). **165 The Walters Art Museum, Baltimore:** Gift of John and Berthe Ford, 2002. **166-167 Alamy Stock Photo:** Dinodia Photos RM. **168 The Cleveland Museum Of Art:** Purchase from the J. H. Wade Fund (tl). **169 Getty Images:** Sepia Times / Universal Images Group. **170-171 Getty Images:** Frédéric Soltan / Sygma. **172 Getty Images:** Hulton Archive / CM Dixon / Print Collector. **173 The Metropolitan Museum of Art:** Gift of Florence and Herbert Irving, 2015 (br). **174 Siddharth Shingade:** KYNKYNY Art Gallery. **176-177 Alamy Stock Photo:** Chirantan Sangrah / State Museum Odisha. **178 Philadelphia Museum of Art:** Stella Kramrisch Collection, 1994. **179 Alamy Stock Photo:** World History Archive (br). **181 Rasa United:** INNI SINGH. **182-183 The Art Institute of Chicago:** Robert Allerton Purchase Fund. **184 Dreamstime.com:** Vasily Gureev. **186-187 Wellcome Collection:** The ten Madavidyas. Chromolithograph. **188-189 Bridgeman Images:** From the British Library archive. **190-191 Getty Images:** IDREES MOHAMMED / AFP. **192 The Walters Art Museum, Baltimore:** Gift of John and Berthe Ford, 2003 (bl). **193 © Asian Art Museum of San Francisco:** The Avery Brundage Collection. **194-195 Asian Art Museum:** Gift of the Ethnic Arts Foundation / Indira Devi. **196 Alamy Stock Photo:** Art Collection 3. **198-199 Getty Images:** Amith Nag Photography. **200 Alamy Stock Photo:** Pictures From History / CPA Media Pte Ltd. **201 Shutterstock.com:** Sagittarius Pro (br). **202-203 Getty Images:** Moment / Feng Wei Photography (tc); Moment / Shu Zhang (b). **203 Dreamstime.com:** Raimond Klavins (tc). **204-205 Getty Images / iStock:** Ivan Wang. **208-209 Unsplash:** João Vítor Duarte. **210-211 Alamy Stock Photo:** Historic Collection. **212-213 Getty Images:** Hulton Fine Art Collection / Ashmolean Museum / Heritage Images. Unsplash: Renee Lin / capsule929 (background). **214-215 Getty Images:** SOPA Images / LightRocket. **217 Los Angeles County Museum of Art:** Gift of Mr. and Mrs. Paul E. Manheim. **218-219 Art by S. Rajam Courtesy Himalayan Academy, Hawaii**. **220-221 Getty Images:** AFP / Dibyangshu Sarkar / Stringer. **222 Dreamstime.com:** Klodien. **222-223 Unsplash:** Mike Hindle (background). **224-225 Dreamstime.com:** Alinamd (t); Aliaksandr Mazurkevich (b). **226 Getty Images / iStock:** Kandarp Gupta. **227 Getty Images / iStock:** Santosh Sinha. **228-229 Alamy Stock Photo:** Dinodia Photos (cb). **Getty Images:** Abdul Munaff (bc); The Image Bank / John Elk III (tc). **229 Dreamstime.com:** Cherylramalho (bc). Getty Images: The Image Bank Unreleased / Dinodia Photo (tc). **230-231 Getty Images:** John Elk III / The Image Bank. **232 Dreamstime.com:** Satish Parashar. **232-233 Unsplash:** Mike Hindle (background). **234-235 Dreamstime.com:** Neutronman. **236-237 Dreamstime.com:** Picsfive (background). **Shutterstock.com:** ReallybeingCreative. **238-239 Shutterstock.com:** ImagesofIndia. **240 Dreamstime.com:** Gbruev (bl). **Getty Images:** Arun K. Mishra / Dinodia (br). Los Angeles County Museum of Art: Gift of Dr. and Mrs. Robert S. Coles (M.81.206.7) (bc). **241 Dreamstime.com:** Anil Dave (bc). **Getty Images:** Pictures From History / Universal Images Group (bl). Shutterstock.com: ShrutiB (br). **242 Wellcome Collection**. **243 Bridgeman Images:** Fototeca Gilardi. **244 Arpana Caur:** Academy of Fine Arts and Literature Museum. **245 Bridgeman Images:** Christie's Images. **246-247 Abhijit Sardar:** @raangtar_araale. **248-249 Abhijit Sardar:** @raangtar_araale. **250-251 Alamy Stock Photo:** Sudip Chanda / Pacific Press via ZUMA Press Wire (cb). **Getty Images:** Janek (b). **Getty Images / iStock:** shylendrahoode (t). **251 Unsplash:** Jannes Jacobs (bc). **252-253 Alamy Stock Photo:** Graham Prentice. **256-257 Unsplash:** João Vítor Duarte. **259 The Art Institute of Chicago:** Bertha Evans Brown Fund (tl). **Bridgeman Images:** © Dirk Bakker. All rights reserved 2025 (tc). **Los Angeles County Museum of Art:** Gift of Dr. Robert C. Majer (56.8) (tr). **261 The Metropolitan Museum

ACKNOWLEDGMENTS

of Art: Purchase, Edward J. Gallagher Jr. Bequest, in memory of his father, Edward Joseph Gallagher, his mother, Ann Hay Gallagher, and his son, Edward Joseph Gallagher III, 1982. **262 Philadelphia Museum of Art:** Gift of Ira Brind, 2012. **263 The New York Public Library:** The Miriam and Ira D. Wallach Division of Art, Prints and Photographs: Photography Collection, The New York Public Library. "Lingayet, Hindoo, Mysore" The New York Public Library Digital Collections. 1868 - 1875. https://digitalcollections.nypl.org/items/b27c4370-c5fc-012f-6a68-58d385a7bc34. **265 Dreamstime.com:** Klodien. **266 The J. Paul Getty Museum, Los Angeles:** Gift in memory of Marie McNabola and Irene Peters. **267 Dreamstime.com:** Mithileshkbadhai (tr). **268 Alamy Stock Photo:** JSM Historical. **269 Getty Images / iStock:** Bambam Kumar Jha. **270 Dreamstime.com:** Alexandra Barbu. **272 Getty Images:** Heritage Art / Heritage Images. **272-273 Dreamstime.com:** Guenter Albers. **273 Los Angeles County Museum of Art:** Gift of Mr. and Mrs. Michael Douglas (M.85.283.10). **274 Getty Images:** Eric Lafforgue / Art in All of Us / Corbis (bl). **274-275 Alamy Stock Photo:** piemags. **276-277 Getty Images / iStock:** AAGGraphics. **278-279 Unsplash:** Heather Green. **278 Internet Archive:** Anon / digitallibraryindia / JaiGyan. **280-281 The Metropolitan Museum of Art:** Purchase, Lila Acheson Wallace Gift, 2011. **282-283 Shutterstock.com:** Filip Jedraszak. **284-285 Getty Images / iStock:** Avishek Das. **286-287 Getty Images:** Subir Basak. **288-289 Alamy Stock Photo:** AP Photo / Niranjan Shrestha. **290-291 Los Angeles County Museum of Art:** Gift of Leo S. Figiel, M.D. (AC1992.170.1). **292 Dreamstime.com:** Gulrez K (tl). **293 Alamy Stock Photo:** Chirantan Sangrah. **294-295 Getty Images / iStock:** ePhotocorp. **296-297 Alamy Stock Photo:** AP Photo / Rafiq Maqbool (tc). Getty Images: Yawar Nazir (bc). **297 Getty Images / iStock:** E+ / guenterguni (tc). **298-299 Alamy Stock Photo:** yawar nazir kabli. **300-301 Getty Images:** Moment Open / Pallab Seth (t). **302-303 Dreamstime.com:** Guenter Albers (background). **Getty Images:** The Image Bank Unreleased / Dinodia Photo. **304-305 Alamy Stock Photo:** Terese Loeb Kreuzer. **306-307 Getty Images:** Herve BRUHAT / Gamma-Rapho. **308 Alamy Stock Photo:** Rajesh Kumar Singh / Associated Press (br). **Getty Images / iStock:** Salvador-Aznar (bl). **Shutterstock.com:** manika kumari (bc). **309 Getty Images:** R. SATISH BABU / AFP (bl); SAJJAD HUSSAIN / AFP (br). **Shutterstock.com:** SushovanPhotography (bc). **310-311 Dreamstime.com:** Saiko3p (c). **Getty Images / iStock:** Saxam Rawat (bc). Shutterstock.com: Kakoli Dey (tc). **311 Dreamstime.com:** Dracozlat (bc). **Shutterstock.com:** ShivamJoshi (tc). **312-313 Alamy Stock Photo:** Aroon Thaewchatturat. **327 Wellcome Collection**

Lead editor Vatsal Verma
Lead art editor Bhavika Mathur
Editorial Janashree Singha
Design Aarushi Dhawan
Picture Research Geetam Biswas, Sumedha Chopra
Pre-production Tarun Sharma, Anurag Trivedi, Nityanand Kumar
Jacket Designers Rhea Menon, Suhita Dharamjit, Harish Aggarwal
Cover Illustrator Priyal Mote
Senior Production Controller Mandy Inness
Managing Editor Chitra Subramanyam
Managing Art Editor Neha Ahuja Chowdhry

Consulting Publisher Aparna Sharma
Publishing Director Stephanie Jackson

First published in Great Britain in 2026 by
Dorling Kindersley Limited, 20 Vauxhall Bridge Road,
London SW1V 2SA

The authorised representative in the EEA is
Dorling Kindersley Verlag GmbH. Arnulfstr. 124,
80636 Munich, Germany

Text copyright © 2026 Nilima Chitgopeker
Nilima Chitgopekar has asserted her right to be identified
as the author of this work.
Copyright © 2026 Dorling Kindersley Limited
A Penguin Random House Company
10 9 8 7 6 5 4 3 2 1
001– 356428–Feb/2026

All rights reserved. No part of this publication may be reproduced, stored in or introduced into a retrieval system, or transmitted, in any form, or by any means (electronic, mechanical, photocopying, recording, or otherwise), without the prior written permission of the copyright owner.
DK values and supports copyright. Thank you for respecting intellectual property laws by not reproducing, scanning or distributing any part of this publication by any means without permission. By purchasing an authorised edition, you are supporting writers and artists and enabling DK to continue to publish books that inform and inspire readers.
No part of this publication may be used or reproduced in any manner for the purpose of training artificial intelligence technologies or systems. In accordance with Article 4(3) of the DSM Directive 2019/790, DK expressly reserves this work from the text and data mining exception.

A CIP catalogue record for this book is available from the British Library.
ISBN: 978-0-2417-9229-2

Printed and bound in India

www.dk.com